The Trumpet of Reform

Studies in German Literature, Linguistics, and Culture

Edited by James Hardin
(*South Carolina*)

About *The Trumpet of Reform:*

This study explores the role that German literature
played in the formation of the minds and imaginations of
progressive nineteenth-century New England intellectuals.
Bauschinger's work focuses on the Transcendentalists of the
Concord circle, presenting five portraits of authors and their
world: Ralph Waldo Emerson, Margaret Fuller, Henry David
Thoreau, Amos Bronson Alcott, and Louisa May Alcott. None of
these Concord Germanophiles ever saw Germany, but each had a
peculiarly productive relationship with the literature and
intellectual traditions of that country.
The contributions of the Concord circle signaled remarkable
innovations in an age when the young republic was searching for
intellectual identity. The revolutionary new thought models these
thinkers presented to America encompassed abolitionism,
opposition to the death penalty, the emancipation of women,
social and educational reform. At the heart of many of their
debates on such causes were ideas and examples drawn from
German letters.

Sigrid Bauschinger teaches at the University of Massachusetts,
and has published widely in the field of German literature of the
twentieth century, with special emphasis on German-Jewish
authors and German exile literature. Her long interest in German-American relations is reflected in the present book, first published in German in 1989.

Thomas Hansen is professor of German at Wellesley College. His
book *The German Face of Edgar Allan Poe* (with Burton R.
Pollin) was published by Camden House in 1995, and won a
Choice Outstanding Academic Book Award.

Sigrid Bauschinger

The Trumpet of Reform

German Literature in Nineteenth-Century New England

Translated by
Thomas S. Hansen

CAMDEN HOUSE

Authorized English edition of *Die Posaune der Reform,*
first published 1989 by Francke Verlag of Bern and Stuttgart.

Translation © 1998 Thomas S. Hansen

First published 1998
Camden House
Drawer 2025
Columbia, SC 29202–2025 USA

Camden House is an imprint of Boydell & Brewer Inc.
PO Box 41026, Rochester, NY 14604–4126 USA
and of Boydell & Brewer Limited
PO Box 9, Woodbridge, Suffolk IP12 3DF, UK

ISBN: 1–57113–176–0

Library of Congress Cataloging-in-Publication Data

Bauschinger, Sigrid, 1934-
    [Posaune der Reform. English]
    The trumpet of reform: German literature in nineteenth-century
New England / Sigrid Bauschinger; translated by Thomas S. Hansen.
        p.   cm. – (Studies in German literature, linguistics, and
culture)
    Includes bibliographical references and index.
    ISBN 1–57113–176–0 (alk. paper)
    1. German literature – Appreciation – New England. 2. German
literature – Influence. 3. German literature – 19th century – History
and criticism. 4. Transcendentalism (New England) 5. American
literature – 19th century – History and criticism. 6. Literature,
Comparative – German and American. 7. Literature, Comparative -
-American and German. I. Title. II. Series: Studies in German
literature, linguistics, and culture (Unnumbered)
PT123.U6.B3813   1998
810.9'003—dc21   98-37817
                                                                CIP

This publication is printed on acid-free paper.
Printed in the United States of America

Contents

Preface

IN THE MIDDLE OF THE 19TH CENTURY, in a small town near Boston, Ralph Waldo Emerson's circle of friends came under the spell of German literature. In the essays that follow I propose to examine just how much the remarkable members of this group in Concord, Massachusetts — five main figures and a few secondary ones — owed to German letters. Rather than paint a complete picture of this vibrant literary culture, I wish to show the animated intellectual lives and personal contacts that made such influence possible. Nathaniel Hawthorne, who lived in Concord for years but did not belong to Emerson's circle, is thus absent from this book. For similar reasons I have not treated the influence of German philosophy on the Concord group; that subject deserves its own specific study.

Any study of the German literary influence on New England authors of the previous century can rely on a great wealth of published material. The works of Emerson and Thoreau, particularly their letters and journals, are all available in exemplary editions. Margaret Fuller's five-volume correspondence has recently been published, as have many works by both the Alcotts. Nonetheless, there is much editorial work that remains to be done. The complete journals of these thinkers and writers, even those of Margaret Fuller, are available only in excerpts. The libraries and archives of New England still contain an untold wealth of material, such as the commonplace books that contain notes by enthusiastic readers of German literature.

Two monumental scholarly works have tackled this subject matter before me: Stanley M. Vogel, *German Literary Influences on the American Transcendentalists* (New Haven: Yale University Press, 1955), and Henry A. Pochmann, *German Culture in America: Philosophical and Literary Influences 1600–1900* (Madison: University of Wisconsin Press, 1957). Despite their efforts, this chapter of America's literary history remains largely unknown to German readers, while Americans have all but forgotten the subject. Nonetheless, this matter deserves to be better known on both sides of the Atlantic. German-speakers ought to be interested in the influence their literature once exerted in America; the reasons for the phenomenon could still be significant today. American readers, on the other hand, might be astonished at what cosmopolitan predecessors they had in those nineteenth century New England intellectuals who, in many cases, never had to leave America to feel at home in Europe or the Orient. When these travellers visited Europe, they brought this culture home with them, or in some cases actually found it first on their back doorsteps, as Emerson wrote in his journal in 1848:

> How impossible to find Germany! Our young men went to the Rhine to find the genius which had charmed them, and it was not there. They hunted it in Heidelberg, in Göttingen, in Halle, in Berlin, (it escaped their pursuit; & then) no one knew where it was. From Vienna to the frontier, it was not found, and they very slowly & mournfully learned that in the speaking it had escaped, and as it had charmed them in Boston, they must return & look for it there. (*Journals*, 11:30–31)

Author and translator are greatly indebted to our editorial assistant, Dr. Karin Obermeier, who retrieved hundreds of quotations from original sources and contributed invaluably to this book. We also acknowledge most gratefully printing subsidies from the University of Massachusetts and Wellesley College.

In preparing this translation for print, the opportunity was taken to consult additional scholarly materials that were not available in 1989, when the original, German edition was published, and revisions were made accordingly.

S. B.
T. H.
August 1998

Works Frequently Cited

Chapter 1

Letters   Ralph L. Rusk, *The Letters of Ralph Waldo Emerson,* 6 vols. (New York: Columbia UP, 1939).

Journals   Ralph Waldo Emerson, *The Journals and Miscellaneous Notebooks,* ed. William H. Gilman, 6 vols. (Cambridge, MA: Harvard UP, 1960–1982).

The Dial   4 vols, (1840–1844).

Chapter 2

Memoirs   Margaret Fuller, *Memoirs of Margaret Fuller Ossoli,* 2 vols., eds. Ralph Waldo Emerson, W. H. Channing, John F. Clarke (Boston: Phillips, Sampson & Co., 1857).

Letters   *The Letters of Margaret Fuller,* 6 vols., ed. Robert N. Hudspeth (Ithaca & London: Cornell UP, 1983).

The Dial   *The Dial* (James Munroe: Boston, MA), 4 vols., quarterly (July 1840–April 1844).

Chapter 3

Journal   Henry David Thoreau, *Journal,* 4 vols., ed. John C. Broderick (Princeton: Princeton UP, 1981).

Chapter 4

Dahlstrand   Frederick C. Dahlstrand, *Amos Bronson Alcott: An Intellectual Biography* (Fairleigh Dickinson UP, 1982).

Chapter 5

Cheney   Louisa May Alcott, *Her Life, Letters and Journals,* ed. Ednah D. Cheney (Boston: Little, Brown & Co., 1928).

Moods   Louisa May Alcott, *Moods* (Boston: Loring, 1864).

Introduction

Transcendentalists and Reformers

IF MODERN EUROPE CAN BE CALLED A child of the eighteenth century, then modern America has to be the child of the nineteenth. It was during this century that the original thirteen states defended and strengthened their initially precarious independence, expanded their number to forty-four, and increased their population from five to seventy-six million inhabitants. Settlement pushed ever more rapidly westward as the continent was covered by a network of roads and rail lines where, at their junctions, homesteads sprang up into metropolises that spawned industry and jobs for the growing numbers of immigrants. As often as not, the tug of the West made these settlers leave and move farther on, for this was a people constantly in flux: from Europe to America; from the cities of the east coast onto the western plains; and from there across the Rockies toward the Pacific. Not even the oldest section of the country back East was spared this activity, change, and expansion. Yet, there were already places in America where the young nation was beginning to define its heritage, where people had roots going back two hundred years and had established institutions that had achieved political independence and were now wresting their cultural autonomy from Europe. The small circle of Ralph Waldo Emerson's Concord friends is a touchstone for this phenomenon.

The life span of this group's oldest member, Amos Bronson Alcott, stretched from the young republic under George Washington (who died a few short weeks after Alcott's birth in 1799), to the industrialized and technologically dominated America of the century's end. It was a century that witnessed the invention of the telephone and the electric chair and the era in which America's strength as a world power emerged.

Alcott and his contemporaries experienced the presidency of Thomas Jefferson and the increasing role of Washington, D.C., which replaced Philadelphia as capital city in 1801. He and his New England society were particularly stung by the hardship of Napoleon's maritime blockade against the British, which cost countless American ships. In 1810 alone France confiscated and sold 132 United States vessels and their cargoes, while England seized even more. Of these, many were from New England, a region that depended upon the sea, and hence experienced great economic difficulty. If some extreme voices had been heeded, the region would have been on the brink of leaving the Union. Hostilities with England between 1812 and 1814, which saw the burning of the Capitol and the White House, was seen as a second war of independence for the republic. America's war effort hardly had popular approval everywhere, and historical annals record anti-war demonstrations in New York. The Monroe Doctrine was to secure European non-intervention in America for the price of American non-intervention in Europe. The next military action of the United States was against Mexico (1846–1848), which resulted in vociferous opposition over the issue of slavery in those territories that the nation stood to win from the encounter. This struggle against the institution of slavery cast a long shadow over decades of the 19th century, leading eventually to the greatest trauma in American history. The Civil War (1861–1865) took a toll of 650,000 — a quarter of a million more lives than America would lose in World War II.

The members of the Concord circle were closely involved with the events that preceded the Civil War. William Lloyd Garrison had held the first speech in favor of emancipation in Boston's Park Street Church in 1829 and in 1833 founded the "Society Against Slavery." The Whig party was re-formed in the following year with an expressly anti-slavery program that opposed Andrew Jackson's presidency, whose powerful Democratic party drew so much of its strength from the southern states and the northern working class. When the Concord group showed any political sympathies — which not everyone did — then it was for the Whig Party.

The Fugitive Slave Law, which was passed in 1850 with the purpose of returning escaped slaves to their owners, entrenched the opposition even more. Concord became a center for this opposition and in 1859 even lent support to John Brown who was hanged after his raid on the military arsenal at Harper's Ferry, Virginia. Concord's citizens not only collected money for Brown, but also received him as an honored guest. After Brown's imprisonment Henry David Thoreau wrote his passionate "Defense of John Brown," which he read first to the people of Concord and then in Boston before the text was printed in newspapers throughout the land. It was reported of Alcott's wife, Abigail, that in her stove she had hidden a runaway slave on his way to Canada (England had abolished slavery in 1807). Incidents surrounding the issue became ever more violent. Senator Charles Sumner of Massachusetts was caned on the floor of the Senate by his congressional colleague from South Carolina; after the secession of this state, war was inevitable. Intellectuals in New England welcomed the conflict with an enthusiasm similar to that of so many German writers at the outbreak of World War I: they expected a catharsis and purification that they hoped would be a catalyst for national renewal.

Once the horrors of Civil War had reached unimaginable proportions and had cost thousands upon thousands of human lives (while simultaneously bringing unimaginable profits from the business side of the war machine), disenchantment spread among New Englanders. Not even Lincoln's Emancipation Proclamation in 1863, nor the thirteenth amendment that abolished slavery two years later, was able to change this feeling. The war had cost America its innocence, and after 1865 the nation would never again resemble the one that had existed before 1860.

In the North there began an industrial revolution with a vengeance. The new western states required railroad tracks, machinery, and textiles. In return they provided the large cities with food from their rich harvests. Exploitation and corruption, of course, went hand in hand with this expansion. Old New England, growing politically and economically weaker, became a region of sheltered enclaves of calm; of quiet college towns and idyllic settings like Concord where a new generation now reaped the fruits of its forebears and, building on those beginnings, brought American culture to its first blossoming of cosmopolitan proportions. That point was ultimately reached when the young Henry James reviewed the first novel of Alcott's daughter, Louisa May.

Who were these people who banded around Emerson and whose small circle was as candidly open to European intellectual currents as to the ancient wisdom of the Orient? Many, like Emerson himself, were trained ministers who had continued their education after Harvard College at the Harvard Divinity School. They had grown up in the Unitarian Church upon which they then turned their backs; some, like Emerson, even left the church officially.

This was an unfortunate development, for Unitarianism (which had its origins in England) had achieved a significant break from the Calvinist Congregationalists who dominated New England in the nineteenth century. Unitarianism, which can be traced to the fifteenth-century Anabaptists, denied the Trinity, preaching instead the doctrine of God in one person in whom Christ, simply the most perfect of men, has no part. In Boston William Ellery Channing, whom Emerson and his friends respected profoundly, gave this doctrine its liberal, ecumenical character. Unitarianism, however, was as an extremely rational religion which seemed to Emerson's generation to be an ice-cold fossil, empty of everything these young ministers sought from religion: spontaneous inspiration and suprasensual, transcendent wisdom — the "divine instincts of the soul." Their ideas displeased conservative theologians for whom the transcendental principle dangerously blurred the boundaries between this world and the next, between definitions of the human versus the divine principle. For them Pantheism, even heresy, lurked in this transcendental chaos.

And so it came to the bitter feud between the young generation of Unitarians and Andrews Norton, one of their most important mentors at the Harvard Divinity School. Norton was editor of *The Christian Examiner,* a journal that labelled them "unbelievers" and condemned everything they had learned from their private studies in European literature, philosophy, and theology. One of the ablest scholars of this period, Perry Miller, has termed the rebellion of the young Unitarians the first revolt of American youth against the philistinism of their fathers, claiming it embodied the greatest concentration of intellectual energy in America prior to the 1920s.

Emerson's closest friends were, for the most part, temporary residents of Concord and anything but theologians. Henry David Thoreau was a case in point, while Margaret Fuller (who as a woman could not yet study at Harvard) earned her living as a teacher, leader of discussion groups, writer, and journalist. Thoreau worked as a teacher and surveyor, though also employed in his family's pencil factory. Alcott was a pure autodidact who became the most renowned pedagogue of his day. Like-minded friends gathered around this small group. Among them were George Ripley, preacher and founder of the Brook Farm community, who had also left the Unitarian church; James Freeman Clarke and Theodore Parker, who remained ministers; and the Reverend Frederic Henry Hedge, who headed a congregation in Maine. Hedge travelled to Boston as often as possible to meet with friends and colleagues in gatherings known as "Hedge's Club," which soon became known as the Transcendental Club. The term derived from Kant's transcendental philosophy, the source of the Transcendentalists' beliefs. From Kant they learned that concepts such as man's idea of God, of the Soul, of immortality, were discernible not by experience, but rather are imparted by the divine instincts of the soul.

The Transcendental Club gave rise to the small but immensely influential journal, *The Dial.* Although this magazine was relatively short-lived (1840 to 1844), it remains one of the most significant American periodicals ever published. One needs to bear in mind that this generation of Americans born after the Revolution was living intellectually in a pre-revolutionary world. Many of the Harvard professors who taught them preached the empiricism of John Locke, which not only Calvinists, but also the modern Unitarians, had accepted. Still, the notion was anathema to the young generation that the human soul could be understood as a blank page registering ideas through sensual impressions, and that consciousness was thus capable of being enslaved by the senses. These thinkers believed in a reality that transcended the world of the senses; they affirmed the power of intuition and poetic imagination which, independent of sensations, could lead man to his full potential. A person experienced the divine not in dogma or in scripture, but first and foremost in nature — that source of greatest inspiration to the Transcendentalists.

The Transcendentalists mark the beginning of something completely different in American history. Their movement was an innovation that began in an age and a place receptive to the new. They saw themselves surrounded by people of all persuasions who desired change across the board. Emerson's report in *The Dial* on "The Chardon Street Bible Conventions" makes clear that one could learn from even the most eccentric of reformers, and that the desired innovations could only be democratic.

"The Friends of Universal Reform," as Emerson's group was called, held several meetings in the Chardon Street Chapel between 1840 and 1842. The public was invited to discuss traditional institutions such as the sabbath, the church, and the clergy. A wide range of believers from the strictest orthodox to the wildest heretics, including "many people whose church had only one member," came to these gatherings. The most different accents and the most varied costumes made an appearance. Even Emerson had to admit that some at the podium seemed a bit mad. Bearded men (wearing facial hair had at one time been outlawed in New England), Anabaptists, Quakers, abolitionists, Calvinists, Unitarians, and philosophers (including some of the country's best minds), women who could measure up to any standard, "including that flea of Conventions, Mrs. Abigail Folsom" — all spoke their minds here. "If there was not parliamentary order," Emerson reported, "there was life, and the assurance of that constitutional love for religion and religious liberty, which in all periods characterizes the inhabitants of this part of America."[1]

The New England desire for reform was not limited to religion. The dawn of this "Age of Newness" featured innovations from all quarters. The most important debates were certainly those concerning the abolition of slavery, the improvement of public education, coupled with hints of women's liberation. All were freedom movements of the most extraordinary sort, and Boston was their center. That city was the site of the first anti-slavery speeches and where the radical feminist Frances Wright also made public appearances. Josiah Holbrook founded the phenomenally successful Lyceum movement which sent public figures of Emerson's stature on speaking circuits to the smallest of rural villages. William Ladd, founder of "The American Peace Society," found his first supporters here; Orestes A. Brownson's journal, the *Boston Quarterly Review*, printed the headstrong notions of a Christian worker's movement.

Whenever possible, these reformers allied themselves with likeminded European contemporaries, or were themselves conduits of European thought. Brownson, for example, owes much to Victor Cousin. Among the European discoveries that quickly spread through New England were Mesmerism (predecessor of hypnosis therapy); phrenology (which deduced character from the examination of skull structure), developed by Franz Joseph Gall and Johann Kaspar Spurzheim who even lectured on his method in Boston. Healthful clothing, vegetarianism, Sylvester Graham's health crackers, as well as the cold water cure imported from Silesia by Vincenz Priessnitz — all were taken seriously in New England in this age of reform.

The Transcendentalists showed keen interest in all these fads. Margaret Fuller had a streak of psychic power and enjoyed taking part in an evening of mesmeric experiments. Alcott was a radical vegetarian and adherent of the cold water cure. Thoreau surely stands for what New Englanders meant by "plain living and high thinking." In this he represented an ideal for which only the poorest Transcendentalists strove, while many considered it theoretically desirable to be free of the burdens of property. The story is told about one of Emerson's ancestors who prayed to God every night that none of his descendants might ever become wealthy.

Emerson, who was by no means rich, was one of the most prosperous of the Concord circle. He knew well that poverty did not further the goals of Transcendentalism. A living example of this principle was his friend Bronson Alcott to whom he continually gave financial support. For Emerson property was always a moral category, in contrast to the doctrines of Saint-Simon, who had New England adherents to his famous definition of property as theft. Property — but not to excess — was the classical golden mean that expressed Emerson's spirit of compromise.

The fact that eccentrics such as Alcott and Thoreau were Transcendentalists shows the level of tolerance in this circle. No one was able to find a common denominator for the highly individual styles of this group; thus the concept of "transcendental" soon became a synonym for "mad," and Alcott's "Orphic Sayings," which were published in *The Dial*, were to provide material for countless parodies. The Transcendentalists bore with dignity this considerable derision to which they were exposed.

For all the confusion surrounding the general term "transcendental," there are enough common traits to help explain how the term gained ground. One of these is the interest that adherents shared for German literature and philosophy. German letters influenced each differently, but was in no case the only factor shaping one's Transcendentalism. For a period of several years German texts were pivotal in the development of Emerson's and Fuller's thinking and writing. Fuller ultimately did most to mediate German literature to American readers. Thoreau's contact with Goethe was brief, yet consequential; Alcott — the only one in the Concord group who knew no German — was repeatedly inspired by translations of German literature. The ministers James Freeman Clarke, Frederic Henry Hedge, Theodore Parker, and George Ripley made considerable contributions to the dissemination of German literature in journals such as *The Dial*, or Parker's *Western Messenger*, or in anthologies and translation series like *Specimens of Modern Foreign Literature*.

In the grand scheme of things, it must be said that ultimately only a few members of the Concord circle worked toward the goals of spreading German literature in America — and then but for a short time. In many cases the selection of German literature to which they had access was limited. While sheer quantity was less important, Goethe was always the principal figure in the whole spectrum. The fact that *The Dial* was printed in runs of only 900 is less significant than the individuals who were actually reading these 900 copies. These readers were the people who infused ideas with the power to influence American thought into the next century. Octavius Brooks Frothingham, author of the first account of Transcendentalism in New England, was struck by the extent to which the influence of the movement encouraged thinkers to accept new ideas, politicians to revise their thoughts, moralists to change their direction, and philanthropists and reformers to gain inspiration. The struggle against slavery and the death penalty, support for women's rights and for social reform — all can trace their origins back to Transcendentalism, which placed individuals over organizations and humanity over human institutions. Referring to Transcendentalism, Bronson Alcott declared that he heard the call: "the trump of reform is sounding throughout the world for a revolution of all human affairs."[2] It is a trumpet that resounds strongly in the writings of the Transcendentalists. To understand better their writings and thoughts we need to know the contribution of German letters to this very significant part of American culture.

General Background Literature

Boller, Paul F., Jr. *American Transcendentalism 1830–1860: An Intellectual Inquiry*. New York: Putnam, 1974.

Frothingham, Octavius Brooks. *Transcendentalism in New England: A History*. New York: Putnam's, 1876.

Hochfield, George, ed. *Selected Writings of The American Transcendentalists*. New York: New American Library, 1966.

Howe, Irving. *The American Newness: Culture and Politics in the Age of Emerson.* Cambridge, MA: Harvard UP, 1986.

Miller, Perry. *The Transcendentalists: An Anthology.* Cambridge, MA: Harvard UP, 1950.

Shi, David E. *The Simple Life: Plain Living and High Thinking in American Culture.* New York: Oxford UP, 1985.

Notes

[1] "Chardon Street and Bible Conventions," *The Dial,* 3:101.

[2] *The Dial,* 1:351.

Ralph Waldo Emerson
Courtesy of Concord Free Public Library

1: The Sage: Ralph Waldo Emerson

THE THIRTY-ONE YEAR OLD RALPH WALDO EMERSON had passed through two major stages of his life before he moved to Concord in 1834. He had first enjoyed a New England youth that had been improved by the best education the country had to offer; and, second, he had had a short career in the Unitarian church. This stint in the ministry ended when he stepped down from his Boston pulpit a short time after the death of his first wife. The second period ended after his nine-month long European trip, from which he returned infused with the ambition to prepare America's way for cultural independence, a path he outlined in his own publications and lectures.

Like generations before him, Emerson had a European education on New England soil. He was born on May 25, 1803, in Boston, the fourth child of William Emerson. His father, although poor, had an affinity for the arts, literature, and philosophy; his appointment to the parish of the First Congregational Church at last improved the family's economic circumstances. William Emerson wore himself out in the service of his church and city. Boston, with its population of 30,000, was a prosperous town with a developing cultural life for which he labored tirelessly, dying in 1811. One year later Ralph Waldo entered the Boston Public Latin School, the institution where he received his comprehensive humanistic education. It is said that he entered school as early as 1805; at least it is known that by his third birthday he could read, if not yet very well. The school calendar was punctuated by long summer visits to Concord in the home of his grandfather Emerson, who was the sixth generation of the family to be pastor in that town. The first pastor, Peter Bulkeley Emerson, had come to Concord from England in 1635. After the death of her husband William, Ralph Waldo's mother took in boarders at the family's various addresses in order to feed the four of her six children that had survived beyond birth. Emerson was later in life to recall religion and poverty as the most important influences on his youth.

He might have named books as the next most important influence, for the Emersons were certainly great readers. William had been one of the founders of Boston's first literary magazine, *The Monthly Anthology*, and later, of the "The Anthological Society," a lending library with reading room, exhibition hall, and laboratory. Among those volumes the Emerson family borrowed from the Boston Library Society were works of Tacitus,

Cicero, Shakespeare, Chateaubriand, and — for the first time — a German author, Klopstock.[1] The German language was at the time still a rare commodity in New England. Harvard College (where Emerson entered as a student in 1817) did not teach the language until eight years later when Charles Follen offered the first small class of German students. By then Emerson was no longer an undergraduate but well into his divinity school studies.

Among Emerson's professors at Harvard were Edward Everett and George Ticknor, the first of the young American scholars who had studied in Europe. Emerson took a course with Ticknor on French literature from 1515–1788. Philosophy, as it was presented to Harvard students in this period, was dominated by followers of the Edinburgh school: the Materialists Thomas Reid and Dugald Stewart with their critiques of Rousseau, Goethe, and the "German sentimentalists" (by which they meant the Romantics).

It was typical for poor students of this period to earn their bread as school teachers, either by interrupting their college study for a year, or taking up such duties after graduation. Emerson's older brother William opened a school for young ladies in Boston in which Waldo (as he called himself after 1821) also taught once he graduated from college. After three years, William had saved enough money to travel to Göttingen, the Mecca of Protestant theology where Johann Gottfried Eichhorn was articulating the newest methods of historical bible criticism. William's German sojourn signalled a new epoch in Ralph Waldo's life as well. The older brother reported back promptly on details of German university life. He was understandably appalled by the bored, drinking, duelling German students; he also labelled the lecture system a "great error." But he considered such particulars superficial and pressed his younger brother to learn German, to read everything by Herder, and to come to Germany. In September 1824 William set off on a hiking tour to Dresden, taking a detour to the small town of Weimar in order to pay a visit to the "great sage." His hope of an audience was fulfilled and the two documents that record the meeting of the young American student with Goethe are especially interesting. Reaching Waldo first-hand, they influenced his image of Goethe well before he encountered Goethe's works.

The first of these manuscripts, now among the William Emerson papers, is entitled *Journal of a Tour from Göttingen to Dresden 1824* and contains the following description of William's visit with Goethe:

> I knew that he was very seldom visible to strangers, but resolved to hazard the attempt. We arrived in the pleasant town of Weimar at noon, and I immediately repaired to his house, and sent up my card, on which I had previously added "Boston, N. America" to my name. He sent me word

that he was then surrounded with company, but if I would call at 4, he would see me. It may be supposed, that I did not forget the appointment. I was shown into a room, that was filled with works of art. A huge bust of Minerva was placed over one of the doors. A large case with books, which from their great size, must have been drawings, stood in one corner. Göthe, the gentle and venerable poet, entered almost immediately. I was so struck with the difference between him who came into the room, and the formidable portrait that is commonly to be seen of this great man, that I almost expected to see another person behind him. His address and manner were perfectly simple and unconstrained. After finding out my profession, he led the conversation immediately upon the state of religion in the U.S. and afterwards upon the state and hopes of our country in general. His tone became gradually that of an instructor, and yet it ceased not to be unassuming, but all was uttered quietly, as a mere private opinion. He said he thought we had nothing to do with the different systems of philosophy, but that the highest aim of life should be for each one to accommodate himself as perfectly as possible to the station in which he was placed. He asked many questions, and talked willingly, yet seemed not loath to be interrupted. The only thing that was American in my possession, a number of the Palladium, I ventured to offer him, as our papers are a great curiosity in Germany. He accepted the trifle very graciously, and said it was 2 years since he had seen one. He shook me kindly by the hand when I took leave. I left Weimar immediately, but I shall not hastily forget this exceedingly interesting visit. He was of the common size, with pleasing but not striking features; his dress was a blue surtout, over a white vest. I should not have judged him to be more than 65, yet he is said to be about 10 years older. (*Letters,* 1:161)

So much for William Emerson's official report. What he did not reveal here — but did tell his younger brother — was the very personal question he had asked Goethe, and the answer he had received. William's faith, it seems, had been shaken in Göttingen by his critical study of the bible, and in his dilemma of skepticism he sought advice from Goethe whether to disappoint his family and give up his profession as a minister. Without hesitation Goethe advised him to preach what the people wanted to hear, saying that the minister's personal beliefs were none of their business. It would be possible, advised Goethe, for William to be both a good preacher and minister without anyone being the wiser about his private views.[2]

Goethe himself — without imagining the consequences his remarks would have on the young American — entered the following dry note in his journal on September 19, 1824: "Will. Emerson from Boston, North America, studying in Göttingen, Protestant theology. I stayed by myself."[3] In the following year the young divinity student was to return to Boston. During a storm on the high sea it became clear to him that he could "never go to the bottom" as long as he intended to follow Goethe's advice. He decided instead to take up law and became a successful attorney in New York where, over the years, he delivered many public lectures on German literature.

When William returned from Europe, his younger brother Waldo (who had just entered Harvard Divinity School) was forced to interrupt his studies due to a weakness of his eyes. Waldo took a post in the nearby village of Chelmsford where he taught school and lived among strict Calvinist farmers. After years of further study, which were also interrupted by ill health and more teaching, he was finally permitted to preach after delivering a sermon on the subject "The Duty of Men to Judge Men only by their Actions."

Waldo must have listened to William's report of his visit with the esteemed German poet with considerable misgivings but nonetheless did borrow Carlyle's translation of *Wilhelm Meister's Apprenticeship* from the Harvard library before travelling to the mountains of New Hampshire. There the book probably lay unread in his suitcase, or at least that is how it sounds from a letter to his brother Charles (*Letters,* 1:254). In 1828, when Emerson was still a newly licensed minister, he borrowed Schiller's *History of the Thirty Years War* as well as Goethe's *Memoirs* from the Boston Library Society; but he continued to show little interest in German letters.[4] In the same year he joked with Frederic Henry Hedge, the Harvard divinity professor who was trying to interest Waldo in German literature, that such a task was probably not worth the effort, reasoning that since he "was entirely ignorant of the subject, he should assume that it was not worth knowing."[5]

What was it that finally led the same Waldo Emerson, after six years of self-study of German, to record in his journal the great joy that grips someone learning a new language? One senses his motivation at the moment when he could suddenly read without the aid of a dictionary. Then "he shuts up his book with that sort of fearful delight with which the bridegroom sits down in his own house with the bride, saying 'I shall now live with you always'" (*Journals,* 4:358).

Carlyle's influence is surely the fundamental cause for this *volte-face*. This Scottish writer and translator was the single most powerful individual driving the dissemination and mediation of literatures across national borders. Carlyle's power resonated far beyond the British Isles, infiltrating the whole English-speaking world and, in translation, even back to Germany and the rest of Europe. Richard Wagner counted himself among the most faithful readers of Carlyle whose essays on German literature he knew well.[6] On the other hand, the prominence of such a mediator can sometimes bring disadvantages. Emerson's curiosity about Novalis, for example, was entirely satisfied by Carlyle's essay on the poet. He took all his Novalis quotations from Carlyle's text and never found it necessary to read the original. Carlyle's authority is even more significant for his choice of those important German authors he discussed and translated in his essays. The New Englanders' enthusiasm for Jean Paul, for example, can be traced to Carlyle. Emerson did not share this taste but did love Carlyle's *Sartor Resartus,* a novel very much conceived in the playful spirit and style of Jean Paul. *Sartor* was a grandiose satire of all that the English taste of 1830 found Germanic: of German poets and thinkers, of German life and manners, and of the labyrinthine syntax of the German language. At the center of the novel is Carlyle's invented protagonist, Diogenes Teufelsdröckh, Professor of Allerley-Wissenschaft ("Omnium scientium") at the University of Weissnichtwo ("Know-not-where"). Carlyle adopts the persona of biographer, translator and editor burdened with the superhuman task of making sense of the life and work of the great clothing-philosopher by excerpting Teufelsdröckh's *magnum opus,* "Die Kleider, ihr Werden und Wirken" ("Clothes, their Origin and Influence" von Diog. Teufelsdröckh, J. U. D.etc. Stillschweigen und Co., Weissnichtwo: 1831). He has to work with a dizzying array of material that includes the pronouncements of a certain Privy Councillor Heuschrecke ("Grasshopper"), as well as Teufelsdröckh's own posthumous papers stored in twelve paper bags labelled with the signs of the zodiac.

The "Tailor Re-patched" gives Carlyle the opportunity to parody all things German. Teufelsdröckh has laughed only once in his life, and that was at a remark by Jean Paul; predictably, he loved but once, and then unluckily. In the one kiss that he has pressed upon the lips of his Blumine one cannot help but hear an unmistakable echo of young Werther. This scholar, who has apparently read every book and visited every country, is presented as a "speculative radical" who ranges in his treatise on clothing from discussions of fig leaves to the highest transcendental heights. He describes man as "handthierendes Tier," a two-legged animal in trousers who is simultaneously a divine figure whose thoughts wear the clothes of language. Countless phenomena — names, customs, religion, symbols, even the pure forms of sense perception as defined by Kant in time and space — are covered under the aspect of clothing.

Yet, *Sartor Resartus* is a far cry from being just a grand joke. Every page of the work proclaims Carlyle's literary and cultural message, especially his reverence for Goethe. "Close your Byron and open your Goethe," he admonishes his readers in Teufelsdröckh's name while condemning the monster of utilitarianism and the false prophets of the empty religions of the age.

These opinions found an enthusiastic readership among New Englanders. Americans were less intimidated than amused by the marvelous Germanisms and linguistic acrobatics with which Carlyle peppered his Teutonically meandering English sentences. It is revealing that the first book edition of *Sartor* was issued in Boston in 1835/1836 after first installments of the work appeared in England in *Fraser's Magazine*. Emerson provided the book's short, anonymously written introduction, although he wrote to Carlyle on March 12, 1835 somewhat less enthusiastically than the numerous lovers of Teufelsdröckh: "I am an icicle to them."[7] Emerson could never warm to the exotic style of this prose, just as he never developed an affinity for the extravagant language of Jean Paul. "I am glad that one living scholar is self-centered & will be true to himself though none ever were before; And 'tis good to have a new eye inspect our mouldy social forms, our politics, & schools, & religion. I delight in the contents," he told Carlyle on May 14, 1834, but confessed that his "defective apprehension for a joke" prevented him from appreciating the form.[8] By September 1836 the first edition of *Sartor Resartus* was sold out and followed by a second the next March; orders even came in from England. Some Americans thought the whole thing true and showed the same preference for German Romantic rapture (even as parody) that they later would endorse in the works of Bettina von Arnim.

Thomas Carlyle was initially an enigmatic and fairly obscure figure. His essays on the life of Schiller, on Jean Paul Friedrich Richter, the state of German literature, Goethe's Helen, and the German dramatists appeared anonymously between 1823 and 1832 in English journals like *The Foreign Quarterly Review*, *London Magazine*, and the *Edinburgh Review*. Young American readers were fascinated with these accounts by Carlyle, which were their first overwhelming encounter with German Romantic literature. In his journal in 1832 Emerson calls Carlyle "my Germanick new-light writer whoever he be" and waxes enthusiastic about his writings (*Journals*, 4:45). Soon thereafter Emerson discovered the identity of the author and, by the time he set off for Europe at the end of the year, was determined to pay Carlyle a visit at Craigenputtock. Their encounter took place in August 1833 before his return home. Emerson wrote to Carlyle the following year at the start of their lifelong friendship and correspondence:

> Drawn by strong regard to one of my teachers I went to see his person &
> as he might say his environment at Craigenputtock. Yet it was to fulfil my
> duty, to finish my mission, not with much hope of gratifying him; in the
> Spirit of "If I love you what is that to you?"[9]

The guiding and calming influence Carlyle exerted on the New England hotspur who was eight years his junior can best be measured by their thoughtful exchanges about Goethe. Carlyle was an unequivocal disciple of Goethe, whom he considered the sage of the century. Emerson, however, took an extremely critical stance against Goethe:

> Far far better seems to me the unpopularity of this Philosophical Poem (shall I call it?) than the adulation that followed your eminent friend Goethe. With him I am becoming better acquainted, but mine must be a qualified admiration. It is a singular piece of good nature in you to apotheosize him. I cannot but regard it as his misfortune with conspicuous bad influence on his genius, — that velvet life he led. What incongruity for genius whose fit ornaments & reliefs are poverty & hatred, to repose fifty years in chairs of state; & what pity that his Duke did not cut off his head to save him from the mean end (forgive) of retiring from the municipal incense "to arrange tastefully his gifts & medals." Then the Puritan in me accepts no apology for bad morals in such as *he*. We can tolerate vice in a splendid nature whilst that nature is battling with the brute majority in defence of some human principle. The sympathy his manhood & his misfortunes call out, adopts even his faults, but genius pampered — acknowledged — crowned — can only retain our sympathy by turning the same force once expended against outward enemies, now against inward, [. . .]. Failing this, it loses its nature & becomes talent, according to the definition — more skill in attaining the vulgar ends.[10]

Carlyle's response was empathetic and conciliatory. He considered Emerson's objections natural, yet it seemed nonetheless only wise for him to learn German for the main purpose of studying Goethe: "his is the only *healthy* mind, of any extent, that I have discovered in Europe for long generations." Emerson was familiar only with Goethe's pagan aspect, but Carlyle assured him that over time he would come to know the man's Christian side. Carlyle advised him to read *Wilhelm Meisters Wanderjahre* and then to decide whether it had been written by a "Parasite or a Prophet."[11]

Emerson followed Carlyle's advice and began his studies by reading works in the language. In September 1836 he reported his great interest in reading the volumes of Goethe's posthumously published works. On the other hand, he could not conceal a hint of *Schadenfreude* when, in 1839, he read Carlyle's *Onyx Ring* and found in this *roman à clef* a deprecation of "the Olympian lover of Frederica, Lili, etc."[12]

For years Emerson tried to persuade Carlyle to visit America. He told him of the innate literary taste of the Bostonians and assured him that the biographer of Schiller, the personal friend of Goethe and honorable Teufelsdröckh himself, would be most welcome. He suggested cities for a potential lecture tour, honoraria, travel expenses. But despite the valuable services Emerson performed in assisting the American publication of many of his works, Carlyle never crossed the Atlantic; Emerson saw him again, however, on his second European trip in 1848. It was probably better this way. Reading the two men's later correspondence — particularly during the Civil War — one hears Emerson's pleas for help to his European friend and supposed savior. Probably at this late date no fruitful encounter could have taken place, for Carlyle had little comprehension of the agony of the young democracy's struggle to free itself from slavery.

Emerson's awareness of German literature can be traced to Carlyle's essays published at the time of his first European trip. Although he did not visit Germany, the sojourn on foreign soil was of particular significance for his relationship to Goethe. After Goethe's death Germany no longer interested him, he claimed,[13] whereas the actual reason for his avoiding German soil was more likely his ignorance of the language. Whereas Emerson could speak Italian and French, he only had a reading knowledge of German; furthermore, his lack of personal ties in Germany may have been a factor.

Still, Emerson was carrying Goethe's Wilhelm Meister's Apprenticeship and Italian Journey in his luggage when he disembarked in Malta on February 3, 1833. In his journal he entered a sentence by Bossuet: "Tout commence." The crossing had been without incident. The captain of the American ship had constantly stressed American superiority on the seas, telling the story of some Sicilians who sailed to America to sell their fruit, but had taken 120 days for the crossing. Even Goethe had sailed in an American craft when he crossed to Sicily: "a ship elegantly and finely built in America, good under sail." He also praised her layout inside which was "fit with spruce little cabins and individual bunks."[14] Emerson's Italian journey led in the opposite direction from Goethe's. He proceeded via Naples to Rome, Florence, and Milan before reaching Paris on July 4th, and London at the end of that month. His visit to Carlyle took place in September before embarking for the return to America on the 17th of that month.

The twenty-nine year old New England minister must have felt some envy when he read the travel description of his predecessor, who fifty years earlier had approached Italy from the North. While the young courtier from Weimar had travelled with companions and come equipped with introductions to the most eminent families, Emerson's trip was, by contrast, quite a lonely one. He seldom visited people privately and even when he did, such visits at the residences of American consuls had a semi-official character. During his sojourn in Paris he complained to his diary that he seldom spoke to people, and were it not for seeing Carlyle, he would leave for home without conversing with anybody but the American painter

Christopher Cranch and the English poet Walter Savage Landor who lived near Rome. A poem written in his journal on the first anniversary of Goethe's death (March 22, 1833) begins with the words "Alone in Rome!"

Following in Goethe's footsteps, Emerson took in Italy's tourist attractions. He visited the Benedictine church in Catania with its famous organ and Museum of Prince Biscari where the prince himself had been Goethe's guide through the coin collection. He saw the public gardens of Palermo (according to Goethe, "the most wonderful spot on earth").[15] Emerson's response to the Monte Reale in the vicinity of the city was: "the world has not many more beautiful landscapes" (*Journals*, 4:140). These are timeless impressions typical of visitors to these spots. Almost fifty years to the day when Goethe climbed Vesuvius, Emerson made the ascent, noting the event with a factual entry in his journal. Goethe, on the other hand, had penned a dramatic account of how he assailed the crater through two rockfalls.

Goethe and Emerson each reacted very differently to life in Italy. Goethe threw himself among the people as into a refreshing bath: "To pass through such numberless crowds and restlessly moving people is strange and therapeutic," he wrote of Naples. "The more the streets roar with people, the more relaxed I become."[16] By contrast, Emerson expected solitude among the ruins, but was constantly being accosted by boys, beggars, and coachmen. In the evenings he stayed in his room in the "Croce di Malta" and read Goethe's *Italian Journey* only to be struck by the stark contrast to his own impressions of Italy:

> Goethe says "he shall never again be wholly unhappy, for he has seen Naples." If he has said "happy," there would have been equal reason. You cannot go five yards in any direction without seeing saddest objects & hearing the most piteous wailings. Instead of the gayest of cities, you seem to walk in the wards of a hospital. [. . .] Whilst you eat your dinner at a Trattoria, a beggar stands at the window, watching every mouthful.
>
> (*Journals*, 4:145)[17]

The contrast between Naples and the prosperity of Boston (which had little poverty at that time) must have been staggering.

By the time Emerson visited Rome during Holy Week of 1833, however, he grasped something that he was to realize again and again through his later years: despite any reservations toward Goethe, and despite all his criticisms of the man, there was a sense of close affinity to an intellect he felt he resembled. Emerson's journal entries are normally fairly sober and objective, but when he left the evening service at Saint Peter's Cathedral to observe the moonlight on the piazza, the church, and the magnificent fountain, he was thoroughly enchanted. His response was to confirm Goethe's remark of February 2, 1787: "No one who has not seen the

sight can conceive of the beauty of walking through Rome by the light of
the full moon. [. . .] Here sun and moon — like the human mind —
have a thoroughly different purpose."[18] On the other hand, Emerson
found the coliseum by moonlight terrifying where Goethe had declared it
"an exquisitely beautiful sight."[19] The Eastertide festivities at Saint Peter's
made Emerson "very melancholy to see an illumination in this declining
church & impoverished country" (*Journals*, 4:157). Goethe, on the other
hand, had seen the same spectacle on the feast of Saints Peter and Paul as
a "gigantic fairy-tale."[20] Both men climbed the "copper ball," as Emerson
called the cupola of Saint Peter's; Goethe had termed it a "copper knob."
They each enjoyed the view of the city and landscape, as well as the view
down into the interior of the church.

Michelangelo was to leave the most lasting impression upon Emerson.
The head of the *Justitia* (Justice) on the monument to Pope Paul III to
the left of the Tribuna in St. Peter's caused him to cry out, "There is a
heaven" (*Journals*, 4:160). Of the Sistine Chapel Goethe wrote "in that
moment [I was] so overpowered by Michelangelo that not even nature
was pleasing to me because I cannot see her with eyes as big as his."[21] Emerson was all but overpowered by Michelangelo's "Moses": "so violent a
type suits not us western Puritans" (*Letters*, 1:379). Emerson seems to
have been trying to trace Goethe's footsteps. He wrote, for example, to
his brother Charles: "Goethe says in a letter from Rome that a man's existence is enlarged is doubled by having seen the head of Medusa, an an-
tique marble in the Rondanini Palace. I am sorry that I must remain only
half myself, for I am told I cannot see that work, but he truly speaks of the
sights of Rome" (*Letters*, 1:373).[22]

Both pilgrims to the holy city had the identical reaction to the services
in Saint Peter's where they were eager visitors. Emerson witnessed Pope
Gregory XVI with twenty-one cardinals bless the palms on Palm Sunday
and saw the pope wash the feet of thirteen pilgrims on Maundy Thursday.
Still, he found Catholic pomp commonplace and complained that the
church had not invented ceremonies that were as good and manly in their
taste as her buildings, art, and music. But he primarily regretted that the
pope was not able to interrupt the prescribed rituals for a moment to
speak from his own heart. Here he echoed Goethe who had been seized
by the longing, "that the head of the Church might open his golden
mouth and, speaking ecstatically of the inexpressible salvation of the
blessed souls, move us to ecstasy." Goethe stated his reason for disliking
the mumbling pope who acted like a common priest: "the familiar Protestant original sin."[23] The sentiment flared up in Emerson as well.

Goethe remained Emerson's companion on the journey northward.
Florence, with its industrious citizens, was clean and spacious and free of

beggars. The city produced in him such a feeling of contentment that he rented a room for a month. In the evenings the landlady would bring him a lamp, ask the question "'Comanda niente Signore?' [. . .] & leave [him] to Goethe & Sismondi" (*Journals,* 4:178). In the town he felt intoxicated with beauty. He had no concept of painting before this time, but the works of Michelangelo sent chills up his spine. He attended the opera where the performance of Bellini's *La Straniera* was so tasteful and dazzling that, as he reported, he was "obliged to rest [his eyes] & look at [his] shoes for half an hour, that [he] might keep them for the last act." The ballet in the entre-actes called upon his reserve of Puritan rejection. After so many weeks of Italy and so much reading of Goethe he was conscience-stricken by the spectacle:

> Goethe laughs at those who force every work of art into the narrow circle of their own prejudices & cannot admire a picture as a picture & a tune as a tune. So I was willing to look at this as a ballet, & to see that it was admirable, but I could not help feeling the while that it were better for mankind if there were no such dancers. (*Journals,* 4:171)

And, as if to soothe his conscience completely, he adds the afterthought: "I have since learned God's decision on the same, in the fact that all the *ballerine* are nearly ideotic" *[sic]*.[24]

Emerson visited Venice, approaching the city by land and being reminded of a vista of New York. He found Venice very uncomfortable, a place fit mainly for beavers because it isolated people, had no large squares for assemblies (except in front of Saint Mark's), and no reading rooms with newspapers. He left Italy by way of Padua, Verona, and Milan.

His Italian journey differed from Goethe's in many ways. To begin with, it was much shorter. Goethe, by contrast, had spent two months in Naples and climbed Vesuvius three times; Emerson, however, stayed there two weeks and made it up the mountain once. As a result, Goethe's accounts of Italy are more far-ranging and enthusiastic than Emerson's who observed the social conditions in the country with a more critical eye. In Naples Goethe noted: "Everything suggests that a happy country that richly offers all the basic necessities also produces people with a happy disposition, who can casually expect that the next day will bring what today brought, and thus live carefree lives."[25] Emerson could never have written such words. Nonetheless, the two travellers resemble each other in their tireless thirst for knowledge about art, nature and technology. During his crossing to Sicily Goethe gathered information on water color painting; on his own ocean crossing Emerson learned about astronomy and navigation. For each, their Italian trips were the most formative journeys of their lives.

Goethe's travel journal was more than just Emerson's *Baedeker;* it was a document that made a crucial contribution to his aesthetic education. After purchasing the Cotta edition of Goethe's works in the summer 1836 (the *Ausgabe letzter Hand*), Emerson reread the *Italian Journey* and filled the text with his annotations. We therefore know directly from Emerson what he found noteworthy in the *Italian Journey*. But this is not to say that Emerson's complete dependence on Goethe is established by his reading, for he also showed considerable independent spirit as a traveller in Italy.[26] His admiration of Michelangelo, which was even more profound than Goethe's, would have been awakened without knowledge of the *Italian Journey*. He ultimately came to see Michelangelo as Goethe's opposite pole, namely the artist characterized by suffering.

Goethe influenced Emerson less on *what* he should see, than on *how* he should devote himself to the observation of humanity, nature, and art. Goethe's aptitude for selecting objects and focussing attention on them (a trait that was to have lasting influence on Thoreau), was highly significant for Emerson. He admired Goethe's "favorite task," as he put it, of finding a unified theory to explain the basis for all observable phenomena:

> Witness his explanation of the Italian mode of reckoning the hours of the day, as growing out of the Italian climate; [. . .] of the Venetian music of the gondolier originating in the habit of the fisher's wives of the Lido singing to their husbands on the sea; of the Amphitheatre, which is the enclosure of the natural cup of heads that arranges itself around every spectacle in the street.[27]

The second realization that Emerson derived from the *Italian Journey,* was Goethe's revelation of natural forms in art. This led Emerson to a new order of perception, as a notebook entry from 1832 reveals: "And so is our eye thro' works of art gradually so tuned that we become ever more eager for the presence of Nature & more susceptible of the beauties which she offers us" (*Journals*, 6:214). Emerson certainly shared with Goethe a primary reason for visiting Italy, namely to study the sculpture and architecture. Italy's art treasures beckoned to both men thanks to the emphasis placed by their classical educations on ancient languages, mythology, and Roman history. Emerson even translated Goethe's description of the aqueduct at Spoleto in which he found architecture described as "a second nature.[28] Emerson was stimulated by such passages in the *Italian Journey* where Goethe observed beauty resulting from necessity, or where he described works of art that, like organic entities, seemed to take on form as if in accordance with laws of nature. Emerson flagged passages in the *Italian Journey* that mention the concept of the *Urpflanze,* that principle of the "One and All," according to which the single leaf contains the possibility of the whole plant and of all plants. He also copied out and translated such passages. When he was leaving Italy, Emerson again ran across a related idea of Goethe's, which at the beginning of his own Italian journey speaks of the lack of new forms in architecture in general. The Christian churches cling to the basilica form, Goethe had noted, despite the fact that "the temple form would be more advantageous for holding religious services; institutions dedicated to science still had a monastic appearance."[29] When viewing the Duomo in Milan, Emerson experienced all architecture as imitation. The comparison applied to American churches as well as European, the latter simply being more opulent. Neither one could provide the sensation he required: rapture (*Journals*, 4:75).

Architecture, Emerson furthermore declared, existed only in the soul; therefore, he said he wished to learn nothing more than the metaphysics of architecture. From here it was but a short step to a question he found posed in the *Italian Journey*, namely whether or not all art had its roots in nature and derived its "organic property" from this source. His collection of translated Goethe quotations made in 1836 contains several statements from the "Zweiter Römischer Aufenthalt" (Second Roman Sojourn) that led Emerson to develop his own idea of a "natural," "inner," "organic," form in art and poetry. Goethe had written: "these greatest works of art resemble the highest works of nature; [. . .] where there is necessity, there is God."[30] Goethe's note about his discovery of the phenomenon "All in One" in botany — the idea of the *Urpflanze* — Emerson applied to art. He also translated the essay Karl Philipp Moritz wrote while travelling with Goethe in Sicily ("Über die bildende Nachahmung des Schönen," [On the artistic representation of beauty]) and quotes from this later in his own essay on Michelangelo. Occupied with these aesthetic ideas, Emerson left Italy over the Simplon Pass on June 12, 1833, stopped in Ferney to pay his respects to the memory of Voltaire, "the king of scorners," and then made his way to Paris (*Journals*, 4:194).

In Paris the idea of "All in One" did not loosen its grip on him. Visiting the *Jardin des Plantes* he found no form that did not relate in some way to the observing man. "I feel the centipede in me — cayman, carp, eagle, & fox. I am moved by strange sympathies." And he promises himself continually, "I will be a naturalist" (*Journals*, 4:200).

A stay in England and Scotland rounded off Emerson's first European trip. In Britain he twice came into contact with Goethe again, albeit indirectly. The most pleasant of these encounters was in Craigenputtock at the home of the Carlyles where letters and gifts from Weimar were proudly on display. At the time of his visit, distress unfortunately prevailed in the household. Carlyle's essays and Goethe translations were selling poorly, which was a disappointment that made visiting Weimar financially impossible.

What a contrast was Emerson's visit to the sixty-three year old Wordsworth at Ambleside. Emerson had to listen to the aged poet in his dark glasses heap disdain upon *Wilhelm Meister*. Wordsworth found the book filled with such indecency of all description that "it was like flies crossing each other in the air." Wordsworth admitted that he had never gotten beyond the first book before finally throwing it across the room. "I spoke *for* the better parts of the book," Emerson noted in his journal (appropriately on August 28th, Goethe's birthday), "& he promised to look at it again" (*Journals*, 4:223).

On the third trip to England Emerson paid a visit to Samuel Taylor Coleridge, seeking out the sixty-one year old poet in London. Coleridge, whose sensually expressive poetry intrigued Emerson, was the translator of Schiller's plays *The Piccolomini* and *Wallenstein*, but when critics rejected these English versions, the unbound pages were sold as scrap paper. More important was Coleridge's contribution to the diffusion of ideas from current German literary criticism and idealistic philosophy. These found their expression in his lectures on Shakespeare's characters and in his philosophical works, *Aids to Reflection* and *The Friend*. Emerson's contact with Coleridge strengthened his belief that an all-powerful spirit was at work through the limited human spirit. Thus, the powerful influence of Coleridge's explication of German transcendental philosophy (especially of Kant and Hegel) reinforced Emerson's growing idealism.

Shortly after his visit to Wordsworth, Waldo Emerson returned home to Boston firmly determined to apply his experience in his publications toward the advancement of America's intellectual independence from Europe. This independence, however, could only be won through an almost universal knowledge of that from which one sought liberation. Only by mastering disparate bodies of knowledge and coming to objective judgments about them, could one use one's own learning to construct new paradigms; at that point the goal would be attained.

A time-worn method of accomplishing this task has always been the systematic collection of quotations. Emerson went about the job meticulously. The commonplace books, which he sometimes bound himself, were treasure troves of countless gems that he later mined when he wrote his essays and lectures. In the notebook that he kept for this purpose between 1830 and 1834, most of the entries come from the period of August through November 1832 — the last months before his departure to Europe. Emerson's German material is prominent among his notes on readings in Latin, French and Italian works. At the time, he was reading *Specimens of German Genius*, a collection of excerpts of modern German literature that appeared in 1830 in the *New Monthly Magazine*. From these he excerpted the thoughts he found most significant. To a large extent these are ethical precepts that he found primarily in *Wilhelm Meister*.[31] The collections include a long translation from the second book of *Wilhelm Meister's Travels* concerning the world's three great religions, as well as quotations from Sarah Austin's Goethe biography, and also Schiller's introductory lecture on universal history. Schiller's plan to contrast the role of the merchant with that of the philosopher was unquestionably in Emerson's own vein; later he would write his most important essays on such themes. During the course of this reading his deeply romantic inclinations were aroused, and by no one more than Novalis, from whom he noted the passage: "Philosophy is properly Home-sickness, the wish to be everywhere at home."[32] Here in a nutshell was a central transcendental idea Emerson derived from the writings of a German Romantic.

But a collection of unsystematic entries from various writers and works did not prove useful for his purposes. Emerson thus assembled his so-called *Encyclopedia* between 1824 and 1836. This collection of 900 quotations was a truly encyclopedic arrangement of 100 categories encompassing death, weather, coffee, horses, etc. that Emerson originally meant as sources for his sermon material. German writers who appeared in Emerson's letters and journals from this period made their way into the *Encyclopedia* among citations of classical, English, and French authors. For example, under the category "Men," we find several quotations from Goethe's *Wilhelm Meister*, a source that proved inexhaustible for Emerson. "Man is properly the *only* object that interests man" (*Journals*, 6:127),[33] or "A man's history paints his character." (*Journals*, 6:128).[34] Under the heading "Names," Goethe appears again with the aphorism from *Poetry and Truth Out of my Life*: "A man's name is like his skin: it just fits him" (*Journals*, 6:155).[35] The section on "Manners" includes Lessing's definition of grace from *Laokoon*: "La Grace peut être considérée comme la beauté mise en action" (*Journals*, 6:160).[36] Under "Women" there is an utterance that goes back to Madame de Staël: "The ancient *Germans* esteemed women to have some divine inspiration!" (*Journals*, 6:188).

Emerson also made long translations from Goethe's *Nachgelassene Werke* (Posthumous works), among which were Goethe's essays and reviews of two works by Ernst Stiebenroth: "Bedeutende Fördernis durch ein einziges geistreiches Wort," (Weighty reassurance in a single clever word) (*Journals*, 6:289),[37] and his *Psychologie zur Erklärung der Seelenerscheinungen*" (Psychology of spiritual manifestations) (*Journals*, 6:289–290).[38] He also excerpted parts of "Einwirkung der neueren Philosophie," (The impact of modern philosophy), (*Journals*, 6:290–291).[39] From Goethe's review of Carlyle's *German Romance* (1827) Emerson copied a paraphrase of "Über die Parodie bei den Alten" (On parody among the ancients) (*Journals*, 6:6:291), and also translated passages from Goethe's letters to Schiller.[40] He translated Michelet's description of the life of Schelling, and from Goethe's "Problem und Erwiderung" (Problem and Response) he derived the assertion that science was just as necessary as art (*Journals*, 6:299–301).[41] He also quoted from the essays "Naturwissenschaft im Allgemeinen: einzelne Betrachtungen und Aphorismen" (Universal natural science: specific observations and aphorisms) (*Journals*, 6:302–303),[42] and quite extensively from "Von deutscher Baukunst" (On German architecture) (*Journals*, 6:303–305).[43]

This harvest contained the fruits of Emerson's reading following his European trip. He was not only reading his newly purchased Goethe volumes containing the posthumously published works, but also books about his true European hero, Michelangelo,[44] whom he compares to Goethe (much to the detriment of the latter). "Are not his struggles & mortifications a more beautiful wreath than the milliners made for Goethe? (*Journals*, 4:259). He also praised Michelangelo's desire for death, noting that one should celebrate not the birth, but the death, of one who has lived a good life.

In the spring and summer months following his return from Europe, Emerson gave Goethe's *Tag- und Jahreshefte* a critical reading, calling them "a book unparalleled in America" (*Journals*, 4:301). The image of Goethe that emerged from the experience was one of:

> an all-sided, gifted, indefatigable student as he is, — to be only another poor monad after the fashion of his little race bestirring himself immensely to hide his nothingness, spinning his surface directly before the eye to conceal the Universe his ignorance. Throughout Goethe prevails the undersong of confession & amazement; the apophthegm of Socrates; the recantation of Man (*Journals*, 4:298)

During this period Emerson laid the foundation of his later lecture on Goethe as the representative writer of his time; he recognized the great importance education played for Goethe's life, although he was not able to recognize the transcendental purpose of this education in the true sense of the word. That would be for Margaret Fuller, another friend from Emerson's circle, to discover. Emerson formulated the question about Goethe thus:

> The problem to be solved, is, How shall this soul called *Goethe* be educated? And whatever he does or whatever befalls him is viewed solely in relation to its effect upon the development of his mind. Even in the arms of his mistress at Rome he says he studied sculpture & poetry.
>
> (*Journals*, 4:301)

In Emerson's view, "self-cultivation" was the "moral" of all that Goethe ever wrote; Emerson continues with his critical assessment: "in indolence, intolerance, & perversion, I think we can spare an olive & a laurel for him" (*Journals*, 4:301).

In the autumn of 1834 — his "Goethe year" — Emerson wrote with even more gravity:

> Goethe is praised as μυριονους (ten thousand minded) or all-sided. And if I understand it this is the apology that is made for his epicurean life compared with his religious perceptions. To praise a man for such quality is like praising an observatory for being very low & massive & a very good fort. It is not more the office of man to receive all impressions, than it is to distinguish sharply between them. He that has once pronounced intelligently the word "Self-renouncement," "Invisible Leader," "Powers of Sorrow," & the like, is forever bound to the service of the Super-human. (*Journals*, 4:302)

Thanks to his intensive work on Goethe, however, Emerson's positive impression of the German poet still predominated. Carlyle's letters from England continually urged him to keep studying Goethe; he consistently finds his own thoughts confirmed by Goethe's. "I was glad to find Goethe say to the same point," Emerson notes in his journal in April 1834 after reading the *Tag- und Jahreshefte* (*Journals*, 4:275).

During the spring and summer months of 1834 Emerson felt the desire for the kind of peace and solitude no longer found in bustling Boston. Thus, he decided to move to Concord, the town he had known since childhood. An inheritance from the estate of his first wife (who had died early) made possible the purchase of a house. As a result, by exercising frugality (a trait familiar to New Englanders) and supplementing his basic capital by lecturing and publishing, he was able to live his remaining forty-eight years in Concord in financial security. His journal expresses a feeling of relief on November 15, 1834:

> Hail to the quiet fields of my fathers! Not wholly unattended by super-natural friendship & favor let me come hither. Henceforth I design not to utter any speech, poem, or book that is not entirely & peculiarly my work. (*Journals*, 4:335)

Concord was a little town of two thousand about 15 miles from Boston and surrounded by woods and lakes. It already had a long history and its own special character. Centuries before, Indians had fished in the rich waters of the Sudbury and Assabet Rivers, which flow together in Concord to form the stream of that name; they had hunted in the river meadows rich with deer, turtles, muskrats, and birds. In 1637 the lush grazing pastures attracted the first settlers who came to establish dairy farms.

These meadows of Concord gained historical significance in the eighteenth century when the colonists drew up their ranks at the Old North Bridge on April 19, 1775 to fire "the shot heard round the world" against the English light infantry.

When Emerson made Concord his home, his grandfather, the Reverend Ezra Ripley, could still remember the event. Ripley was minister of the only church in town for sixty-three years, which made him head of this little New England theocracy. Like all educated men of Concord, he had studied at Harvard and was as tolerant in his views as the new arrival Ralph Waldo, who two years earlier had terminated his affiliation with the church and was devoted to everything new that emanated from European intellectual life. Emerson was determined to spread this secular intellectual gospel from Concord to all America and the little town with its daily mail to Boston was well suited to his mission. Letters, books, and over the years a growing stream of visitors, found their way to Concord, which changed its character as a result of Emerson's presence. Still, the pastoral tranquility of the place that Emerson savored remained unaltered. The lives and tasks of the farmers in the area did not change much; those who visited Concord, be it briefly or for longer stays, may have influenced the intellectual climate, but not the bucolic charm. This was a vision of peaceful social balance without stark contrasts between rich and poor, nearly lacking any socially marginalized individuals (exceptions being Indians who were never integrated into the social fabric, or Irish Catholics who had recently arrived). This social and intellectual configuration has led to the claim that Concord was a town even more open to the best of what had been said and thought by the civilized world than most American university towns in the twentieth century.[45]

Emerson made it his business to convey this intellectual broadmindedness to the world at large. For this purpose the best vehicle was the so-called Lyceum movement that was taking New England by storm. In 1826 Josiah Holbrook had hit upon a plan to satisfy the New Englanders' thirst for knowledge. The scheme involved establishing Lyceum offices at the parish, state, national, and even the international level for the purpose of organizing lectures, establishing libraries and natural history collections, and supporting publications of a popular yet serious nature. In 1828 Holbrook, with the collaboration of Daniel Webster, founded the "Society for the Improvement of Schools and Diffusion of Useful Knowledge" and chose as its head administrator a cousin of Ralph Waldo Emerson. Lyceums were soon founded in Concord and Salem from which the movement spread throughout New England. The meetings usually took place in church vestries. A committee chose the speakers and subjects while a curator arranged practical details. Patrons could purchase an entire course

of lectures given by one or several different speakers. Local lecturers —
ministers, professors, laymen — usually spoke for no fee, whereas invited
guest speakers were paid between one and twelve dollars. For Ralph
Waldo Emerson it was an advantage that he had studied at Harvard College and Harvard Divinity School and been an ordained member of the
clergy in Boston. Such credentials meant he could count on attracting an
interested audience. Shortly after his return from Europe he held four lectures on scientific subjects beginning with "The Uses of Natural History,"
which was addressed to the "Society for the Improvement of Schools and
Diffusion of Useful Knowledge" in Boston. This lecture was followed by
"The Relations of Man to the Globe" and "Water," which he addressed
to various other learned groups before he again appeared before the
"Natural History Society" with his lecture "The Naturalist," which according to Van Cromphout (who has a scholar's flair for detecting traces
of Goethe in these lectures) is "riddled with references to Goethe's scientific opinions.[46] In 1834 he delivered two addresses on Italy that he put
together from material collected from journals; in the following winter he
then gave five talks on great men in arts and letters, starting with Michelangelo and followed by ones on Luther, John Milton, the statesman and
historian Edmund Burke, and John Fox, the founder of the Quakers.
When Emerson was considering becoming a lecturer, he wrote in his
journal: "We want lives. We want characters of worthy men, not their
books nor their relics" (*Journals*, 2:54). This ambition is unquestionably
noticeable in his early lectures, although he had to resort to a great amount
of biographical description when treating a life as dramatic as Luther's.

The lecture on Michelangelo, which shows Emerson's method of de-
ducing an artist's character from his biography, is a good example of his
thought process. Michelangelo's life, according to Emerson, had developed unusually harmoniously for such a great man. He was devoted to
only one goal: beauty. This question "What is beauty?" provided Emerson
an opportunity to mine his collection of quotations that he had accumu-
lated over the years. He consulted the essay by Karl Philipp Moritz, "Über
die bildende Nachahmung des Schönen," but cites Boileau for the answer,
"Rien de beau que le vrai: nothing is beautiful but what is true."[47] Emerson used his own Italian journey to illustrate these lectures, for without
that experience he never would have discovered Michelangelo. The enthusiasm of this recent exposure suffuses the lecture with short but penetrating descriptions of Michelangelo's works. A passage at the end of the
lecture conveys Michelangelo's ubiquity in Florence. It is a city where
portraits of the artist gaze from shop windows, where his works are
prominently displayed in public, where his house is open to visitors, and
where buildings and works of art call to mind his words, "Santa Maria

Novella is my bride." The image of Emerson himself standing before the grave of the artist in Santa Croce conveys a powerful emotion to the speaker before his American audience. With this intensity of ardor and quality of personal delight in his subject, Emerson was able to captivate his listeners.

Audience reaction was similar when listening to the lecture on Martin Luther, the longest from the series entitled "Biography." Emerson prepared this speech with particular care, although he used only English-language sources to describe the reformation figure. These included several biographies and a translation of Luther's *Table Talk* which, he claimed, "has left a deeper impression of his presence in the modern world than any other except Columbus."[48] Emerson interpreted Luther's character in light of the reformer's central life experience, the nailing of the ninety-five theses to the church door in Wittenberg. This had inspired Emerson to imitate Luther's act of defiance by nailing his own theses against the religious formalism of the day on the door of the Second Church in Boston. The lecture on Michelangelo and the three that followed on the three great Englishmen make it clear just what it was that fascinated Emerson about Luther. The tenet — which was to become a life principle for him and to which he would devote much thought and writing — was that of self-reliance, or the trust in one's self that can only come of absolute independence from all institutions. Just as Luther had broken with the church, Emerson did the same, for he was by nature a man who later could barely even tolerate a guest professorship at Harvard.[49] Luther, as a scholar and man of the spirit, became a leader of a great revolution while remaining true to his convictions to the end. In spite of the dangers and threats that surrounded him, and despite his own volcanic temper, he resorted to no weapons except those of the mind.

Although Emerson did not read Luther's texts in the original German, he was quite aware of Luther's linguistic genius, his humor, his wit, and cleverness of mind. Emerson devoted particular verve to describing Tetzel, the seller of indulgences in Wittenberg, and at the end of the lecture reached a crescendo with a description of Luther as: "this enraged Poet, who did not write his visions in sonnets, but believed them, spoke them, and acted them, [...] and [...] shook to the centre [...] the whole fabric of tyranny in the world.[50]

Emerson's lectures became ever more carefully crafted over time. It was his intention to probe areas of knowledge systematically as, for example, when he announced a series on English literature in 1835, or in the following year on "The Philosophy of History." This latter subject was, as Emerson well knew, the same that Friedrich Schlegel had undertaken in Vienna in 1828. He was also familiar with Victor Cousin's work, similarly titled "Introduction to the Philosophy of History," and apparently felt that it was time to present the American public with his own concept of the philosophy of history.

The lectures in this series are filled with quotations from Emerson's favorite German authors, with Goethe's ideas on natural history enjoying a particularly central position. He presented German intellectual efforts as colossal, even though not consistently exemplary. In the lecture of January 5, 1837 entitled "Literature" we read that the voice of reason sounds "deepest and loudest out of Germany where it is not the word of a few but of all the wise." He characterized German professors as:

> a secluded race, free to think, but not invited to action, poor and crowded, [who] went back into the recesses of consciousness with Kant [. . .]. All geography, all statistics, all philology, was read with the great distinction of Reason and Understanding in view, and hence the reflective insight of their research, — of Niebuhr, Humboldt, Müller, Heeren, Herder, Schiller, Fichte, Schlegel, and greater than all in literary fame and in universal power, Goethe.[51]

The twelve lectures entitled "The Philosophy of History," which explore art, literature, politics, religion, society and ethics, are devoted to human nature and all its limitations. In these Emerson shows the "Individual" (as stated in the title of the final lecture) as the focal point of society and history. These lectures are linked to the lecture series he gave the following winter (1837/38) on one of the great topics that gripped New Englanders of the day, that of "Human Culture." This idea he viewed as closely allied to the German concept of *Bildung*.

Emerson's predecessors had defined a concept of culture commonly known in New England as "self-culture." The spiritual father of the term was William Ellery Channing (1780–1842), the Boston Unitarian who had struggled to liberate the church from the Calvinist doctrines of election and predestination to damnation. These Channing countered with his doctrine of the possibility of human perfectibility, which was taken up not only by Emerson but also by many of his friends, particularly Margaret Fuller and Amos Bronson Alcott.

But in the meantime Emerson had become acquainted with German idealism. He had read *Wilhelm Meister's Apprenticeship,* the *Bildungsroman* par excellence, and had filled his journals and notebooks with countless quotations from this and Goethe's *Italian Journey.* These references contained a wide range of statements on education that served to broaden Emerson's own notion of the concept.

Emerson had reached the conclusion in Concord "not to utter any speech, poem, or book that is not entirely & peculiarly my work" (*Journals,* 4:335). His intention was clearly to avoid saying what had already been said and thinking what had already been thought, for to do so meant reconstructing Europe in America. This meant a rejection of the educational standards of the eighteenth century from which New England was radically beginning to free itself. On June 8, 1838, one of those New England summer days drenched in such sunshine that every object stood out in sharp outline and nothing seemed impossible to the human spirit, Emerson took a walk through his woodland and noted in his journal:

> I would say to the young scholar: [. . .] you are greatly obliged to them as you are to all the History, to the pyramids, & the Authors, but now are we here, now our day is come, we have been born out of the Eternal silence, & now will we live, live for ourselves & not as the pallbearers of a funeral but as the upholders & creators of an age & neither Greece nor Rome nor the three kings of Cologne nor the three Unities of Aristotle nor the College of Sorbonne nor the Edinburgh Review is to command any longer. Now we are come & will put our own interpretation on things & moreover our own things for interpretation. (*Journals*, 7:7)

This defiant stance, noticeable in Emerson even as a young traveller in Europe, was still not diminished after five years. Now when he discussed the subject of human culture, he inevitably dug deeply into his journals and notebooks, his "savings books," as he called them, in order to invest the capital accrued there in his lectures. But the actual text shows surprising little use of this material, and especially little by German authors. Part of the explanation is certainly Emerson's gradual emancipation from the repetition and reproduction of European culture. For this ideal he substituted instead his own critical judgment and achievement, which were enhanced in turn by older material. In his journal entry for April 22, 1837 Emerson wrote: "Culture — how much meaning the Germans affix to the word & how unlike to the English sense." And several days later, on Germans and their search for truth, he wrote:

> What have these German Weimarish Art friends done? They have rejected all the traditions & conventions, have sought to come thereby one step nearer to absolute truth. But still they are no nearer than others. I do not draw from them great influence. (*Journals*, 5:306)

The journals and lectures make clear that this attitude toward European culture was not merely one of simple rejection. On the day after the self-confident remark about his own intellectual independence Emerson wrote:

> Goethe certainly had good thoughts on the subject of female culture. How respectful to woman & hopeful are the portraits in Wilhelm Meister, — Natalia, Theresa. (*Journals*, 7:10)

One cannot help noticing that even the introduction to the new lecture series contains far more of Goethe's spirit than mere literal quotations can convey. Indeed, Emerson's definition of culture is thoroughly in the tone of *Wilhelm Meister*: "His own Culture, — the unfolding of his nature, is the chief end of man." "Since my youth it had been my dark wish and intention to educate myself just as I am," says Wilhelm.[52] Emerson found this potential for personal education — "self-culture," as he too called it — in its derivation from an ability within human nature that philosophy calls "the Ideal." The striving for perfectibility is impossible without an idea of perfection. Thus the Ideal does not exist in opposition to the Real, but rather is identical to it. The Ideal is not identical to the Actual, i.e., present existence, which represents only that which is transitory.

Herein lie the roots of Emerson's subsequent conflict with Goethe. In his later essay from 1840, "Thoughts on Modern Literature," Emerson would accuse Goethe of being interested more in the Actual than the Ideal.[53] The reason for this emphasis, he claimed, was that Goethe did not accept the challenge of living in nature. By virtue of man's superior position, on the other hand, Emerson saw the means of education precisely in the myriad relationships possible between human nature to nature in general. Thus, it is the role of culture ultimately to confirm man's sovereign status above nature. Several lectures address this theme, among them those on work ("Doctrine of the Hands"), on thinking ("The Head"), on the perception of beauty ("The Eye and Ear"), on feeling ("The Heart"), on ethics ("Being and Seeming"), and finally, those entitled "Prudence," and "Heroism and Holiness."

In the lecture on "The Eye and Ear," in which Emerson for the first time attempts to formulate aesthetic principles, his ideas coincide again with those of Goethe. The perception and creation of beauty must arise from a thought system ultimately devoted to the perfectibility of man. Such a man will be elevated above his own individuality by the perception of the beautiful — as Goethe had sensed when he viewed the casts of classical statues in the French Academy in Rome. About that moment he wrote: "In such a presence one becomes more than one is."[54]

Emerson's intellectual disposition during these early years was remarkably similar to Goethe's. From intensive work on the German writer, the American developed an independence from the very object of his scrutiny — an independence ultimately from Goethe, German literature and European literature as well. He found himself confirming much he discovered, but rejecting other aspects. It was altogether a vibrant intellectual process.

Rüdiger Els has pointed out convincing similarities between Emerson's thoughts on nature with those of Goethe on the same subject. These are most evident from a comparison of Emerson's first book publication, *Nature* (1836), with the fragment "Die Natur" by Georg Christoph Tobler.[55] Goethe included this fragment in 1783 in the *Tiefurter Journal*, writing the following note about it to chancellor von Müller in 1828: "I cannot in fact recall that I wrote these observations, yet they correspond with the ideas I had arrived at at that time."[56] At the time he wrote his book on nature, Emerson did not yet know Tobler's fragment; when he discovered it soon thereafter in volume ten of Goethe's *Nachgelassene Werke*, he must have thought Goethe the author of the work. Tobler and Emerson, as naturally Goethe himself, were knowledgeable readers of Plato, Plotinus, the Orphic Hymns, and the bible. Building on such a tradition, they were able to evolve an idea of nature that overwhelmed them.

Emerson's *Nature* is no fragment, but rather a hymn-like prose text that was followed by such famous essays like "Self-Reliance," "The Over-Soul," "The Poet," and "Friendship" which assign to nature the divine function of redemption. Compared to nature, man is a child who experiences death but also transcendence. Particularly in the final portions of the works of Tobler and Emerson there are obvious parallels for the themes of unity in the multiplicity of nature, humility and exaltation before nature, and childlike trust in nature. After buying the fifteen volumes of Goethe's posthumously published works, Emerson wrote an eight-line verse into volume ten (which contained the fragment "Die Natur"). The lines reveal that he carried this volume around in his jacket pocket, but seldom had time to study the contents, for he "had too much to think,/Heaven and earth to eat and drink."[57] Finally he did turn his attention to the volume. John S. Dwight's fine translation of the fragment "Nature" was soon published with his own *Select Minor Poems* (Boston, 1838); the second version of Emerson's *Nature* (1847) shows the influence of Tobler's text.

In addition to the book *Nature,* two further lectures from the years 1836–1838 established Emerson's fame. One of these, however, cost him severe disapproval, which came in 1837 when he spoke to the Phi Beta Kappa chapter at Harvard on the topic of "The American Scholar." In the speech he delineated a great future for scholars if they would only free themselves from the fetters of academic tradition. "Our day of dependence, our long apprenticeship to the learning of other lands, draws to a close. The millions that around us are rushing into life, cannot always be fed on the sere remains of foreign harvests."[58]

Emerson defined it as the American scholar's duty to learn from nature, to be inspired by books, and to engage actively in life. The old adage "know thyself" had to be amplified by the modern charge, "study nature" — by no means only through books. "The one thing in the world of value, is, the active soul, — the soul, free, sovereign, active."[59] One should recall Emerson's lecture on literature and his description of the fairly lamentable conditions of German professors, though this sentiment may be an echo of Carlyle's *Sartor Resartus*. The American scholar, stated Emerson, should lead a different life from that of the solitary loner whom the world associates with scholars. "The office of the scholar is to cheer, to raise, and to guide men by showing them facts amidst appearances."[60] To be sure, by "facts" Emerson here refers to quotidian events. The discussion then takes on a mood worthy of Adalbert Stifter:

> I ask not for the great, the remote, the romantic; what is doing in Italy or Arabia; [. . .] I embrace the common, I explore and sit at the feet of the familiar, the low. Give me insight into to-day, and you may have the antique and future worlds. What would we really know the meaning of? The meal in the firkin; the milk in the pan; the ballad in the street; the news of the boat; the glance of the eye; the form and the gait of the body.[61]

Emerson was unfamiliar with the Austrian novelist Adalbert Stifter, with whom he nonetheless shared a similarity. Both derived from Goethe the idea that man and nature were intimately interconnected and that knowing mundane details was to make fresh discoveries. Emerson notes: "Goethe, in this very thing the most modern of the moderns, has shown us, as none ever did, the genius of the ancients."[62]

In July 1838 Emerson gave the second lecture before the graduating class of the Harvard Divinity School where he himself had studied. The effect was so revolutionary that for many years he could not set foot in this institution; nor did he preach much after the incident. With the speech he separated himself radically from the Unitarian church of his day. He found this denomination of Protestantism weak, lacking a love of good, and a fear of evil. He charged these "newborn bards of the Holy Ghost"[63] to abandon all attachments to traditional liturgical institutions and to lead mankind directly to God. The lecture again expressed, albeit indirectly, Luther's influence on Emerson in its suggestion that the young New England ministers should stand — like the German reformer himself before the Imperial Diet of Worms — independent and self-reliant. At the end, the speech rises to a powerful climax typical of the Emersonian lecture style. There surfaces, perhaps unconsciously, a thought from Schiller when he adjures his listeners to link together the fragmentary teachings of Hebraic law and Greek writings to form a unified whole in order to perceive "the world to be the mirror of the soul." These will demonstrate that the principle of "the Ought, that Duty, is one thing with Science, with Beauty, and with Joy."[64]

Emerson had retired to Concord to dedicate himself to his great mission — laying the foundations of a "self-reliant" American culture — but it was never his intent to become a hermit. His family was there, source of so much pleasure and anguish as well. His second wife's health declined, his oldest son Waldo died of scarlet fever at age six, and two brothers succumbed to tuberculosis. His aged mother lived and died under his roof. The unmarried sister of his father, Mary Moody Emerson, was an arch-Puritan who watched over her nephew's spiritual state. From her secluded farm in Maine she corresponded with Ralph Waldo about Kant and Goethe, often visiting Concord to wield the righteous sword of orthodoxy before finally moving to the town for good.

Considering himself a citizen of the town of Concord, Emerson by no means withdrew from civic duties. He served a long term on the school committee and frequently spoke at the Lyceum. It was also the custom that he, being a newly-married recent arrival in town, should be elected hog-reeve, thereby assuming the nominal duty of assessing fines against the owners of marauding pigs. His lecture visits to Boston and other towns kept him in contact with the world and soon he was travelling more widely, to New York, Philadelphia and Baltimore. His circle of correspondents also broadened and with it his circle of friends, many of whom visited Concord, some to settle there.

In his early years in Concord, Emerson's foray into German literature is evident not only in the correspondence with Thomas Carlyle, but in his far-ranging search for books and information. He also needed a forum where he could discuss the authors and the books of this new-found culture. Correspondents who knew more German than Emerson were ideal for this purpose. His situation was parallel to that of his younger colleague from Divinity School days, James Freeman Clarke, who had also attended Harvard College and been among the students in Charles Follen's first German classes.

Clarke had written an essay on Goethe and Carlyle that Emerson wished to see published. But when he suggested this in 1835, Clarke had just taken his first post as a minister in a parish in Kentucky and was busy publishing a new journal, *The Western Messenger*. At the frontier of American civilization Clarke was preaching the new Unitarian beliefs mixed with large doses of German literature and philosophy from his pulpit as well as the pages of *The Western Messenger*. Clarke wrote to Emerson declining to revise his Goethe article, but asking whether Emerson wanted him to write a piece on Schleiermacher, the German theologian whose work combined Plato, Calvin and Spinoza, yet who seemed thoroughly neglected. All Berlin had been in tears at the death of this thinker who had rejected the obsessiveness of rationalism and had renounced the hypocrisy of Pietism. In the same letter Clarke recommended to Emerson a possible author who might contribute an article to the discussion of Goethe. This author was a young lady, who lived not far from Concord in the town of Groton. She had, as Clarke reported, drunk "very deeply of the spirit of German Literature" — her name was Margaret Fuller (*Letters,* 1:425). This remarkable twenty-five year old was to exert immense influence upon Emerson's knowledge of German literature, which she made accessible to the growing circle of New England readers and through them indirectly to all educated Americans.

The first meeting between Ralph Waldo and Margaret Fuller was ar-ranged by the English writer Harriet Martineau. This formidable author, armed with her prodigious ear trumpet, impressed the intellectuals when she travelled through New England. When she returned home, however, she penned an arrogant book criticizing American intellectual life, which nonetheless did not diminish her stature among New Englanders.[65] In July 1836 Margaret Fuller accepted the Emersons' invitation to spend two weeks as their house guest in Concord. She was, as Emerson later recalled, ladylike but far from attractive and her constant nervous eye twitching and nasal voice annoyed him. He thought to himself, "we shall never get far."[66] Yet, this impression was by no means universal. Robert D. Richard-son, for example, gives a much more positive picture of Margaret Fuller's impression on her friends.[67]

Emerson could not escape the fascination of Margaret Fuller's person-ality any more than could the large circle of friends that surrounded her at this period. From then on she visited the Emersons for a week every four or five months until she finally moved to New York in 1846. These Con-cord afternoons were usually spent reading together and taking walks; in the evenings hosts and guests gathered in the library.

Emerson's descriptions of Margaret Fuller eventually softened and changed. There developed between the two a friendship characterized by mutual esteem that at times waxed rhapsodic. In one letter he called her a "divine mermaid or fisher of men, to whom all gods have given the witch-hazel-wand" with which to discover "an Immortal under every disguise in every lurking place" (*Letters,* 2:336). She is "the Concord River Muse" (*Letters,* 3:252), and Emerson wrote to her: "I thought you a great court lady with a Louis Quatorze taste for diamonds & splendor, and I find you with a 'Bible in your hand'" (*Letters,* 2:337). Emerson evidently wished Margaret Fuller had been his neighbor in Concord. He wrote to her: "Then instantly came the poor exhausted Lidian's tragic letters. — but I mean yet to coax you into Mrs. Brown's little house opposite to my gate" (*Letters,* 4:28). "Lidian" refers to his sickly wife, who sometimes was forced to spend weeks in darkened rooms while Waldo and Margaret traipsed across the countryside with a crowd of friends reciting poetry, making music, or boating on Walden Pond.[68]

The correspondence between Emerson and Margaret Fuller from the years after 1837 is the best measure of their intellectual exchange. At first they avidly traded books back and forth. Margaret Fuller, being the one who obtained the newest titles soon after their publication, usually furnished Emerson with them. In April 1837 Emerson returned her copy of Eckermann's *Gespräche mit Goethe* with the question: "Cannot a biography of this minutely faithful sort be written without self-destruction?" (*Letters*, 2:64). He borrowed Goethe's correspondence with Zelter, as well as the *Briefe an Johann Heinrich Merck von Goethe, Herder, Wieland und anderen bedeutenden Zeitgenossen* (1835), calling the Merck book "inestimable" for any Goethe biography and for understanding "the inside of Germany." "Wieland is the charm of the book" (*Letters*, 2:70–71). Emerson read "Goethe's Life" (or *Dichtung und Wahrheit*); Eckermann's *Gespräche* got passed on to the well-read Sarah Ripley in Concord; he intended to pass along the Merck volume too. A lending library network was beginning in and around Concord.

Soon, however, there appeared on the scene a new sensation from the realm of German literature that caught Emerson in its grip, not to let him go. The name first appeared in May 1838 in a letter to Margaret Fuller in which he requested "the letters of Bettina" on behalf of John Sullivan Dwight who had just published an extensive volume entitled *Selected Minor Poems of Goethe and Schiller*. In the following year Emerson then wrote:

> I have Bettina in English & treat it as gingerly as one would a large butterfly. She is a wonderful genius & yet these creatures all wing & without any reserve make genius cheap & offend our cold Saxon constitution.
>
> (*Letters*, 208–209)

As soon as *Goethe's Correspondence with a Child* appeared in the three-volume London edition in 1839, Emerson obtained a copy. Werner Vordtriede has unraveled the extraordinary story of how the English translation came about.[69] Without ever having learned English, Bettina herself worked on this translation between 1834 and 1838. Her goal was the simultaneous publication of an English version of *Goethes Briefwechsel mit einem Kinde* in order to collect money abroad for a Goethe monument. The result was a new work with an original foreword and thirty-five additional pages of text. Vordtriede has called it "an extraordinary linguistic feat in which the stammering of a child blends with the silence of an unusually talented poetic nature."[70] He cites one letter of Bettina's in which she herself confessed that the work was "teeming with voluptuousnessholyghost, accompanied by a procession of walking amphibians somewhere between fish and flesh."[71] Sarah Austin was to have translated the book and Bettina could not have found anyone better for the task. But Austin's English version of the first part (lacking Goethe's sonnets) was too bland for Bettina's taste, and so with the help of two advisors she set out to do the job herself. These advisors were probably two English students living at the time in Berlin, whom Bettina called "das Kembridschmember" and "das Ochsfordmember." But not even these native speakers met her high expectations, for the first two volumes appeared in London to little acclaim. During this time Bettina was busy translating the third volume, which she decided to dedicate to Queen Victoria — a gesture that was prevented by German diplomats at the Court of St. James. The entire undertaking was a bad business venture that damaged Goethe's stature in England, while at the same time, as Vordtriede recounts, completely ruining Bettina's own reputation there.

Not so in America. The reception of *Goethe's Correspondence with a Child* is a sign of the intellectual independence of New England readers from their mother country. On the other hand, it should be stressed that the book luckily fell first into the hands of the open-minded circle of Emerson and his friends.[72]

It was certainly Goethe's name on the title page that initially attracted the attention of these readers always eager for facts about him and other prominent Germans. The image of Goethe they had been able to glean so far was corroborated and elaborated by this fascinating book. Bettina indulged in formulations such as "thou art like the streaming moon-beams. Thou art great and splendid, and better than all which I have yet known, seen, or heard."[73] Such phrases correspond to Margaret Fuller's own rhapsodic characterizations, at least in the early stage of her knowledge of Goethe. Even the aura of chilly reserve, of which Bettina repeatedly accused the poet, had been detected in New England. Readers there could sense an affinity when she compared Goethe to a winter's night "cold and friendly and clear and still;"[74] similarly, her comment, "yet your brow was never clouded with unhappiness."[75] Her description that she had heard from Goethe's mother of the poet ice skating on the Main River "like a god's son" was quoted throughout New England as a characterization of Goethe. Bettina's description of their first meeting in Weimar even had reverberations in American popular fiction.

But Goethe was not the only reason that Bettina's *Correspondence* had such repercussions in America. Bettina was recognized as an incomparable phenomenon and talent. A bold, free spirit like Margaret Fuller appreciated Bettina's brashness, identified with her stories of rides on runaway horses, her climbing exploits in chasms, or in the highest trees, on the crags of Goetz von Berlichingen's ruined castle in the Odenwald forest, over the roofs of Frankfurt, and over the window arches of the

Cologne cathedral. Margaret admired Bettina for her recovery of her baggage from the waters of the Main when her coach overturned, and for her
nocturnal journey through the forest carrying sabers and loaded pistols. In
sympathy with the struggle of the Tyroleans against Napoleon, Bettina
had written from Munich in 1809:

> Oh if I but had doublet, hose and hat, I'd run to the straight-nosed,
> stout-hearted Tyroleans and wave their green standard in the breeze."[76]

With their own War of Independence in the very recent past, Americans
were inspired by the freedom-fighting Tyroleans almost as much as Bettina was. Ralph Waldo Emerson was probably struck most profoundly by
Bettina's enthusiasm for nature, which she at times raised to the level of
nature religion. "Ah, how has Nature tried in love, to imitate the spirit of
God," she wrote.[77] It was in statements such as these, or in the following,
that Emerson must have recognized a kindred spirit:

> Bountiful Nature grants to be understood; and that is her wisdom that
> she paints such images, which are mirrors of our inner world; and he who
> contemplates her, penetrates into her depths, to him she will reveal the
> answers of hidden enigmas.[78]

Ever since writing the book *Nature*, Emerson's thoughts had revolved
around correspondences between nature and the human soul. That work
contains one of the most famous and most strikingly formulated definitions of the mode of thinking commonly understood as transcendental
thought. The oft quoted (and parodied) passage runs thus:

> Standing on the bare ground, — my head bathed by the blithe air, and
> uplifted into infinite space, — all mean egotism vanishes. I become a
> transparent eye-ball. I am nothing. I see all. The currents of the Universal
> Being circulate through me; I am part or particle of God. [. . .] I am the
> lover of uncontained and immortal beauty.[79]

The author of these lines must have felt considerable surprise upon
reading Bettina's transcendental fervor which so resembled his own:

> All sensual nature becomes spirit, all spirit is sensual life of the divinity, —
> eyes ye see! — ye drink light, hues, and forms! — O eyes, ye are nour-
> ished by divine wisdom, but ye offer all to love, ye eyes.[80]

Bettina's aphorisms are conceived in an equally transcendental spirit.
When she writes, "the sensual is symbol of the spiritual, is the mirror of a
truth, not as yet born in spiritual experience,"[81] it is a sentiment that corresponds with Emerson's: "[nature] always speaks of Spirit. It suggests the
absolute."[82] By the same token, Bettina's philosophy of art was illuminating for Emerson. She found in the work of art a symbol of revelation:
when the divine breath inhaled, it meant for her creation; when it exhaled,

birth and nurturing. Her view of the human body was one of art gener-
ated into the life of the spirit.[83]

After Emerson had read Bettina's *Correspondence with a Child,* he
wrote to Margaret Fuller of his admiration for the book:

> What can be richer and nobler than that woman's nature. What life more
> pure and poetic amid the prose and derision of our own time. So pure a
> love of nature I never found in prose or verse. What a lofty selection in
> character! What unerring instinct in action. If I went to Germany I
> should only desire to see her? Why do you not write to her? She must be
> worth all the Jamesons and Müllers on earth.[84] It seems to me she is the
> only formidable test that was applied to Goethe's genius. He could well
> abide any other influence under which he came. Here was genius purer
> than his own, and if without the constructive talent on which he valued
> himself yet he could not have disguised from himself the fact that she
> scorned it on the whole — though I think he appears sometimes to great
> advantage under the sharp ordeal — he is too discreet and cowardly to be
> great and mainly does not make one adequate confession of the trans-
> cendent superiority of this woman's aims and affections in the presence of
> which all his Art must have struck sail. (*Letters,* 2:210)[85]

No other female writer ever moved Emerson to such Romantic effu-
sion of feeling as Bettina. In the same letter to Margaret Fuller he wrote
that he placed the inspiration of women higher than men's thanks to the
female inclination to:

> add religion to talent, and so give our hope an infinite play until society
> gets possession of them [women] and carries them captive to Babylon.
> [. . .] if they would not subdue their sentiments, the age of heroes
> would come at once!" (*Letters,* 2:210–211)

With such an advocate Bettina's reputation in America was made. Emerson sent both volumes of the *Correspondence* to Jane Tuckerman, who
was asked to pass them along to a certain Mr. Adams because, as Emerson
put it, "The book is greatly in request here & I have promised it on its
return to several friends" (*Letters,* 2:212).[86] He announced his own visit to
Margaret Fuller in early September 1839 by promising, "I will bring with
me Bettina or, otherwise, send it by stage" (*Letters,* 2:220). In another
letter to Fuller from September 9, 1839, he made it clear that a Mr.
Theodore Parker, who was a Unitarian minister well-read in German literature, "may have it [Bettina's *Correspondence*] after you, if he will not
keep it over a few days; but if he wishes to sit upon it, let him not touch it
now and he shall have it after it returns from one or two earlier applicants
(*Letters,* 2:223). And so it went for weeks. Emerson finally made his personal copy available for a reprint edition to be published in 1840 in nearby
Lowell, Massachusetts.

Emerson's encouragement of Margaret Fuller to write Bettina did not fall on deaf ears. On November 7, 1840, referring to her letter to Bettina as "the most important event of the week," Fuller writes:

> Anna Shaw's brother takes the letter and I hope she may be induced to answer it. I will tell you what it said when we meet. I sent "Nature," (and lamented I had not your book proper for the occasion) John Dwight's volume and "the Dial." But I told her [. . .] that she must consider the despatch only as a token of respect. (*Letters*, 354)

                                        Boston, US.
                                        22d Novr 1840

Dear Bettine,

For how can I address you by any title less dear than that by which you have become so familiar to our thoughts. I write to you in the name of many men and many women of my country for whom you have wrought wonders. How many have read the records of your beautiful youth and ceased to distrust the promptings of their own young hearts! How many have looked back from maturer years and wondered that they also did not dare to *live!* How many have counted each pulse of your heart of love, how many more been kindled into flame at the touch of your genius!

We want to know more of you, Bettine. In your youthful ideal we see such promise! Your childhood was so prodigal a May-time, we want to know that you have bloomed into an eternal youth. Since you have trusted us with the secret of your love, will you not trust us farther? We have read again and again the manifold records of those early years of inspiration. We drink deep of the nectar cup, and yet long for more. We ask all men who come from your land, Have you seen Bettine? — What know you of the Child? — Is she weeping beside the monument of Goethe, or has she ascended a pedestal of her own? — But they do not speak intelligently of thee! They do not tell us what we want to hear. Thou art dear to us, thou art the friend of our inmost mood. We do not wish to hear street gossip about thee. We will not hear it. Speak to us thyself. Give thyself to us still further. There lives none perhaps now who could speak fitly of thee but many who would listen intelligently.

I do not believe you will refuse to gratify our desire. Though expressed by an obscure individual it is the desire of many hearts, I would say of a new world, — but all worlds are new to ardent natures like yours. Write to me or print it in a book. Tell us how the years have flown, what brought on their wings. There is one question above all we would fain ask. You will divine and, I trust, answer it. —

I give my name, though it will be a word without significance, in hope that you will address yourself to me and thus enable me to give the great pleasure to others of hearing more from their friend. We have written here no book worthy to send you; should any printed leaves accompany this, it will be merely as a token of respect.

But you are wise, you have the spiritual sight, the breath of our love will be wafted to you and you will see whether we are yours. The bearer of this will tell you how to direct if you are disposed to fulfill the hope of yours in faith

S. Margaret Fuller

My messenger may miss you. Address to care of Hilliard, Gray and company and I shall receive the letter. Or to that of Rev. George Riply, Boston. (*Letters*, 6:328–329)[87]

We do not know whether Bettina ever received the young Mr. Wood. At any rate, nothing is known of any answer to Fuller's letter.

The journal that Margaret Fuller included in her letter to Bettina was none other than *The Dial*. This had just begun to appear as the Concord circle was deciding the best method for disseminating transcendental notions to a wider audience; there were hardly any possibilities of publishing such ideas in the journals already on the market. *The Christian Examiner* was too conservative, the *Unitarian Review* too erudite, and the *North American Review* was inimical to the aims of the Transcendentalists.

There was an obvious need to found a journal and *The Transcendental Journal* was considered as a possible title. Emerson even offered the editorship to Carlyle, but when he turned this down, Margaret Fuller served for the first two years as editor of the journal that Amos Bronson Alcott had christened *The Dial*. In the last two years of the journal's life Emerson himself took over the editorship under protest.[88]

Emerson, Fuller, Alcott and George Ripley (who managed the financial affairs of *The Dial* in its first year), all had literary preferences that were too strong to permit the magazine from taking a purely theological or philosophical direction. Emerson introduced the first number in July 1840 with a foreword from "The Editors to the Readers," as it was entitled. In this opening statement he declared that he and his friends had submitted to the pressure of "many sincere persons" in New England who had new expectations for literature and were demanding a break with current religious and pedagogical conventions that were, as he put it, "turning us to stone."[89] He noted that the present revolution in New England had been brought about by people who may be poor, and may never meet each other, yet who were united by their love of truth. Each may have a different goal — one wanting to reform the state, the other to reform literature. Readers felt the higher tone of the influential literary criticism in *The Dial*. Emerson closed with the apodictic statement, "All criticism should be poetic; unpredictable; superseding, as every new thought does, all foregone thoughts, and making a new light on the whole world."[90] Margaret Fuller's piece in the same tone, "A Short Essay on Critics," then followed in which her awareness of the theories of the German Romantics was evident.

In the pages of *The Dial* Waldo Emerson expressed himself repeatedly on the topic of German literature — and with greater deliberation and precision than in his letters or journals. He was determined that the magazine, which has been called "the first really independent and original journal published in this country,"[91] should not become "too literary." Rather, he saw its role as treating such various themes as law and property, government, education, art, literature and religion, in short, what constituted for Emerson the "Art of Life, — The Scholar's Calling." This he distilled into the three concepts of work, form, and reform (*The Dial*, 1:175–182).

Emerson's first elaborated statements on German literature are contained in the essay "Thoughts on Modern Literature," printed in the second number of *The Dial*. His designation of Shakespeare as "the first literary genius of the world" confirmed the Transcendentalists' preference for English literature. Shakespeare merits this role, according to Emerson, because of his reliance upon the Bible, that "most original book."[92] Among the books of the modern era, which include new editions of all the select pieces of the first of mankind,"[93] Shakespeare's influence in the past 150 years has been immense. German literature offers Emerson his prime example, for it was Shakespeare who awakened "the genius of the German nation into an activity, which [. . .] has made theirs now at last the paramount intellectual influence of the world (*The Dial*, 1:142).

The basis for this influence is primarily the historical-critical orientation of German scholarship that is brought to bear on philosophy and literature. This reference suggests that Emerson had in mind historically-grounded source studies, for he expressly mentions the *Nibelungenlied*, the poems of Hans Sachs, Henry of Alkmaer, and English and Scottish ballads. The value this methodology placed on precision and facts — as demonstrated by Humboldt's investigations in Mexico — had once and for all put an end to scholarly superficiality and foolishness, to such "ghost stories" or "sky-full of cobwebs" (*The Dial*, 1:142–5).

Emerson judged the result of this innovation in scholarly method a "bold and systematic criticism" that scholars such as Berthold Niebuhr could apply to Roman history, Pestalozzi to education, and Schelling, Kant, and Fichte applied in their new "analysis to nature." Goethe's technique, on the other hand, was to inspect the whole spectrum of human knowledge and to label each category "true" or "false" (*The Dial*, 1:145).

This essay must be viewed as the precursor to Emerson's later lecture on Goethe in the series "Representative Men." For Emerson, Goethe perfectly united all the forces of his age: from the storehouses of the world he gathered knowledge, and as a resolute realist was able to observe the world as no one else before him. His observations of nature, which all Transcendentalists admired, showed this trait best. In Emerson's eyes Goethe's love of nature had lent new meaning to the word, for Goethean analyses always led to syntheses. Emerson replicated here the experience he had when reading the *Italian Journey,* concluding again that Goethe always found an explanation for every phenomenon.

Yet, Emerson exempted neither modern literature nor Goethe from criticism. He found the contemporary writer to be subjective, one who judges people and things solely in relation to what they mean for him. Subjectivity is but the cultivated name for intellectual egotism, which separates the great from the small minds. Great men always direct us to facts and to nature; small ones lead back to themselves. The great minds include Byron and Jean Paul Richter, who impatiently desire to break through the boundaries of modern life in their wild striving to express the infinite. Goethe, on the other hand, who was simply all things, certainly had (in Emerson's eyes) a "vicious subjectiveness" about him (*The Dial,* 1:153). Emerson found a passage in Wieland's letters to Johann Heinrich Merck in which Wieland reports on an occasion at which Goethe read aloud from his Swiss travel journal. Emerson recognized in this what it was that differentiated Goethe (the subjective poet) from Homer and Shakespeare, namely that "the Me, the *Ille ego,* everywhere glimmers through." Viewing this as the reason for Goethe's isolation, Emerson noted that "no man was permitted to call Goethe brother" (*The Dial,* 1:153). David M. Robinson observes that "Emerson's dialogue with Goethe was thus one of his most rigorous exercises in self-criticism," chiefly because he realized that his "own pursuit of self-culture was exposed as a limited and even potentially dangerous enterprise, whose very object of concern, the self, threatened its foundation."[94]

Goethe's subjectivity was an aspect of the man that Emerson interpreted as characteristic of the dawning age. In *Wilhelm Meister* he found a representation of the real as it would be depicted years hence, showing man in all his weakness. Emerson interjects at this point, "Yes, O Goethe! but the ideal is truer than the actual" (*The Dial,* 1:155). It was the same flaw of which Emerson had accused Goethe in his journal during his Italian journey. Because he missed in Goethe the representation of the ideal, he did not succumb to his spell. But this aspect is precisely what interested the Transcendentalists. The poet on the highest peak was a creator, savior of the human spirit, and because Goethe certainly inhabited such heights, they were doubly disappointed that he had not reached those transcendental regions of Homer, Dante or Shakespeare. "We feel that a man gifted like him should not leave the world as he found it. [. . .] Being so much, we cannot forgive him for not being more," wrote Emerson at the end of his essay (*The Dial*, 1:157).

These words express an absolute demand placed on literature such as could only grow from the religious soil of Transcendentalism. Yet, such infinite demands that Transcendentalism placed on art contained the seeds of its own limitations. The Transcendentalists developed an exquisite sensibility for all poetry. In the areas of criticism and translation they were capable of creative representation, but not capable of individual poetic creativity. Emerson is again an exception. His first contributions to *The Dial*, which he had written prior to the magazine's publication, contained some of the most significant American poetry written in the 19th century. These poems include "The Problem" from the first number; "Woodnotes," from the second; and "The Snow Storm," and "The Sphinx" from the third.

Not only did Emerson write for *The Dial*, but he did not shy away from the drudgery of publishing the journal. He wrote book notices and was probably a contributor to the long "Select List of Recent Publications" in the second number. The interest on the part of *The Dial* in German literature is evident from this list. We find a *Faust* translation by A. Hayward, Esq. that was first published in Lowell, Massachusetts, followed by Gustav Pfizer's biography of Luther, translated in London. There are notices of Goethe's *Theory of Colors*, translated by Charles Lock Eastlake, as well as the second London edition of *The Protestant Exiles of Zillerthal* by Dr. Rheinwald of Berlin. The work *Geschichte des Urchristentums* by A. Fr. Gfrörer (Stuttgart 1838–1840) received the comment:

> It appears to be a work of great pretensions and little merit, if we may judge from two able articles upon it, one in the *Berlin Jahrbücher*, and the other in the *Halle Allg. Literatur Zeitung.* (*The Dial*, 1:272)

Emerson did not write any more contributions on German literature to *The Dial* during the two years Margaret Fuller edited the journal. Her own articles covered this specialty more than adequately. When he took over the editorship from his overworked predecessor in 1842 to prepare the July number, his interest in German literature had peaked. He did, however, publish a piece on "Europe and European Books" in the number for April 1843, which he had left to the editorial care of his assistant Henry David Thoreau in order to go on a three-month lecture tour. His text emphasized again the necessity for America to achieve intellectual independence from Europe: "We go to school in Europe. [. . .] we write on English culture and to an English public, in America and Europe" (*The Dial*, 3:511). "The centre of population and property of the English race

[. . .] will [. . .] certainly fall within the American coast, [. . .] and then will the great Yankee be born (*The Dial*, 3:512).

He of course remained grateful for the contributions of European civilization, but saw the "man-hunting" among American writers and scholars as a kind of self-deception that only led them to complain about their newly-acquired riches. "Seeing Herschel or Schelling, or Swede or Dane, satisfies the conditions, and "we can express ourselves happily" (*The Dial*, 3:512). He complained that too many cheap novels were imported from Europe, but none was so exemplary as *Wilhelm Meister*. This noble book had proven that a novel's ending could succeed without "a castle and a wife [. . . as the] indispensable conclusion." *Wilhelm Meister* was a work based on the "power to do what was necessary" (*The Dial*, 3:520). Each of its characters, he argued, performed some useful task. Justice was the primary element of the novel and beauty lent dignity to all characters within its pages.

Emerson gave his collaborators on *The Dial* as much room for German topics as they needed. He even invited Margaret Fuller to his house for two weeks where he reserved a desk and an inkwell so that she could write her rhapsodic, nearly fifty-page long article, entitled the "Romaic and Rhine Ballads" (*The Dial*, 3:137–80), which Karl Simrock had collected. He published a biographical study by Theodore Parker on the pioneer of German studies in America, Charles Follen, reviews of a Jean Paul biography, a selection of Schiller's letters, the story "The Sleepwalker" by Heinrich Zschokke, and Henry Hedge's translation of Uhland's poem "The Castle by the Sea." The last numbers of *The Dial* contained two more translations of poems by Ferdinand Freiligrath, "The Emigrants" and "The Moorish Prince." On his second trip to England Emerson met the exiled poet Freiligrath, who was greatly admired in New England. The issues of *The Dial* that Emerson edited contained several essays about German philosophical debates, research, and the teaching of philosophy in Berlin or Heidelberg. Much energy has been expended in an effort to trace a direct descent of the American Transcendentalists from the German idealists, especially since their name was expressly borrowed from the philosophy of Kant. Yet, much argues against viewing the Transcendentalists as the children of Kant, Schelling, and Hegel. Transcendental elements can be found in Cotton Mather's Puritan sermons from the collection *The Key to the Heavenly Kingdom* (1644). The Quakers too, especially William Penn, showed tendencies toward Transcendentalism in their thought. One hundred years before the influence of German idealism was felt in New England, there occurred the religious revival known as "The Great Awakening," inspired by the sermons and writings of Jonathan Edwards. Edwards had a mystical conversion in his youth which led him to interpret the visible phenomena of nature as symbols of divine truth. This teaching gave rise to a new idealism that harmoniously united pantheism and mysticism. Emerson's patron, William Ellery Channing, as well as others, developed these ideas further into a belief in the perfection of man. It is to this tradition of Transcendentalism in New England that such interest among Emerson and his friends in contemporary philosophy can be traced.

Emerson himself emphasizes this in his lecture "The Transcendentalist" from the series, "Lectures on the Times," printed in 1843 in *The Dial* (3:297–313). He notes that the innovative attitudes in New England are not really so new, and then traces Transcendentalism back to deeper and older roots than the Great Awakening or the Puritanism of John Cotton. "What is popularly called Transcendentalism among us, is Idealism" (*The Dial*, 3:297), Emerson proposed in his essay, and as such was to be understood as a mode of thinking in contrast to materialist philosophy based on experience. Transcendentalism can be found to be present in a long tradition of historical thinking: in the writings of the Roman Stoics and such patriots as Cato and Brutus who opposed despotism; during periods of superstition in the teachings of prophets and apostles; among the popes, ascetic monks, and the preachers who decried salvation through good works; in the Puritans, Quakers, and finally, the Transcendentalists themselves.

Among the Transcendentalists can be counted many intelligent religious thinkers and believers who can be remarkably radical in their idealism. Sometimes they even retreat from a normal working life (Emerson was clearly thinking of Thoreau with this characterization) and are therefore not always ideal citizens of the state. Some even choose not to vote. For them the highest principle is beauty, and in a society of farmers, seafarers and weavers these thinkers have an indisputable function as measures of character (*The Dial* 3:312).

Nonetheless, Emerson was intent upon advertising in *The Dial* new developments in German philosophy as well as news about the philosophers themselves. He therefore welcomed the letters of a young American student, Charles Wheeler. In 1842 Wheeler reported from Berlin, "The City of Criticism," where the King of Prussia had assembled the stars of modern scholarship: Humboldt, Bettina von Arnim, Raumer, and Ranke were active there and Waagen directed the Royal Gallery. Wheeler reported that the fresco painter Cornelius, the poet Rückert had arrived, and the greatest mind of all, Schelling, had come from Munich. He reported that the king was dissatisfied with Hegelian influence, noting "we regret to say [the king has] set himself to suppress the 'Hallische Jahrbücher'; [. . .] With this view, also, he summons the great Schelling, now nearly seventy years old, to lecture on the Philosophy of Revelation" (*The Dial*, 3:136). Wheeler continues his report in a personal, dramatic tone as he describes the lecture hall, filled to overflowing — almost to suffocation — and the thunderous welcome accorded the pale professor, whose visage resembled Socrates, yet who seemed not to notice that he was opening a new era in German history.

For *The Dial* Henry Hedge translated Schelling's inaugural university lecture, which was held under these political conditions. The text appeared in the January issue of 1843 with the following comment: "One good thing we note, *Das Heil der Deutschen ist in der Wissenschaft.*"[95] In the meantime Charles Wheeler had travelled to Germany to study; from Heidelberg he reported his impressions in detail. He applauded the restoration of the churches on the Rhine, but noted of the Cologne Cathedral that it was "a pity that its interior should be defiled with the nonsense of the skulls of the three kings, the bones of St. Matthew, &c. &c" (*The Dial*, 3:388). In Bonn he paid a visit to August Wilhelm Schlegel, an impressive old gentleman who inquired about friends in America and was delighted at the publication of his writings in the United States. Wheeler was genuinely impressed by the torchlight parade with which the Berlin students honored Schelling. He sent back to Concord not only Schelling's words of thanks, but texts of several speeches given by dignitaries in his honor. Wheeler's "Letters from Heidelberg"[96] appeared in *The Dial* after the author had literally studied to death in Leipzig in June 1843. He was deeply mourned by Emerson and by his Harvard roommate Henry David Thoreau.

Wheeler's reports include a remarkable amount of detail. He wrote how many students Schelling had in the summer semester at the Berlin University — 60 in all, down from the 300 during the winter semester, a fact that pleased the Hegelians who wished to see him decamp back to Munich, the place of "the inaction of previous years" (*The Dial*, 3:390). But Wheeler knew that Schelling would go to Berlin "as his home for the rest of his life; [. . .] in the capacity of a member of the Academy of Sciences [. . .] a salary of 2000 Thalers a year, and the considerable addition thereto arising from lecture-fees" (*The Dial*, 3:391). Thus, Wheeler communicated to readers of *The Dial* facts such as Tieck's improved health since his stroke, as well as the death of Clemens Brentano. The most important features of Wheeler's reports are his growing awareness of the restrictions upon academic freedom in Berlin. The Hegelians, for example, were forced to concede that Hegel's philosophy, correctly understood, conformed to Christian doctrine. In Heidelberg Bruno Bauer was even removed from his professorial post for his radical critique of the bible. Wheeler described the controversies between the allies of Schelling versus those of Hegel with the verve of a modern sports announcer, and Emerson felt obliged to delete from Wheeler's reports more than just the exclamation marks. At one point his dry editorial comment reads, "We omit many interesting details on the German Universities, furnished by our correspondent, especially on the University of Berlin" (*The Dial*, 3:397).

Wheeler was very conscientious about listing important new German publications and announcing scholarly meetings in Strassburg, Mainz and Ulm. He also cited American translations into German, but could not understand German scholars' ignorance of America and was puzzled by the low esteem Goethe enjoyed in Germany. When Wheeler told Germans that Goethe was read with interest in America, he was met with a frigid response, unlike the response to news of lesser literary lights:

> But when the fact is mentioned, that the letters of Bettine and Günderode have admirers beyond the Atlantic, many persons are forward to express their indignation, as if they felt a personal responsibility for whatever came from the German press. Some young people, whom I know, are sufficiently enthusiastic in regard for Goethe. But for Schiller all profess unbounded reverence and admiration; and Jean Paul is spoken of much in the same way except that the praise is sometimes qualified by criticisms on his style. [. . .] Cooper seems to be the only American who is really read here, but they do not know that he is an American.
>
> (*The Dial*, 3:393)

The German image of Americans lay somewhere between that of an Indian and a Negro. Wheeler found that one could surprise the staff in bookstores and print shops with the news that Americans speak English. There were even some professors who believed that only the educated classes in America spoke English while the rest of the population communicated in a mixture of Indian dialects.

Emerson was able to publish another letter from Wheeler in *The Dial* in April 1843 in which he discussed primarily German philosophical debates. (*The Dial*, 3:541–544). The numerous cliques of Hegelians caught the attention of the correspondent: "Hegelians of the right, of the centre, of the left; of the extreme left and of the mountain." Wheeler wrote that the right, left and center were prepared to find common ground for cooperation, while the Young Hegelians still remained highly critical of the philosopher (*The Dial*, 3:543).

Had Wheeler not died, Emerson probably would have published further letters by him in *The Dial*, for these certainly contributed to a clearer understanding of German intellectual life. Over time he found himself searching for articles for the journal as early contributors busied themselves with other projects or travelled to Europe themselves. He had to fill out the October 1843 issue with material of his own and a long excerpted review of Bettina von Arnim's new book, *This Book Belongs to the King*, from the September 1843 issue of the New York German newspaper, *Deutsche Schnellpost*. Emerson published "A Letter" in *The Dial* (see 4:267–270) reproaching the *Schnellpost* writer, whose review was written "plainly from no very friendly hand" about "that eminent lady, who in the silence of Tieck and Schelling, seems to hold a monopoly of genius in Germany." According to the *Schnellpost*, Bettina's new work, in which she criticized the miserable living conditions of the poor, showed "her eccentric wisdom," while the realization of her ideas could only plunge Germany into deeper misery.

Nonetheless, there appeared in the following number of *The Dial* (which was also the penultimate issue) a very positive review of the *Schnellpost* by Margaret Fuller who recommended the literary discussions in that paper to her readers. In the final number Emerson printed a further essay on philosophy, this one about Kant by James Elliot Cabot who had begun his law studies at Harvard after returning from a three-year stay at the University of Heidelberg where he had studied Kant. Cabot would have had more valuable contributions to make to *The Dial*, but financial difficulties brought the publication to an end in April 1844. The mere three hundred subscribers were not enough to protect Emerson from having to dig into his own pocket to support the venture. New England frugality led many readers to borrow each other's copies rather than to subscribe. The reception the individual numbers received from readers and in other American and English publications was always mixed. Furthermore, Emerson's work on his own books and lectures, as well as his speaking engagements, left him little time for the project. In his eulogy for this singular journal he wrote:

> I have just done with the Dial. Its last number is printed; & having lived four years, which is a Presidential term in America, it may respectably end. [. . .] In New England its whole quadrennium will be a pretty historiette in literary annals.[97]

The closing of this chapter actually had greater significance than Emerson's description suggests. The number of actual readers of *The Dial* was less important than the fact that it was read by writers, theologians and other dynamic and socially active people who were able to glean stimulating ideas from the journal and pass these on to others. German literature had no greater friend in America than this little magazine, especially when Margaret Fuller was its editor. Despite Emerson's attempts to treat more philosophical topics in its pages, *The Dial* was primarily a conduit for the powerful literary influence of Germany on the Transcendentalists and their circle, and not for philosophical influences.

It seems as if the Transcendentalists had followed Goethe also in this regard: "For philosophy in the actual sense of the word, I had no faculty," wrote Goethe in 1820 in his essay on the "Influence of Modern Philosophy."[98] He confessed that only with the help of a method that taught him to grasp the ideas of philosophers like objects, did he begin to be interested in philosophy. In Rome he had discussed aesthetic issues with Karl Philipp Moritz who had written on "The Nature of the Beautiful." This little essay, which Emerson had translated for himself, characterizes the Transcendentalists' occupation with German philosophy. They were, of course, familiar with — and for the most part, fascinated by — the works of Kant, Fichte, Schelling and Hegel. Yet, despite their best efforts, they were not able to penetrate the works of these thinkers. René Wellek has shown the invalidity of the persistent myth of Transcendentalism's German origins. Even Emerson was seeking confirmation of his own thought, and found it in Schelling's philosophy of identity. But, as Wellek comments, the Transcendentalists did not basically need German idealism to support their own convictions.[99] Emerson, like most of the Transcendentalists, was much more conversant with the Platonic and pre-Socratic philosophy he had studied systematically as a student, while German idealism was presented to the students by empiricists at Harvard College — even by Charles Follen — with considerable hostility. Although one cannot call Emerson a mystic, he had a much more intimate relationship to Jacob Böhme, who was admired by many New England utopians, than to any other German philosopher. Emerson even considered Böhme as significant as Goethe. It is Goethe, however, who finds a place in Emerson's successful lecture series entitled "Representative Men." He considered Plato the philosopher of his age and Homer, Dante and Shakespeare the representatives of their times. For the modern age Emerson chose Napoleon as the man of action who put into motion the extreme energies of his day. Goethe was the influence behind the contemporary intellectual and spiritual powers, but he saw Jacob Böhme as the religious inspiration of the modern period. Emerson reiterated this canon in a poem that he published in 1861 in *The Atlantic Monthly,* but did not include in his own *Selected Poems*. He added an additional name to this poem, which consists of two parts and is entitled "The Test," subtitled "Musa loquitur." The muse relates that she has "hung [her] verses in the wind," all of which have been blown away except five. The second part of the poem, entitled "Solution," solves the riddle of the authorship of these five lines that have outlasted five hundred other poets. They are from Homer, whose song made "the earth grow civil"; Dante, "moulding Nature at his will"; Shakespeare, whose "wit" was not surpassed in "sequent centuries"; and Swedenborg who "leads the soul." Emerson characterizes the modern age as the Napoleonic era in which France — "where a poet never grew" — divided and redivided the world, a world in which science and commerce are in the service of war. Into this world, says Emerson, came Goethe and brought wisdom from Olympus for all humanity: "his finger wrote in clay/The open secret of to-day."[100]

The text of "Goethe: Or, The Writer" represents the culmination of Emerson's Goethe experience.[101] The nature of the summation explains why Emerson furnished no new insights on the German poet, but rather presented an expanded version of his *Dial* article of 1840 with somewhat different emphasis. This lecture, which is Emerson's most extensive discussion of Goethe, had the greatest impact, largely because he took it on an extended tour in 1845 and 1846.

Goethe was the second youngest, and in Emerson's eyes the most modern, representative in his collection of "Representative Men." He used the opportunity to present the writer as a man of intellect so very different from his American contemporaries caught up in the anti-intellectual pursuits of trade and politics. This emphasis shows that Emerson was not addressing fellow Transcendentalists, but a wider audience outside New England. In his lecture "The Transcendentalist" Emerson had evoked the extreme of someone who can distance himself from daily life so radically that he no longer votes because no candidate meets his standards.

Those who are hard-working and zealous, however, like the Quakers and Shakers in their communal societies, pay too high a price in Emerson's eyes, for they have lost a sense of balance between practical and spiritual activity. Great deeds need a spiritual basis and therefore society should have no more pressing interest than the "wellbeing of the literary class." According to Emerson, the modern writer is to blame for having lost his former position of leadership. Today he is forced to "sustain with shameless advocacy some bad government, or must bark all the year round in opposition."[102]

But Goethe best represented for Emerson the power as well as the duties of the writer in the modern age. In contrast to earlier times, culture manifests itself in countless areas. Goethe is the modern "philosopher of this multiplicity"[103] — master of stories, philosophies, mythologies, which he accomplished with the unique encyclopedic technique of modern research.

The work by Goethe that best demonstrated for Emerson this universality of the poet was "Helena." He was referring to Carlyle's partial translation of *Faust II* (that appeared in 1828 in the *Foreign Review),* which was all he knew of that part of the drama. In an essay, "Nominalist and Realist," he noted that when one criticized a genius like Burns or Goethe, one was whipping a false image of the man:

> If you criticise a fine genius, the odds are that you are out of your reckoning, and instead of the poet, are censuring your own caricature of him. [. . .] After taxing Goethe as a courtier, artificial, unbelieving, worldly, — I took up this book of Helena, and found him an Indian of the wilderness, a piece of pure nature like an apple or an oak, large as morning or night, and virtuous as a brier-rose.[104]

And so Emerson cited *Faust* in his lecture to prove that Goethe was "the soul of his century,"[105] reasoning that it was in this work that he showed his mastery most clearly. Basically, Emerson felt that since Goethe assumed that nothing was certain, it mattered little what he wrote about — whether it be "the leading idea of modern Botany in "The Metamorphosis of Plants," or his rejection of the artificial theory of the seven colors in the field of optics. He takes nothing for granted; therefore, whatever he says "refuses to be forgotten."[106] Goethe is for Emerson the prototype of the realist who states boldly: "I have never heard of any crime which I might not have committed."[107]

But that is not the way Goethe actually put it. In 1961 this "forged" quotation was the occasion for a lively debate in the pages of the yearbook of the Goethe Society as scholars tried to ascertain the true author of the quotation. It had surfaced most recently in Thomas Mann's novel *Lotte in Weimar* (1939) (*The Beloved Returns*), but can actually be traced back to a published lecture on Goethe by Herman Grimm. Grimm must have found it in Emerson's own lecture, which he translated into German himself in the mid-nineteenth century. Wolfgang Herwig describes the interesting array of authors who make use of this quotation over the subsequent years. The list stretches from Peter Altenberg via Stefan Zweig to Egon Friedell and Paul Hankamer.[108]

Goethe's actual idea can be found among his *Maxims and Reflections:* "Man darf nur alt werden, um milder zu sein; ich sehe keinen Fehler begehen, den ich nicht auch begangen hätte."[109] The sixth book of *Wilhelm Meister's Lehrjahre* closes with a similar thought:

> Denn niemals werde ich in Gefahr kommen, auf mein eigenes Können und Vermögen stolz zu werden, da ich so deutlich erkannt habe, welch Ungeheuer in jedem menschlichen Busen, wenn eine höhere Kraft uns nicht bewahrt, sich erzeugen und nähren könne.[110]

Even the "Beautiful Soul" speaks of the unavoidable weaknesses of human nature, of the horrors that lurk deep in the soul. Thus, by radically reformulating Goethe's thought, Emerson coined a phrase that was picked up by German writers who willingly assumed that Goethe was the source. It should be added that Thomas Mann surely found the quotation in Emerson, whose lecture on Goethe he used in his own essay "Goethe's Career as a Man of Letters" (1932), and in an introduction he wrote for the 1948 volume of translations, *The Permanent Goethe*.

Emerson introduced his readers to *Wilhelm Meister,* the work by Goethe he had gotten to know first and the one he knew better than any other. He sweeps away the old reservations about the supposed immoral episodes in the novel, defining the main theme to be the transition of a democrat to an aristocrat. Then he uses *Wilhelm Meister* to compare Goethe's intellect (and therewith the German *per se*) with the Anglo-Saxon and the French. In England and America one finds greater delight in intellectual brilliance for its own sake. "What distinguishes Goethe for French and English readers is a property he shares with his nation, — a habitual reference to interior truth."[111] This quality Emerson contrasts with the superficiality of mere talent:

> Goethe, the head and body of the German nation, does not speak from talent, but the truth shines through: he is very wise, though his talent often veils his wisdom. [. . .] The old Eternal Genius, who built the world, has confided himself more to this man than to any other.[112]

The passage shows how Emerson's admiration prepares an American image of Germany that was to determine Goethe's reception through the end of 19th century. But not much more than a feeble, clichéd imitation of Emerson's original idea endured. He had seen the German spirit visible through Goethe, but what he perceived was not a nebulous, poorly defined phenomenon at the depths of the German personality. On the contrary, he felt that German intellect lacked French sprightliness as much as it did the practical understanding of the English and the American sense of adventure. German intellect, in Emerson's view, is not satisfied with categories based on superficial performance, but steadily asks "To what end?"

Emerson was far enough removed from the German character, as well as from Goethe (despite his deep admiration), so as not to see the shortcomings of German intellect or its highest representative. He was also enough of an American not to be puzzled by the otherworldliness of German scholars. The entire nation seemed to him to preserve "the most ridiculous good faith" in Greek and Latin literature[113] while the professors seriously believed that philosophical truths could actually be applied to daily life on the streets of Berlin and Munich.

Even Goethe did not escape the high standards of Emerson's American morals. The New Englander never changed his mind about the rank and quality of Goethe's genius, although he certainly did not place him on the highest rung reserved for Shakespeare and Dante. What he missed earlier in the *Italian Journey* he never found again in Goethe: self-mastery, that "selfsurrender to the moral sentiment." He criticized Goethe for always having posed the same challenge to his fellow man: "*What can you teach me?*"[114] As proof he quotes Goethe himself: "Piety itself is no aim, but only a means, whereby through purest inward peace we may attain to highest culture."[115] This aspect of Goethe's autobiography helps explain why the work was such a novelty in both old and New England: "That a man exists for Culture; not for what he can accomplish, but for what can be accomplished in him."[116] For Emerson, "that a man exists for Culture," seemed to exhibit a monstrous egotism. Thus, he denied the representative writer of his age the title "artist" and instead, called him "this lawgiver of art."[117]

If one views the general transcendental attitude toward Goethe, and the specific attitude toward art, it is understandable why the American Transcendentalists did not produce the great works of art in their generation. Emerson's ideas on art and culture were not identical with those of his like-minded friends, who harbored a confusing multiplicity of views. The significant literary works of the 19th century, at any rate, did not come out of Emerson's circle. Nathaniel Hawthorne, who had lived for years in Concord, was not among Emerson's closest friends and made clear what he thought of Transcendentalism in his satire *The Celestial Rail-Road* (1843).[118] In Hawthorne's work the movement appears in the form of a giant who captures respectable travellers and then fattens them up for his table with a rich diet of smoke, fog, moonlight, raw potatoes and sawdust. He is by birth a German and is called "Giant Transcendentalist." When it comes to the facial features and the substance of "this huge miscreant," the most remarkable thing is "that neither he for himself, nor anybody for him, has ever been able to describe them."[119]

Herman Melville had few connections to Concord except through Hawthorne; Walt Whitman was closer to the Concord group because Emerson and Thoreau and other visitors from Concord enjoyed meeting him in New York. The affinity lay in his poetry, which although not exactly transcendental thought in a strict sense, still expressed poetic enthusiasm in an entirely new language. This language immediately gripped the Transcendentalists who were open to such modern impulses. There are very specific reasons why they did not know the great lyrical genius of the century, Emily Dickinson, who had withdrawn to a life of relative solitude only sixty miles away in western Massachusetts. Still, they all wrote poetry, though it was again Emerson who left behind an enduring work. This assertion is legitimate despite his own admission within the poem "The

Poet," that the high muse had "directly never greeted [him]," but that he "was free to overhear," to listen to what others had said.[120]

Emerson's poetic *oeuvre* consists primarily of reflective poems and nature lyrics. His verses reflect his high aesthetic standards, his sublime moral criteria, and his love of the New England landscape with its drama of seasonal change. A comparison to the poetry of Goethe or of German Romanticism shows that Emerson also wanted to maintain his independent voice. The complete text of the poem (mentioned above) that he wrote in the volume of his Goethe edition is as follows:

> "Written in a Volume of Goethe"
>
> Six thankful weeks, — and let it be
> A meter of prosperity, —
> In my coat I bore this book,
> And seldom therein could I look,
> For I had too much to think,
> Heaven and earth to eat and drink.
> Is he hapless who can spare
> In his plenty things so rare? [121]

The lines illustrate Emerson's progressive development away from literary models — imitation was never his method — toward intellectual autonomy. In his poem "To J. W." Emerson admonishes John Weiss, a young theologian, who was consumed by criticism of Goethe's flaws:

> Set not thy foot on graves;
> Nor seek to unwind the shroud
> Which charitable Time
> And Nature have allowed
> To wrap the errors of a sage sublime.[122]

Rather than wasting time on fruitless criticism and sterile imitation, he advises Weiss not to disturb Goethe's deserved repose, but to earn his own "trophies" by living and observing life and the world to the fullest, much as Goethe had done: "Go, get them where he earned them when alive."[123]

Emerson was unquestionably knowledgeable about German poetry. Yet he rarely expressed himself on the subject, not even more specifically on Goethe's poetry. But his profound comprehension of German Romanticism is evident in a poem that he wrote in 1857 on the little island of Naushon near Cape Cod. The poem is entitled "Waldeinsamkeit" and uses the form of the German *Lied* with its short quatrains and abab rhyme scheme.[124] This celebration of the forest, so thoroughly imbued with the spirit of Eichendorff, is again evidence of the spiritual affinities between German and New England Romanticism.[125]

A further parallel between Emerson and Goethe deserves mention. Emerson's admiration for Goethe's encyclopedic knowledge would not have been as great if he himself had not harbored a similar passion to experience new and different arenas. His exploration of foreign cultures and literatures often led him to where Goethe had been, and it can be assumed that he owed many a creative stimulus to the poet who was for him a representative of modernity.

So motivated, Emerson entered in his notebooks (between 1837 and 1840) some remarks from Goethe's *Noten und Abhandlungen zum besseren Verständnis des West-Östlichen Diwans* (Notes and essays for the better understanding of the *West-östlicher Diwan*). We can assume that he was also reading Goethe's poetry at this time, for in 1841 he read Persian poetry in English translation and in 1843 discovered his "ideal poet," Saadi, author of the collection *Gulistan* ("The Rose Garden"). Emerson would write a new preface to the collection in 1865. In 1846 he bought the two volume translation of Persian verse by Joseph von Hammer-Purgstall, a collection Goethe also owned.[126] These anthologies were Emerson's most important access to Persian poetry and the chief inspiration of his own creativity during this period. The oriental poets opened imaginative vistas before him, giving poetry meaning as a medium of sensuality, allying it to music and dance. Emerson was to be the mediator of this force in America. On July 6, 1841 he wrote in his diary that he was actually called to be "professor of Joyous Science" (*Journals*, 8:8), an expression that comes from the Provencal *gai saber*. He used the term again in the lecture called "Prospects," which is probably Nietzsche's source for the concept. Nietzsche cites Emerson's essay "History" for his tract *Die Fröhliche Wissenschaft (The Gay Science* or, *The Science of Joy):* "To the poet, to the philosopher, to the saint, all things are friendly and sacred, all events profitable, all days holy, all men divine."[127]

The Persian poet Hafiz must have delighted Emerson as much as he had Goethe, for he translated more than 700 verses of Hammer-Purgstall's German into English (over 150 of these are from "Sakiname, the Book of the Cup Bearer"). In so doing, he followed his German originals so closely that he often produced syntax quite foreign to English. The cryptic style and metrical awkwardness of his own poems from this period have been traced to the influence of this translation work from Hammer-Purgstall's German.[128]

For the most part Emerson only translated excerpts of Persian poems to use in his lecture "Persian Poetry." But he also recombined disparate parts of various poems and translated nine poems in their entirety. Furthermore, some of his own poems owe their inspiration to short Persian quotations; others seem to be quite independent of any source and are taken to be Emerson's own verses.

In imitation of Hafiz, who was Goethe's oriental alter ego, Emerson chose for himself the Persian poet Saadi, whose name he also gave himself. In the October 1842 issue of *The Dial* he published a long poem entitled "Saadi." From then on Saadi, Seyed or Said is the name that concealed his own persona in poems and journal passages: Saadi who loves solitude, but also mankind; who rejects the fakirs with their mournful eyes and bitter sermons; who — as his name proclaims — is a happy one. Emerson most likely applied to himself the words that Goethe wrote in the notes to the *West-östlicher Diwan* about this poet who died in 1291 at the age of 102: "He lives and weaves within a wide-ranging breadth of experience and is rich in anecdotes which he embellishes with maxims and verses. It is his express intent to teach his readers and listeners."[129]

From this period on, Emerson's attraction to eastern culture began to compete with his interest in the West. His last ocean voyage took him, consequently, beyond Europe into Egypt. The civilization of India appealed to him at least as much as the Persian, and in 1844 he followed Thoreau's recommendation and read the *Bhagavad-Gita*. Here, too, there was such a clear spiritual affinity that an Indian scholar later proclaimed in Concord in 1884 that some Indians considered Emerson a "geographical mistake." His work *Nature,* they felt, contained the entire body of Indian religious truth, which expressed the infinite through the symbolism of nature.[130]

Emerson's fame reached not only India. In 1861 the scholar Herman Grimm first called German readers' attention to the American sage. This son of the philologist Wilhelm Grimm was active in Berlin as an art and literary historian. In his essay entitled "Ralph Waldo Emerson" he reported how an American friend had shown him part of an essay by Emerson, how he had read a page and was astonished "to have understood nothing, although I was fairly certain of my English. I asked about the author and was told he was the premier writer in America and very brilliant, though sometimes a bit mad, and sometimes could not even explain his own sentences."[131] Grimm was undeterred and, with the aid of his *Webster's Dictionary,* kept on reading. "I soon discovered the secret: these were true thoughts, this was a true language, a real human being that I had before me. [. . .] Since then I have not stopped reading Emerson's works.[132]

Reading alone did not satisfy Herman Grimm's curiosity about Emerson. He contacted the American writer whose response may possibly have been induced by blandishments like the following: "When I think of

America, I think of you, and America seems to be the foremost country on earth. [. . .] I have tried to write my book on Michelangelo with your sensibility."[133] A year later Grimm made a propitious marriage to Gisela von Arnim, a daughter of Bettina. Gisela was herself a writer of dramas who sent samples of her art to Concord. Emerson replied with the comment: "Certainly it requires great health and wealth of power to ventriloquize (shall I say?) through so many bodies; [. . .] But, in Germany, I can well see, the drama seems to cling about the intellectual heart."[134] When Bettina died in 1859 Emerson wrote to her son-in-law, Grimm:

> I mourned that I could not earlier have established my alliance with your circle, that I might have told her how much I and my friends owed her. Who had such motherwit? such sallies? such portraits? such suppression of commonplace?"[135]

Herman Grimm was the only German with whom Emerson corresponded. To be sure, their letters cannot be compared in intellectual quality with those that Emerson exchanged with Carlyle. Sometimes years separated the infrequent letters sent between 1856 and 1871, in which Grimm wrote German and Emerson English. Emerson's son had visited Grimm in Berlin when he was studying medicine in that city; Emerson himself met Grimm personally in Florence on his return visit from Egypt in 1873 and recognized in him one of the leading German admirers and scholars of Goethe. Emerson's daughter Ellen captured the details of the encounter in a letter written to her mother, who had remained in Concord.[136] Her account tells how Emerson and she spent a very pleasant evening with Gisela and Herman Grimm in Emerson's hotel. Grimm could not contain his amazement at Emerson's healthy appearance and "such fresh cheeks" and "bright coloring which is all lost, of course, in the photographs."[137]

Grimm did all in his power to make Emerson known in Germany, writing in his essay: "Emerson, the free, republican American, who bows to nothing but his own wants and the glory of the Germanic race,"[138] also calling him "this perfect swimmer in the element modern life."[139] But the task of popularizing his subject was remarkably difficult. It was not merely the lack of language skills — for Grimm was prepared to translate Emerson into German — but rather what he called "the lack of inner freedom"[140] that stood in the way. Grimm's explanation involves differences between the educated public in America versus that of Germany. He characterized Americans as "people who know practical life and have a concrete idea of the past and future of their fatherland. This is a remarkable contrast to our country. We are extremely learned — but only for our examiners."[141] Likewise, he saw the difference between the American social system where "birth, money, talent, exuberance of spirit" could bring a man to the top of society. He perceived that a further obstruction to Emerson's message in contemporary Germany was "the artificial class of people who feel superior to others and separate themselves by imaginary barriers."[142] Nevertheless, Grimm did not feel "blind devotion" to Emerson. He wrote:

> Emerson is an American; the stern nationality of his people will need a long time before it approaches ours. We stand higher than the Americans: that which serves them well is not necessarily useful to us. Emerson's character seems to me more significant than if I were to think of him solely as a writer."[143]

In 1867 Grimm wrote a novel, entitled *Unüberwindliche Mächte* (Insurmountable Forces), which explores questions of nationality and the role of the aristocracy in a modern Germany soon to be united under Prussia. The United States, in its post-Civil-War period, serves as a model of this literary evocation of vitality and perseverance, particularly in the strength of certain individuals whose families have lived and worked there for generations — the American aristocracy. A constellation of German, American, and German-American figures is developed in the story in order to offer various perspectives on the life-story of the main character, an impoverished German nobleman named Arthur. Among the many secondary characters is the figure of the wise Mr. Wilson, an American who leaves his solitary life in the American forests to travel to Europe where he is needed. Emerson, no doubt, was the model for Grimm's American sage.[144]

On the other side of the Atlantic Emerson was quite responsive to Grimm's increasing sense of national identity during the period of Prussia's growing domination. "I give you joy, the new year, on these great days of Prussia," he wrote on January 5, 1871, two weeks before Wilhelm I had been proclaimed German Kaiser from Versailles.[145] The letter also contains an expression of Emerson's hope for Prussia's political role in Europe: "You will have seen that our people have taken your part from the first, and have a right to admire the immense exhibition of Prussian power. Of course, we are impatient for peace, were it only to secure Prussia at this height of well-being."[146]

Emerson spent the last years of his life in Concord as a respected figure, loved by the nation. When his house burned down in 1873, the citizens of Concord not only rescued all his books and papers, but friends and admirers took up a collection for rebuilding his house, during which time Emerson and his daughter were sent on their trip to Egypt. Before his return to America he was greeted in London by scholars, politicians and aristocrats who showered him with accolades. On this visit he was also able to see Carlyle for the last time.

Emerson returned to Concord to find his new house and be greeted by a small town decked out in flags in his honor and throngs of townsfolk to meet him at the railroad station. Amidst the strains of a band playing "Home Sweet Home" he drove home and walked into his front door between rows of singing schoolchildren. One cannot help sensing a resemblance between this honorific spectacle and the stature accorded his analogue, the German intellectual icon of Weimar.

In his last years Emerson's memory deteriorated and his public appearances became infrequent. He lived in bucolic repose surrounded by his books before dying on April 22, 1882 of a lung condition. He had brought this upon himself walking in the chill spring air in the hope of curing a cold. Among the objects that received particular mention in his will was one that had been brought to him from Germany by the abolitionist Charles Sumner: a small drinking glass that had once belonged to Goethe.[147]

Notes

[1] On Emerson's reading habits, see John A. McCarthy, "Emerson, Goethe und die Deutschen," *Goethe-Yearbook* (Columbia SC: Camden House, 1994), 8:177–193.

[2] Ralph L. Rusk, *The Life of Ralph Waldo Emerson* (New York: Scribner's, 1949), 113.

[3] "Will. Emerson aus Boston, Nordamerika, in Göttingen studierend, protestantischer Theolog. Blieb für mich." Johann Wolfgang von Goethe, *Tagebücher* (1823–1824), in *Goethes Werke,* herausgegeben im Auftrage der Großherzogin Sophie von Sachsen (Weimar: Hermann Böhlaus Nachfolger, 1897), part III, vol. 9:271.

[4] Ralph L. Rusk, *The Life of Ralph Waldo Emerson,* 143.

[5] James Elliot Cabot, *A Memoir of Ralph Waldo Emerson,* 2 vols. (Boston: Houghton Mifflin, 1887), 1:139.

[6] Dieter Borchmeyer, *Das Theater Richard Wagners* (Stuttgart: Reclam, 1982), 387, note 165.

[7] *The Correspondence of Emerson and Carlyle,* ed. Joseph Slater (New York and London: Columbia UP, 1964), 120.

[8] *The Correspondence of Emerson and Carlyle,* 98.

[9] *The Correspondence of Emerson and Carlyle,* 97–98. Emerson quotes from Goethe's *Wilhelm Meister's Apprenticeship* in a speech of Philine to Wilhelm. The

remark on "environment" refers to Carlyle's first use of the term in its present sense.

[10]   *The Correspondence of Emerson and Carlyle*, 107–108. The censorious remark about Goethe's arranging of gifts refers to the celebration in honor of a half century of his civil service to the state of Sachsen-Weimar. Sarah Austin's *Characteristics of Goethe* contains an account of this event (3:105).

[11]   *The Correspondence of Emerson and Carlyle*, 114–115. For differences in Carlyle's and Emerson's appreciation of *Wilhelm Meister*, see Anders Holengren, *The Code of Concord: Emerson's Search for Universal Law* (Stockholm: Almquvist & Wiskell Intern 1994), 125–129.

[12]   *The Correspondence of Emerson and Carlyle*, 218. In his thorough study of Emerson's relationship to Goethe, Gustaaf Van Cromphout gives an overwhelming number of examples to the contrary. Emerson's great admiration for the German poet, the similarity in both Emerson's and Goethe's thought on the most various subjects from the theory of nature and art to their rejection of epistemology and lack of any sense of system, whether in the works of others or in their own. Indeed, it is fascinating to follow Emerson's development from the first critical pronouncements on Goethe to his later, very different judgments. See Gustaaf Van Cromphout, *Emerson's Modernity and the Example of Goethe* (Columbia and London: U of Missouri P, 1990), 26.

[13]   Rusk, *The Life of Ralph Waldo Emerson*, 192.

[14]   Goethe, *Italienische Reise* (Hamburg: Christian Wegner Verlag, 1954), "Hamburger Ausgabe," 14 vols., ed. Erich Trunz *et. al.*, 11:222, 225.

[15]   *Hamburger Ausgabe*, 11:240.

[16]   *Hamburger Ausgabe*, 11:211.

[17]   The Goethe quotation is as follows: "so konnte man umgekehrt von ihm [Goethe's Vater] sagen, dass er nie ganz unglücklich werden konnte, weil er sich immer wieder nach Neapel dachte" (*Hamburger Ausgabe*, 11:186).

[18]   *Hamburger Ausgabe*, 11:168.

[19]   *Hamburger Ausgabe*, 11:168.

[20]   *Hamburger Ausgabe*, 11:353.

[21]   *Hamburger Ausgabe*, 11:145.

[22]   *Hamburger Ausgabe*, 11:372.

[23]   *Hamburger Ausgabe*, 11:127.

[24]   *Hamburger Ausgabe*, 11:127.

[25]   *Hamburger Ausgabe*, 11:199.

[26]   See Vivian Hopkins, "The Influence of Goethe on Emerson's Aesthetic Theory," *Philological Quarterly*, 27 (October 1948), 325–344.

[27]   "Thoughts on Modern Literature," *The Dial*, 1:152–153.

[28]   *Hamburger Ausgabe*, 11:121–122; see also Hopkins, 328.

[29] *Hamburger Ausgabe,* 11:109.

[30] *Hamburger Ausgabe,* 11:395.

[31] The *Wilhelm Meister* quotations are all from Carlyle's translation.

[32] *Journals,* 6:202. Novalis, *Werke,* 4 vols., ed. Edwald Wasmuth (Heidelberg: Lambert Schneider, 1953–1957), 2:42.

[33] *Hamburger Ausgabe,* 7:101. "Der Mensch ist dem Menschen das Interessanteste und sollte ihn vielleicht ganz allein interessieren."

[34] *Hamburger Ausgabe,* 7:443.

[35] *Hamburger Ausgabe,* 9:407. The passage in *Dichtung und Wahrheit* runs as follows: "denn der Eigenname eines Menschen ist nicht etwa wie ein Mantel, der bloss um ihn her hängt und an dem man allenfalls noch zupfen und zerren kann, sondern ein vollkommen passendes Kleid, ja wie die Haut selber ihm über und über angewachsen, an der man nicht schaben und schinden darf, ohne ihn selbst zu verletzen."

[36] Lessing's original German is as follows: "Reiz ist Schönheit in Bewegung." *Lessing's Laokoon,* ed. A. Hamann (Oxford: Clarendon Press, 1878), 159.

[37] *Hamburger Ausgabe,* 13:37–41.

[38] *Hamburger Ausgabe,* 13:41–43.

[39] *Hamburger Ausgabe,* 13:25–29.

[40] *Der Briefwechsel zwischen Goethe und Schiller,* ed. Emil Staiger (Frankfurt: Insel, 1977), 2:813–814; *Journals,* 6:291–292; 294–295.

[41] "Da im Wissen sowohl als in der Reflexion kein Ganzes zusammengebracht werden kann, weil jenem das Innere, dieser das Äussere fehlt, so müssen wir uns die Wissenschaft notwendig als Kunst denken, wenn wir von ihr irgend eine Art von Ganzheit erwarten." *Goethes Nachgelassene Werke* (Stuttgart: Cotta, 1833), 10:85.

[42] *Hamburger Ausgabe,* 13:7–52.

[43] *Hamburger Ausgabe,* 12:7–15.

[44] Thomas Roscoe, *The Life of Michelangelo,* London: 1833. The citation represents a bibliographical puzzle and comes from Emerson's own journal.

[45] Henry Seidel Canby, *Thoreau* (Boston: Houghton Mifflin, 1939), 12.

[46] Gustaaf Van Cromphout, *Emerson's Modernity and the Example of Goethe* (Columbia and London: U of Missouri P, 1990), 26.

[47] Ralph Waldo Emerson, "Michel Angelo Buonarotti." *The Early Lectures of Ralph Waldo Emerson,* 3 vols., ed. Stephen E. Whicher and Robert E. Spiller (Cambridge, MA: Harvard UP, 1959–1972), 101–102. Henceforth cited as *The Early Lectures.*

[48] Ralph Waldo Emerson, "Martin Luther." *The Early Lectures,* 1:119.

[49]   In 1869 Emerson was a member of the University Lectureship at Harvard, where he lectured on the "Natural History of the Intellect." He also gave a total of sixteen lectures in 1870. Overall, he considered this period at Harvard to be an unhappy experience.

[50]   *The Early Lectures,* 1:143.

[51]   "Literature," *The Early Lectures,* 2:67.

[52]   *The Early Lectures,* 2:215; "Mich selbst, ganz wie ich da bin, auszubilden, das war dunkel von Jugend auf mein Wunsch und meine Absicht" *(Hamburger Ausgabe,* 7:290).

[53]   "*Thoughts on Modern Literature,*" *The Dial,* 1:155–156.

[54]   *Hamburger Ausgabe,* 11:542.

[55]   Rüdiger Els, *Ralph Waldo Emerson und "Die Natur in Goethe's Werken: Parallelen von Nature (1836) und "Natur" (1844) mit dem Prosahymnus "Die Natur" und sein möglicher Einfluss* (Frankfurt/M.: Peter Lang, 1977; Mainzer Studien zur Amerikanistik 8).

[56]   *Hamburger Ausgabe,* 13:48.

[57]   "Written in a Volume of Goethe," *Complete Works,* 9:373.

[58]   "The American Scholar." *The Collected Works of Ralph Waldo Emerson,* vol. I: Nature, Addresses, and Lectures. Introd. Robert E. Spiller (Cambridge: Harvard UP, 1971), 52.

[59]   "The American Scholar," *Collected Works,* 1:56.

[60]   "The American Scholar," *Collected Works,* 1:62.

[61]   "The American Scholar," *Collected Works,* 1:67.

[62]   "The American Scholar," *Collected Works,* 1:68.

[63]   "An Address," *Collected Works,* 1:90.

[64]   "An Address," *Collected Works,* 1:93.

[65]   Harriet Martineau, *Retrospect of Western Travel* (London: Saunders & Otley, 1838).

[66]   *Memoirs of Margaret Fuller Ossoli,* 2 vols., ed. Ralph Waldo Emerson, W. H. Channing, John F. Clarke (Boston: Phillips, Sampson & Co., 1857), 1:202.

[67]   Robert D. Richardson, *Emerson. The Mind on Fire* (Berkeley, Los Angeles, London: U of California P, 1995), 338–339.

[68]   The tensions created by Margaret Fuller's visits are described in Joel Myerson, "Margaret Fuller's 1842 Journal at Concord with the Emersons," *Harvard Library Bulletin,* 21 (July 3, 1973), 320–340.

[69]   Werner Vordtriede, "Bettinas englisches Wagnis," *Euphorion,* 51 (1957), 271–294.

[70]   Werner Vordtriede, "Bettinas englisches Wagnis," 271.

[71] *Ibid.*

[72] For a thorough study of this phenomenon, see Hildegard Platzer Collins and Phillipp Allison Shelley, "The Reception in England and America of *Goethe's Correspondence with a Child,*" in *Anglo-German and American German Cross Currents,*" vol. 2, ed. by Shelley and Arthur O. Lewis, Jr. (Chapel Hill: U of North Carolina P, 1962), 2:97–174.

[73] *Goethe's Correspondence with a Child,* 2 vols. (Lowell, MA: Daniel Bixby, 1841), 1:97.

[74] *Goethe's Correspondence with a Child,* 2:234.

[75] *Goethe's Correspondence with a Child,* 2:89.

[76] *Goethe's Correspondence with a Child,* 1:257.

[77] *Goethe's Correspondence with a Child,* 1:216.

[78] *Goethe's Correspondence with a Child,* 2:165.

[79] "Nature," *Collected Works,* 1:10.

[80] *Goethe's Correspondence with a Child,* 2:202.

[81] *Goethe's Correspondence with a Child,* 2:249.

[82] "Nature," *Collected Works,* 1:37.

[83] *Goethe's Correspondence with a Child,* 2:202.

[84] The references are to the Irish writer Anna Jameson and the Swiss writer Anna Rothpelz. Rothpelz published a popular collection of tales under the pseudonym Rosalie Müller in 1839–1840.

[85] This letter, in Margaret Fuller's hand, is incomplete. The first page contains a note: "Extract from RWE's letter to me which I sent to Bettine." We can assume that she enclosed the first page of Emerson's original letter with the papers she sent to Berlin.

[86] Jane Tuckerman had been a pupil of Fuller's and visited Concord in September 1839. Mr. Adams has not been identified.

[87] Nationale Forschungs- und Gedenkstätten der klassischen deutschen Literatur in Weimar. Arnim, 302a: Margaret Fuller to B. von Arnim, 22.11.1840.

[88] For the most recent treatment of *The Dial,* see Joel Myerson, *The New England Transcendentalists and The Dial. A History of the Magazine and its Contributors* (Rutherford, NJ: Fairleigh Dickinson UP, 1980).

[89] "The Editors to the Reader," *The Dial,* 1:1–4.

[90] "The Editors to the Reader," *The Dial,* 1:3.

[91] See George Willis Cook, *A Historical and Biographical Introduction to Accompany the Dial,* vol. 1 (New York: Russell and Russell, 1961), 56.

[92] "Thoughts on Modern Literature," *The Dial,* 1:139.

[93] "Thoughts on Modern Literature," *The Dial*, 1:142. The following seven references to *The Dial* are to this essay.

[94] David M. Robinson, *Emerson and the Conduct of Life. Pragmatism and Ethical Purpose in the Later Works* (Cambridge, New York: Cambridge UP 1993), 111.

[95] "The salvation of the Germans lies in scholarship." F. Henry Hedge, "Literary Intelligence," *The Dial*, 3:387; 398–404.

[96] *The Dial*, 3:388–397.

[97] Myerson, *The New England Transcendentalists and The Dial*, 98.

[98] *Hamburger Ausgabe*, 13:25.

[99] René Wellek, "The Minor Transcendentalists and German Philosophy," in *New England Quarterly*, 15 (1942), 652–680.

[100] *Complete Works*, 9:220–223.

[101] "Goethe, or the Writer," *Collected Works*, 4:149–166.

[102] "Goethe, or the Writer," *Collected Works*, 4:155.

[103] "Goethe, or the Writer," *Collected Works*, 4:156.

[104] *Complete Works*, 3:241–242.

[105] "Goethe, or the Writer," *Collected Works*, 4:157. For Emerson's "love-hate" attitude toward *Faust*, see Van Cromphout, *Emerson's Modernity and the Example of Goethe*, 73–74.

[106] "Goethe, or the Writer," *Collected Works* 4:158–159.

[107] "Goethe, or the Writer," *Collected Works*, 4:159.

[108] Wolfgang Herwig, "Das falsche, aber verbreitete Goethe-Zitat vom 'Verbrechen.'", in: *Goethe, Neue Folge des Jahrbuchs der Goethe-Gesellschaft* (Weimar, 1961), 352–352. See also W. Herwig, "Nochmals zum Zitat vom 'Verbrechen'" *Jahrbuch* (1962), 292; Also, W. Herwig. "Das 'Verbrechen' und kein Ende," *Jahrbuch* (1963), 359–362. My thanks to Katharina Mommsen for the reference to miscellanies by Herweg and to the context of the *Maximen* with the *Lehrjahre*.

[109] *Hamburger Ausgabe*, 12:542 (number 1332), "One may only grow old in order to become gentler; I see no error committed that I could have not committed myself."

[110] *Hamburger Ausgabe*, 7:420. I shall never be in danger of feeling pride in my own proficiency and competence, for I have seen so clearly what a monster can be born and nurtured in every human breast when a higher power does not protect us.

[111] "Goethe, or The Writer," *Collected Works*, 4:161.

[112] "Goethe, or the Writer," *Collected Works*, 4:163.

[113] "Goethe, or the Writer," *Collected Works*, 4:162.

[114]   "Goethe, or the Writer," *Collected Works,* 4:163.

[115]   *Hamburger Ausgabe,* 8:295. Also, "Goethe, or the Writer," *Collected Works,* 4:164.

[116]   *Ibid.*

[117]   "Goethe, or the Writer," *Collected Works,* 4:165.

[118]   See *The Centenary Edition of the Works of Nathaniel Hawthorne,* 23 vols., ed. William Charvat, *et. al.* (Columbus: Ohio State UP, 1962–1997), 10:186–206.

[119]   *The Celestial Rail-Road,* in *Works of Nathaniel Hawthorne,* 10:197.

[120]   Emerson, *Complete Works,* 9:324.

[121]   *Complete Works,* 9:373.

[122]   *Complete Works,* 9:29–30.

[123]   *Complete Works,* 9:30.

[124]   "Waldeinsamkeit," *Complete Works,* 9:249–251.

[125]   Elaborating on the findings of Carl Strauch, Van Cromphout discusses this aspect of Goethe's influence on Emerson's "poetry of ideas," calling the poem "The Sphinx" the "most Goethean" of all of Emersons's poems. *Cf.* Carl F. Strauch, "The Year of Emerson's Poetic Maturity: 1834", in *Philological Quarterly,* 34 (1955), 353–3 77; also: Van Cromphout, *Emerson's Modernity and the Example of Goethe,* 81–97.

[126]   Goethe's German edition was *Der Diwan von Mohammed Schemeseddin Hafis* (Stuttgart and Tübingen, 1812–13). He also owned *Geschichte der schönen Redekünste Persiens mit einer Blüthenlese aus zweihundert persischen Dichtern* (Vienna, 1818).

[127]   *Collected Works,* 2:8.

[128]   J. D. Yohannan, "Emerson's Translations of Persian Poetry from German Sources," in *American Literature,* 14 (1943), 407–420. See also the chapter "Persia and Poetry" in Richardson, *Emerson: The Mind on Fire,* 423–428.

[129]   *Hamburger Ausgabe,* 2:157.

[130]   Protap Chunder Mozoomdar, "Emerson as Seen from India," *The Genius and Character of Emerson: Lectures at the Concord School of Philosophy* (Boston: J. R. Osgood, 1885), 367.

[131]   Herman Grimm. "Ralph Waldo Emerson." in *Fünfzehn Essays; Erste Folge* (Berlin: Dümmlers, 1884), 426.

[132]   "Ralph Waldo Emerson," in *Fünfzehn Essays,* 426–427.

[133]   *Correspondence between Ralph Waldo Emerson and Herman Grimm,* ed. Frederick William Holls (Boston, New York: Houghton, Mifflin, 1903), 50.

[134]   *Correspondence between Ralph Waldo Emerson and Herman Grimm,* 43.

[135] *Ibid.*

[136] *The Letters of Ellen Tucker Emerson,* 2 vols., ed. Edith E. W. Gregg (Kent, OH: Kent State UP, 1982). 2:65–67.

[137] *The Letters of Ellen Tucker Emerson,* 2:67.

[138] "Ralph Waldo Emerson," in *Fünfzehn Essays,* 436.

[139] "Ralph Waldo Emerson," in *Fünfzehn Essays,* 444.

[140] "Ralph Waldo Emerson," in *Fünfzehn Essays,* 438.

[141] "Ralph Waldo Emerson," in *Fünfzehn Essays,* 432.

[142] "Ralph Waldo Emerson," in *Fünfzehn Essays,* 436.

[143] "Ralph Waldo Emerson," in *Fünfzehn Essays,* 445.

[144] Helmut Kreuzer, "Unüberwindliche Mächte. Deutschland und die Vereinigten Staaten in einem Adelsroman des bürgerlichen Realismus," in: *Amerika in der deutschen Literatur; neue Welt, Nordamerika,* eds. Sigrid Bauschinger, Horst Denkler, Wilfried Malsch (Stuttgart: Reclam, 1975), 205–217.

[145] *Correspondence between Ralph Waldo Emerson and Herman Grimm,* 85.

[146] *Correspondence between Ralph Waldo Emerson and Herman Grimm,* 85–86.

[147] Rusk, *The Life of Ralph Waldo Emerson,* 505.

Margaret Fuller
Courtesy of Schlesinger Library, Radcliffe College

2: Germanico: Margaret Fuller

> Tieck, who has embodied so many Runic secrets, explained to me what I
> have often felt toward myself, when he tells of the poor changeling, who,
> turned from the door of her adopted home, sat down on a stone and so
> pitied herself that she wept. Yet me also, the wonderful bird, singing in
> the wild forest, has tempted on, and not in vain. (*Memoirs,* 1:11)

THIS OBSERVATION ON TIECK'S NOVELLA "Der blonde Eckbert" from
a letter by Margaret Fuller to William Channing was chosen as an
epigraph to her two volumes of *Memoirs*. These writings, which are actually a posthumous compilation of autobiographical texts, letters, journals,
and commentary, were brought out in 1852 by three editors, William
Henry Channing, Ralph Waldo Emerson, and James Freeman Clarke two
years after Fuller died.

The magical bird in Tieck's story truly lured her farther from her origins than any of her other friends in the Concord circle — far beyond the
obstacles placed before a nineteenth century American woman of no
means. Sarah Margaret Fuller was born on May 23, 1810, in Cambridge-
port, today part of Cambridge, Massachusetts. Timothy Fuller was a very
protective father who kept his daughter extremely sheltered in her early
youth. Fuller had received his law degree from Harvard and was sent to
Washington from his district in 1817 as a Republican congressman. During the six months of each of those following eight years that he spent in
the capital, his model daughter Sarah Margaret regularly sent him letters.
The eldest of his nine children, Margaret showed early intellectual interests that were nothing short of astonishing. "Dear Father," writes the
eight-year old, "why do you not write to me. I want to read letters if I
cannot books" (*Letters,* 1:82). Her letters report on her studies in Latin
and arithmetic, music, and drawing. The precocious girl wrote enthusiastically to the Marquis de Lafayette in 1825, and as a twenty-year old described her "whole being" as "Byronized" (*Letters,* 1:164). Yet the youthful memories as later recorded by the thirty-year old adult do not describe
these early years as particularly happy. She recalled her father as a hard-
working man who lacked a sense of higher things. Furthermore, his desire
to make Margaret the inheritor of all his knowledge led him to develop
her mind too early, a decision for which she later reproached him. She was
thus given as much instruction and study as would fill a day. In the even-

ing she was then forced to recite the day's lesson, usually staying awake
longer than was healthy for a growing child. When it was finally time to
sleep, she was often visited by nightmares or sleepwalked through the
house. To this oppressive burden of early learning she later attributed her
severe headaches and poor health that plagued her all her life.

Timothy Fuller's educational ideal was by modern standards quite conservative. He felt one ought to amass as much knowledge as possible and
then regurgitate it as clearly as possible. He especially valued precise expression and forbade the use of phrases like "may be" or "if I am not mis-
taken." Sarah was taught Latin and English grammar when she was only
six, and for years the child's daily reading consisted of Latin authors. Her
father's library contained the best French writers of the 18th century, but
one Sunday afternoon at the age of eight, when she was not supposed to
be playing or reading novels, she discovered Shakespeare. Before bed that
evening she had finished half of *Romeo and Juliet.*

When she was eleven Sarah Margaret entered one of the many private
schools for young ladies in the vicinity of Boston. The school was run by
Dr. John Park, a medical man and former newspaper publisher who
placed language study at the core of his educational objectives. Later,
from age 14 to 16, Margaret's father sent her to Miss Prescott's Young
Ladies' Seminary in Groton, west of Concord, though she would have
preferred to be a pupil of William and Ralph Waldo Emerson at their
school in Boston.

In Groton the somewhat exalted Margaret encountered difficulties
with the other girls, read a great deal, and acted in plays. At home during
the holidays she would lead a Spartan life devoted solely to learning.
"Having excused myself from accompanying my honored father to
church, which I always do in the afternoon," she wrote on July 11, 1825
to Susan Prescott, "when possible, I devote to you the hours which Ariosto and Helvetius ask of my eyes." The following passage from the same
letter offers a description of her truly impressive regime:

> I rise a little before five, walk an hour, and then practise on the piano, till
> seven, when we breakfast. Next I read French, — Sismondi's Literature
> of the South of Europe, — till eight, then two or three lectures in
> Brown's Philosophy. About half-past nine I go to Mr. Perkins's school
> and study Greek till twelve, when, the school being dismissed, I recite, go
> home, and practise again till dinner, at two. Sometimes, if the conver-
> sation is very agreeable, I lounge for half an hour over the dessert,
> though rarely so lavish of time. Then, when I can, I read two hours in
> Italian, but I am often interrupted. At six, I walk or take a drive. Before
> going to bed, I play or sing, for half an hour or so, to make all sleepy,
> and, about eleven, retire to write a little while in my journal, exercises on

what I have read, or a series of characteristics which I am filling up according to advice. Thus, you see, I am learning Greek, and making acquaintance with metaphysics, and French and Italian literature.

(*Letters*, 1:151)

The rigors of these school years injured Margaret as much as they helped
her. During this period she found solace only in the garden of her gentle
mother, whom she described as "one of the fair and flowerlike natures,
which sometimes spring up even beside the most dusty highways of life"
(*Memoirs*, 1:12). On the one hand, she certainly read too much too early,
which damaged her health; on the other, her enormous learning and remarkable powers of judgment were increasing by leaps and bounds. Thus,
once her schooling was finished, she was superbly prepared to conquer
new worlds when in 1826 her family moved to Cambridge, not far from
Harvard. When James Freeman Clarke edited Fuller's *Memoirs*, he pref-
aced the difficult struggles of her Cambridge years with the following lines
from Theodor Körner's poem "Durch" (Through). Fuller's own translation, which contains the ideals that guided her in this period of her life,
runs:

> Through, brothers, through, — this be
> Our watchword in danger or sorrow,
> Common clay to its mother dust,
> All nobleness heavenward! (*Memoirs*, 1:59)[1]

Clarke, who was a distant cousin of Margaret, graduated from Harvard
College in 1829 where he studied German with Charles Follen, the first
instructor of German at the institution. Follen had come to America via
Switzerland in 1824 after being arrested in Jena for his involvement with
the political circle around Karl Ludwig Sand, the assassin of the playwright
Kotzebue. This first Germanist in exile had to produce all his own pedagogical tools, first writing a grammar and then a collection of literary texts
in which the freedom-loving, anti-Napoleonic poetry of Körner had a prominent place. His classes must have been very inspiring. Not only was he
made the first German professor at Harvard, but he also introduced gym-
nastics at the College. He would certainly have exerted even greater influence on the emerging field of German Studies if he had not left to go to
Watertown, New York, to be an educator and guardian for several boys.
He met an untimely death in 1840 when the ship burned on which he
was crossing Long Island Sound.[2]

Among Follen's students was a son of a Harvard professor, Frederic
Henry Hedge, who at the age of thirteen was sent by his father along with
his tutor George Bancroft to Germany for four years. Bancroft was later to
make a considerable reputation for himself in the fields of education, his-

tory, and diplomacy. When he returned from Germany he (along with his friend from Göttingen, Joseph Cogswell) founded the Round Hill School in Northampton, Massachusetts. The school was modelled on the German *Gymnasium*. His patriotic history of the United States won him great fame, and from 1867 to 1874 he served as ambassador to Berlin.

Hedge first attended boarding school in Ilfeld and later in Schulpforta. His memoirs give an amusing account of his life at Ilfeld where the discipline was lax, Latin was the official language, and nobody knew anything about America. The high point of the humdrum school life was the occasional hot chocolate treat or a visit by an elephant to a nearby town. At Schulpforta, however, he found higher standards, writing, for instance, "Here I came to know Goethe."[3] Hedge, who later became a Unitarian minister, was the only one of Margaret's Harvard friends who had first-hand experience of Germany and who could speak the language to which she devoted herself with such zeal.

Margaret Fuller, like so many of her contemporaries, first had her interest in German culture piqued by Madame de Staël's *De l'Allemagne*, which appeared in English in 1814. Indeed, this seminal work touched an entire generation, launching a Germanophile craze in the English-speaking world. American readers, and especially Margaret Fuller, must have discovered in the descriptions of Germany many a familiar trait described by the French critic. This was a land covered by forests, crossed by rivers, and beset by freezing winters — all familiar features that suggested her own New England. The "young culture" that the French traveller found there hardly seemed older than the one on the American east coast. "Civilization and nature seem to be not yet sufficiently amalgamated together,"[4] wrote Madame de Staël about a phenomenon that was beginning to engage Americans at the same time. New Englanders also strove for a firm moral purpose, a trait she ascribed to the Germans, while Saxony and northern Germany, seen as "the cradle of Protestantism," could be felt as a kind of spiritual home. De Staël's description of the German love of scholarship, as well as her accounts of the love of German women and the courtliness of German men — in short, love as a religion in Germany — put an indelible stamp on Margaret's image of this nation. It was a picture of a fantastic land with barren fields, smoke-charred houses, and gothic churches, which "are all so many preparatives for stories of ghosts and witches."[5] This was a culture whose poets and philosophers had contributed to that body of thought that in New England was to be called "transcendental." One could find in Madame de Staël suggestions of "this secret alliance of our being with the wonders of the universe, which gives to poetry its true grandeur."[6] She produced the first canon of German literature for American readers, encompassing works from the *Nibelungenlied* through Jean Paul — and Margaret Fuller made every effort to read the works she recommended. Beyond the influence of Madame de Staël, Margaret was certainly also inspired by the "wild bugle call" of Thomas Carlyle that reached her by 1830. In 1838 cousin James wrote in his journal, *The Western Messenger,* of the unforgettable hours spent together in the Boston Athenaeum sitting at the feet of the Laokoon group, reading and re-reading Carlyle's essays in the *Foreign Review:* "It was as if we saw the angels ascending and descending in a Jacob's dream."[7]

Margaret began the year 1832 with her systematic study of German. Clarke reports in the *Memoirs* that she was reading the masterpieces of German literature with ease in about three months. Within a year she had read Goethe's *Faust, Tasso, Iphigenie, Hermann und Dorothea, Die Wahlverwandtschaften,* and *Dichtung und Wahrheit.* In addition, she also read among other things by Tieck, his *William Lovell* and *Prinz Zerbino,* as well as works by Novalis, Jean Paul, and all the poems and major dramas by Schiller. "Her mind opened under this influence, as the apple-blossom at the end of a warm week in May" (*Memoirs,* 1:114).

A letter to James makes clear how early she began to form independent opinions. When she returns a copy of *Die Wahlverwandtschaften* she writes:

> It pains me to part with Ottilia. I wish we could learn books, as we do pieces of music, and repeat them, in the author's order, when taking a solitary walk. But, now, if I set out with an Ottilia, this wicked fairy association conjures up such crowds of less lovely companions, that I often cease to feel the influence of the elect one. I don't like Goethe so well as Schiller now. [...] That perfect wisdom and *merciless* nature seems cold, after those seducing pictures of forms more beautiful than truth.
>
> (*Memoirs,* 1:117)

Cousin James is Margaret's most important correspondent during this period. "I have not anybody to speak to, that does not talk common-place, and I wish to talk about such an uncommon person, — about Novalis!" (*Memoirs,* 1:118). Novalis brought an immense relief after the overpowering force of Goethe's mind, which for her "had embraced the universe" (*Memoirs,* 1:119). When reading his poetry she finds all her emotions understandable and perfectly expressed, but she seems to sense a loss of identity in the process. She suddenly sees herself allied with a host of other beings, but she overcomes her aversion to the titanic Goethe and ploughs onward in her reading of "the great sage" while experiencing mixed feelings of attraction and rejection (*Memoirs,* 1:119).

While reading Theodor Körner, she is enchanted because she comprehends all the emotions he excites in her. Novalis, on the other hand, ("good Novalis," as she and Clarke call him, following Carlyle), conveys something completely new. She has only a fragmentary understanding of the poem "Die Lehrlinge zu Sais," but she thinks she comprehends the novel *Heinrich von Ofterdingen* as a representation of the development of poetry in a human spirit. The response to Lessing is similar. Whereas his *Miss Sara Sampson* she judges almost unreadable, *Emilia Galotti* is praised as "good in the same way as Minna [. . .] strong, but not deep" (*Memoirs*, 1:121).

Her experience of German literature was much more than a mere reading frenzy and simple accumulation of knowledge in the style of her father's early training. Clarke writes how Margaret was inspired by a deep longing for the perfect development of her entire nature: "Very early I knew that the only object in life was to grow" (*Memoirs*, 1:133), she wrote to him, which sounded like an echo of Wilhelm Meister's purpose "to educate myself just as I am." As such, she realized the American answer to Goethe's ideal of education: self-culture.

Margaret Fuller's correspondence with James Freeman Clarke shows how difficult it was for her to find her way to self-culture. Those German writers to whom she had been spontaneously attracted also presented obstacles, but she never compromised her own nature to their teachings. Novalis, whom she termed "a wonderous youth," is a good example (*Memoirs*, 1:118). His rejection of those "unbelievers" who merely use philosophy as a system that substitutes for thinking, provokes a contradiction from Margaret:

> Now this is just my case. I *do* want a system which shall suffice to my character, and in whose applications I shall have faith. I do not wish to *reflect* always, if reflecting must be always about one's identity, whether "ich" am the true "ich," &c. I wish to arrive at that point where I can trust myself, and leave off saying, "It seems to me," and boldly feel, It *is* so to ME. [. . .] This is the philosophy *I* want; this much would satisfy *me*. (*Memoirs*, 1:123)

Here speaks the self-assured, pragmatic American who, though at first fascinated by the German metaphysicians, later turned from them with irritated impatience — a process that repeated itself again and again among New England readers of German literature.

At this period Margaret had the good fortune to have James as a soulmate. Thanks to their correspondence, their reading of the same books, and their visits together, she participated in a serious exchange of ideas. "Three or four afternoons I have passed very happily at my beloved haunt in the wood, reading Goethe's 'Second Residence in Rome.' Your pencilmarks show that you have been before me" (*Memoirs*, 1:121).

James was an ardent admirer of Goethe, so much so that he seems to have sought advice in Goethe's writings at every juncture in his life. For example, upon receiving his degree from Harvard and having to interrupt his studies at the Divinity School, he wrote to Margaret that he was seeking a position at a school, "on Goethe's principle of doing the duty that is nearest."[8] In August 1832, when he was staying at a particularly beautiful spot in Maine, he sent back an ode to Goethe and a long translation from *Hermann und Dorothea*. He wrote that the landscape of Maine reminded him of a region in "Leonardos Tagebuch der Entsagungen" (Leonardo's Journal of Renunciations). Clarke refers to a lady living nearby as a "Gute-Schöne," an allusion to Goethe's novel *Wilhelm Meister* in which Leonardo keeps a journal and a woman is called "Beautiful Soul." His influence was immensely important for Margaret. "I desire, Margaret, that you would edit my posthumous works and write a life of me. [. . .] Margaret, you are destined to be an author. I shall yet see you wholly against your will and drawn by circumstances, become the founder of an American literature!"[9] He ends his declaration with a vision of an age tempered and gilded by art. Lines from Goethe's poem "Zueignung" close the letter: "Every life-billow shall sink to repose/The day become lovely and the night serene. "I exclaim with Schiller's Don Carlos," he writes in 1833, "Three and twenty years! /And nothing done for immortality." Clarke continues in this vein: "nor for anything else. I have *done* nothing. Real action lies all before. But next year at its close sees me free, and an independent agent in creation, or I shall go to my grave a nothing — a cipher."[10] And he also promises to finish his translation of Schiller's *Die Jungfrau von Orleans* as soon as possible.

James and Margaret were certainly not the only ones in New England to converse in this manner. Clarke's unpublished diary, which he sent to Margaret, suggests the high level of intellectual life of the period.[11] "Last night I smoked a cigar with W. Allston." So begins the long report of a conversation in 1832 among Clarke, the painter Washington Allston, and Elizabeth Peabody. In that lively debate Clarke undertakes a defense of Goethe who comes under heavy criticism from the other two. "What does Miss Peabody mean by calling him Epicurean in his W. Meister?" Allston, an admirer of Schiller who procured for himself all translations of his work (whether good or bad), found much fault with Goethe's views of art, which to him did not seem to penetrate the heart of a work. He even finds the judgment of Winckelmann "meager and worthless." James suspected that Allston lacked analytical power as well sympathy for those who possessed it. Could he, in this case, ever admire Wilhelm Meister or "indeed any part of the *prose side* of Goethe"? The conversation focussed mainly on the novel:

I told Miss Peabody that the book was full of knowledge, nothing else —
that which the Imagination looked at a thing as a whole, the understanding took it to pieces — that all thinking was of necessity separation
[...] We murder, to dissect. Therefore, as the object of Meister was
strictly didactic, his object required Goethe to put out of view all high
moral power, which is an action of the whole soul, not a single tendency
or striving. The thought that it was never justifiable to omit it, for it
should be the object of all exertion. That, said I, is a narrow view of
life — making one idea, the ruler of human nature. She said that one idea
should rule [...] I demurred still, I said that there was no all-compre-
hending idea. Every man [...] carried before him his own flag. One
said, my Profession — another, my Country — another Mankind. [...]
All are excellent ideas — very well to lean on them & gather strength
from faith & action. But why make your watchword, the scale of all excellence?

James reported questionable things about the great Unitarian authority
William Ellery Channing. He reported that Channing was incapable of
reading *Romeo and Juliet,* and that he found Dante's and Petrarch's conduct necessarily incomprehensible for the English sensibility. "Do you
think," James asked Margaret, "he deserves the name of Philistine?"[12]

As a student James kept a routine similar to Margaret's: 6:00–8:00
a.m., dress, pray, breakfast; 8:00–1:00, German; 1:00–2:00, travel to
Boston; 3:00–7:00, Athenaeum. In addition, he devoted himself to translating Schiller, Goethe, Schleiermacher and wrote Margaret his thoughts
on the Germans and their literature. The portraits of Goethe and Schiller
("No doubt where lies the mental supremacy") inspire him to expostulate,
"If these were men what are angels or archangels?"[13]

He claimed that the Germans had a wonderful literature that acquired
ever stranger forms the longer one studied it. By applying the German
method of self-discipline one could acquire a truly "cosmic reputation."
He wrote that Germans as a nation seemed to be under a profound influence that made them into original and productive minds. [...]
"Whether that is the influence from Goethe I will not say."[14] He draws
the conclusion in the following sentence: "The maxim of German philosophy is not I think, therefore I am, but I feel therefore I believe."[15]

But the happy years of Margaret's and James's youth were over soon
enough. In 1833 Margaret's father decided to withdraw from public life
and to settle on a farm in Groton, far from the cultural centers of Boston
and Cambridge. The move cost Margaret her indirect connections to
Harvard, made so enjoyable by friendships with students and professors
and by the opportunity to visit libraries and exhibitions. Such circles and
events had become important to her voracious quest for knowledge. In

Groton she was tied to her mother and obligated to teach three younger siblings and three other children for several hours a day.

James, on the other hand, removed to Louisville, Kentucky, where he took a pulpit. The young Unitarian with his head full of Goethe had a very hard time in this undeveloped frontier region. His letters are filled with homesickness for New England where he had been able to wander through nature; in Kentucky he was confronted with wilderness. His church was small and his parishioners had little understanding for his sermons. Thirty-five souls, including children and slaves, came to church on Sundays, but one after the other they deserted during the sermon. "I wonder what Goethe would do in my place," Clarke exclaimed in despair, but then sought solace in his advisor:

> In the Wanderjahre we must renounce — renounce half of our nature [. . .] that is a final trial of the character [. . .] thus proving as with a steel hammer the temper of each link of the chain of our nature. In this spirit I did indeed think of my being to you as Wilhelm was to Natalia.[16]

Thus he resolved to put aside literature, painting, and philosophy, and to fulfill the "necessity of the day" ("die Forderung des Tages") by becoming a powerful preacher. Schiller's advice from the poem "An einen Weltverbesserer" offered some guidance:

> Für Regen und Tau und für's Wohl der Menschengeschlechter
> Lass du den Himmel, Freund, sorgen, wie gestern so heut.

> (For the rain and the dew and the good of mankind,
> Let heaven, take care, my friend, yesterday as today.)

Yet, Clarke's sermons did not become less challenging. In November of 1834 he reported connecting the "ideas of Reverence held by the Three [characters] from" Goethe's *Wanderjahre* with Timothy II, 1:7–8. Religion could thus be seen being born out of reverence. Margaret was to remain his constant correspondent during these thought processes. "Write to me as often as you can. Be my Goethe and I will try to be your Schiller and go on with you."[17] The correspondence during Clarke's first years in Kentucky was particularly lively. Margaret wrote long letters, and in order to save expensive postage, after covering the sheets with tightly written lines, she would turn the paper ninety degrees and fill the pages with just as much again. There was always something to add, as on April 28, 1835: "Did you ever hear of Henri Heine? I have seen some extracts from a work of his on modern German belles lettres which are highly amusing. Have been fascinated into reading Richter's *Flegeljahre* and cannot resist the *original* mind when I am with it though not of the kind I naturally like. Hard to get into the stream and harder to get out as somebody in Blackwood said about Rabelais" (*Letters*, 6:261).

Around this time several friends of Margaret Fuller's conceived of creating a forum that would spread their ideas to an interested New England reading public. Henry Hedge and George Ripley were the first to plan such a publication that was to be different from all existing magazines; all "Germanic-philosophical-literary talents" were to contribute to the venture. Names for the journal such as "The Transcendentalist" or "The Spiritual Inquirer" were considered and Margaret Fuller was asked if she wished to participate. Flattered, she answered Hedge in March 1835: "I shall feel myself honoured if I am deemed worthy of lending a hand albeit I fear I am merely 'Germanico' and not 'transcendental'" (*Letters*, 1:226–227).

At the same time, however, the ever active James Clarke was promoting his own similar ideas. "I think with Fichte," he proclaimed, "that Transcendentalism and Spirituality can be made perfectly intelligible to any simple, untrampled minds."[18] And to this end the first number of *The Western Messenger* appeared under his editorship in Cincinnati, Ohio, in June 1835. His journal — predating *The Dial* by five years — began to advance the influence of the Concord intellectuals. This monthly publication focussed on religion and literature, defining its goal as the spread of "rational and liberal religion," and taking up the progressive, anti-Calvinist position of the Unitarians.

Clarke's influence is evident in the literary contributions of the first three volumes of *The Western Messenger*. He translates Theodor Körner's poem "Durch, Brüder durch!" for the first issue, and for the seventh, the elegy upon the death of Euphorion from the third act of *Faust II*. In the second year of publication he printed his translation of Goethe's "Urworte. Orphisch" and notes with satisfaction the intellectual revolution in England and America that had made Goethe, who had previously been unknown, almost a household word. Clarke was obviously pleased at people's surprise in finding in Goethe a great poet of the genius of Shakespeare, for he considered Goethe truly an eclectic philosopher, as his poems testified.[19]

For the December 1836 issue Clarke translated the extremely moral tale of Ferdinand from Goethe's *Unterhaltungen deutscher Ausgewanderten (Conversations of German Emigrés)*. He also employed Charles Timothy Brooks, who had been three years his junior at Harvard, and had taken a parish in Rhode Island. Brooks, the translator of *Wilhelm Tell* and Jean Paul's *Titan*, is represented in *The Western Messenger* with the opening monologue from *Die Jungfrau von Orleans*. Clarke's good friend and classmate James Sullivan Dwight contributed a translation of Schiller's poem "Hoffnung." In November 1836 Clarke reprinted "The Atheist's Dream; from the German of Richter" (from Jean Paul's *Siebenkäs*) from the *Foreign Review*. Even Schiller's *Philosophical Letters* appeared in two issues of *The Western Messenger*.

Margaret had some critical remarks on Clarke's translation activity. In her letter of January 30, 1836 she writes:

> It is a shame to degrade such a very transparent and flexible style into English whose literalness makes it unfaithful. Surely we should consult the idiom of our own language if we want to do justice to a writer who valued form so highly. [. . .] how many beautiful ideas marred for want of a proper finish. (*Letters,* 6:276)

Margaret Fuller's first piece was printed when *The Western Messenger* published her long article on Theodor Körner in January and February of 1838. The essay is remarkable for its unerring critical power. She recognizes that the figure of the twenty-one year old Körner, who had died in the wars against Napoleon, was not a genius central to the understanding of German literature. Furthermore, she cannot discover anything typically German in works that lack philosophical content. Rather, she felt, Körner's "beautiful moral nature,"[20] with which he expressed the feelings of the German nation, made his poetry belong to the whole world.

In her essay Margaret describes Körner's life based on his father's biographical description of his son. "This spotless Christian hero"[21] whose hand was equally capable of wielding a sword as playing a lyre. Unsparing in her criticism, however, she calls Körner's dramas stiff and his prose light-weight, leaving only to his lyric poetry of value. She translates the poem "Missmut" ("Dissatisfaction") and rejects Heine's caricature of Körner as the poet of "sweet melody and uncouth verses, which enthused the Germans so."[22]

As a cursory glance at *The Western Messenger* shows, the figure of Goethe dominated Clarke's imagination. "How can we escape from the influence of such intellect, once having come under it" he writes to Margaret on July 17, 1835. "We must go on reproducing Goethe, I suppose to the end of our natural lives, either consciously or unconsciously,"[23] and he acknowledges that he "stole" from Goethe, this time from the *Unterhaltungen deutscher Ausgewanderten,* a "moral tale." This must refer to the aforementioned story of Ferdinand, which he had printed two years earlier in the journal.

Even Margaret had already translated Goethe. The first piece of hers that Emerson ever saw was her 1833 translation of *Torquato Tasso* (published posthumously), which was passed among friends in manuscript form. Fuller did not translate the drama word for word, but in places

paraphrased monologues. She was especially good at rendering the apho-
ristic *sententiae* (which were favorites of the classically educated New
Englanders) into widely admired English versions. Compare Goethe's

> Ein Edler Mensch zieht edle Menschen an
> Und weiss sie festzuhalten, wie ihr tut.

with Margaret's English:

> Only the noble can attract the noble
> And hold them firmly bound as you have done. (Act I:59–60)[24]

She also conceived of the idea of "interpreting him [Goethe] satisfactorily
to others"[25] by describing his life. During her years of exile in Groton
Goethe had become her most important guiding figure — sorely needed,
one might say, in light of the fact that during the course of one day in
1835 her father died of cholera, leaving his family of eight poorly provided
for. There were brothers to be educated and the uncle who was made
ward of the children brought to the task little understanding of his niece's
intellectual interests. For two years Margaret had been looking forward to
a European trip on which she was to accompany the Harvard mathemati-
cian John Farrar and his wife. The English writer Harriet Martineau, who
had met Margaret in Cambridge, wanted to introduce her into the best
literary circles in London. Now the trip had to be canceled.

    The incalculable disappointment cast Margaret back upon literature for
solace. She translated Uhland's poem "Rechtfertigung" (Justification):

> Our youthful fancies, idly fired,
>   The fairest visions would embrace;
> These, with impetuous tears desired,
>   Float upward into starry space;
> Heaven, upon the suppliant wild,
>   Smiles down a gracious *No!* — In vain
> The strife! Yet be consoled, poor child,
>   For the wish passes with the pain.
>
> (*Memoirs,* 1:160)

On her twenty-sixth birthday Margaret read Goethe's "Lebensregel"
(Rule of life):

> Willst du dir ein hübsch Leben zimmern,
> Mußt du dich ums Vergangene nicht bekümmern;
> Das wenigste muß dich verdriessen;
> Mußt stets die Gegenwart geniessen
> Besonders keinen Menschen hassen
> und die Zukunft Gott überlassen.

(Wouldst make thy life go fair and square?
For the Past, then, thou must have no care:
Must let the very least annoy thee,
Must in the Present still enjoy thee,
Above all, hate no human being,
And all the Future leave to the All-Seeing.)[26]

On the same day she writes in a letter, "It is easy to say 'Do not trouble yourself with useless regrets for the past; enjoy the present, and leave the future to God.' But it is *not* easy for characters, which are by nature neither *calm* nor *careless*, to act upon these rules. I am rather of the opinion of Novalis, that 'Wer sich der höchsten Lieb ergeben Genest von ihren Wunden nie'" *[sic]*.[27]

Despite all external opposition, and the necessity of finding a teaching position, Margaret did not abandon her plans for a Goethe biography. The recently discovered letters to James Freeman Clarke show the extent of her reservations toward the project. On April 28, 1835 she suggests to her friend that he write a two-volume life of Goethe and include critical essays on Goethe's works. "This vision swims often before mine own eyes, but I know too many are swimming there of the kind and would gladly see this one realized by a friend. — If I do it — there shall be less eloquence perhaps but more insight than in De Staël" (*Letters*, 6:269). Again and again she begs James to keep the plan a secret, even from his wife, although George Ripley expressed readiness to include such a work, entitled "The Life of Goethe" in his series of modern foreign literature.

Margaret Fuller no doubt wanted to create an American counterpart to Sarah Austin's English *Characteristics of Goethe* (1833), which was the first portrayal of the writer. Another model was Mrs. Anna Jameson's *Studies, Stories, and Memoirs* (1859) in which she discussed Goethe's dramas, the conversations with Eckermann, "Goethe's last love," and his table-talk. Anna Jameson had visited Weimar in 1833 and met Goethe's daughter-in-law Ottilie. Her *Visits and Sketches at Home and Abroad* (1834) report the impressions Ottilie's family left upon her.

Margaret, however, would not begin her project without the most thorough preparations. Even before her father's death she wrote to James complaining of the lack of material. She had no information whatever about the ten years between Goethe's arrival in Weimar and his departure for Italy. Furthermore, she wanted to consult the books on the subject written in Germany "by friend and foe." The following comment makes clear her own desire to produce a new, independent study: "I wish to look at the matter from all sides. [. . .] And I think it possible I shall come out from the Carlyle view, and perhaps from yours [Clarke's], and distaste you, which will trouble me" (*Letters*, 1:244).

Margaret asks Clarke for suggestions of what to read about German society. Using histories of philosophy she wants to make herself charts of the most important philosophical schools and their representative thinkers. She writes her cousin, "Tell me exactly what is meant by *Transcendentalism* and why it is called the critical philosophy. Is Goethe united to any philosophical school? He only speaks of Spinosa" (*Letters*, 6:282).

As her letters intimate, she has been harboring the suspicion for some time that no intellect is up to the task of systematizing and summarizing knowledge without first mastering metaphysics. Her aversion to this philosophical direction, however, kept her away from this study for a long time. It finally became clear that she needed to be acquainted with the history of German philosophy in order to assess its influence upon Goethe. Thus, she wrestles with Fichte without in the least understanding him. She comprehends details from Jacobi, but not as a system. Should she read Spinoza? Before doing so she reads her way through five histories of philosophy. Such thoroughness places Margaret far above Sarah Austin whose anthology of Goethe's autobiographical writings was a compilation of third-hand (albeit interesting) reports, especially those by the chancellor von Müller, mingled with excerpts of Goethe's own texts. Mrs. Jameson's *Studies* were, by contrast, much more subjective and sentimental.

James fulfilled Margaret's request for enlightenment by writing her a long letter summarizing the history of German philosophy since Kant. He tells her that Schiller had studied the German idealists as a metaphysician; Goethe had done so as a philosopher. James gave Margaret an illuminating definition of the concept of transcendentalism as understood by Kant, and encouraged her to read the *Critique of Pure Reason*, which he recommended as very comprehensible. He suggested also that she should concentrate on a characteristic idea in Goethe's thought and then follow and illustrate this concept throughout his life. For every original thinker, he maintained, there can be found just such a key. Margaret ultimately asked Clarke to make the unprecedented sacrifice of the loan of his Goethe edition, possibly even for a whole year, for even Miss Martineau was encouraging her to work on the Goethe biography. James, the soul of goodness, fulfilled this wish.

For her preliminary research on Goethe's life Margaret relied principally on printed sources, on Goethe's own autobiography *Poetry and Truth*, and Bettina von Arnim's *Goethe's Correspondence with a Child*. The folders of her excerpts and notes reveal with what refreshing independence she went to work. She neither adopts Carlyle's attitude of Goethe adoration, nor is she influenced by her countrymen who dismiss Goethe as immoral. The Friederike episode from Goethe's Strassburg period illustrates her attitude: "Love-affair with Frederica identifies the character of Goethe as well as any part of his history. It excites no moral indignation in my breast, but it shows clearly how everything in this nature was subordinated to the intellect."[28] She can muster empathy for the experiences of Goethe's life and his environment. Goethe's sister Cornelia represents a particularly kindred spirit who had also had to suffer under a tyrannical father. "In this sister I see, *leider*, many traits of myself."[29]

She also tries to get her hands on new sources of material, a role for which Henry Hedge seemed predestined. "I want to know the facts about Goethe and Lili, can you give them me?" Margaret wrote to him. "This somewhat passée affair troubles me; I want to know did he give her up from merely interested (ie selfish) motives" (*Letters,* 1:226). Two years later she begged Hedge again for details: "Will you, Henry, can you tell me all the scandal about Goethe — about his marriage and so forth?" (*Letters,* 1:292–293). Hedge pleaded ignorant of Goethe's "liaisons" and suggested that Margaret approach Carlyle, or the philosopher Francis Lieber who had immigrated to the United States in 1827 and was teaching in South Carolina. Margaret even asked Anna Jameson for information, but without success.

In 1836 Margaret discovered in an English publication that Goethe's son was illegitimate. She confided to James that, "I confess this has greatly pained and troubled me. I had no idea that the mighty 'Indifferentist' went so far with his experimentalizing in *real life*" (*Letters,* 6:287). She had never been able to believe Charles Follen's tales about Goethe's private life, thinking that such behavior would have been impossible at court. Still, unperturbed by such discoveries, she writes, "Of course, my impressions of Goethe's works cannot be influenced by information I get about his *life*."[30]

During this period Margaret first met Ralph Waldo Emerson. As discussed earlier, the Emersons invited Margaret to visit for two weeks in Concord after having become curious about her from reports by Harriet Martineau and Hedge (who had lent Emerson Margaret's *Tasso* manuscript). Fuller and Emerson thus met each other at a time of her most intense interest in German literature, especially in Goethe. In the *Memoirs* Emerson gives a lively picture of the visits in Concord. "She could hold them all with her honeyed tongue" (*Memoirs,* 1:215), and thus there developed a cult of true friendship that Margaret certainly encouraged.[31] Emerson found "that there was somewhat *[sic]* a little pagan about her" (*Memoirs,* 1:219), particularly her habit of identifying people with precious stones, or of giving birthdays and names particular significance. She derived these practices from her Goethean belief in a personal *daemon:*

When Goethe received a letter from Zelter, with a handsome super-
scription, he said, "Lay that aside; it is Zelter's true hand-writing. Every
man has a daemon, who is busy to confuse and limit his life. No way is
the action of this power more clearly shown, than in the handwriting. On
this occasion, the evil influences have been evaded; the mood, the hand,
the pen and paper have conspired to let our friend write truly himself."

(*Letters*, 3:163)

Margaret wrote these words to Emerson in a letter from December 1843,
quoting, as she notes, from memory. They were, to be sure, far from Goethean in temperament, but nonetheless applied to her. For weeks and
months, as she put it, the daemon would work its will with her.

The text betrays familiarity with a passage in Eckermann's *Conversations with Goethe,* which she knew well.[32] For as it became increasingly impossible for her to complete the Goethe biography, she turned to a new
project. She had not gotten far with her search for materials, despite Emerson's request for information from Carlyle about Goethe's first ten years
in Weimar. The information, Emerson had written, was needed to help a
friend studying Goethe's life.[33] Except for Jördan's *Lexicon,* Carlyle could
not recommend anything new; he also mentioned an essay by Schubarth,
which he deemed critical and ethical,[34] and he recommended Goethe's
correspondence with Zelter and Schiller, which were crucial if also unin-
formative about the period of Goethe's life in question. He also recommended the Leipzig journal *Zeitgenossen,* which specialized in contemporary biography. Being an avowed admirer of Goethe, Carlyle warned
against the "Blackguard" Heine's critical parody, *Die Romantische Schule.*
Wolfgang Menzel's *Deutsche Literatur,* with its sharp attacks against Goethe, he described as being "duller, decenter, not much wiser." But then
he referred to a "very curious Book, Eckermann's *Conversations with
G. — just published."[35]

This was a book that would henceforth engage Margaret Fuller, for
her new circumstances made a translation more feasible than a biography.
Most of all, she lacked time, yet she continued to collect biographical
material on Goethe, writing to Emerson in 1839:

> I find daily new materials and am at present almost burthened by my
> riches. I have found for instance all the Frankfort particulars in letters to
> Meyer. And Goethe's Darstellunggabe [*sic*] lends such beauty to the
> theme that I shall often translate, and string rather than melt my pearls. I
> do not write steadily for the subject keeps fermenting and I feel that the
> hour of precipitation is not arrived. Often a study is suggested and I pass
> several days in the woods with it before I resume the pen. It would make
> quite a cultivated person of me, if I had four or five years to give to my

task. But I intend to content myself with doing it inadequately rather than risk living so long in the shadow of one mind. (*Letters,* 2:68–69)

In 1838 she replied to a question from cousin James about her Goethe project, saying that the answer would either be "a book or a billet-doux from my coffin" (*Letters,* 6:302). Her letter was sent from Providence where she was so busy with her duties at the Green Street School that she had not a moment's time to think of working on the biography.[36] Two months later she writes James that she has received her own copy of Goethe from Germany (the *Nachgelassene Werke*). As a result, she could return his volumes with a thousand thanks — at a point when it had become too late to continue with the project. Margaret's copy, which is today in the Houghton Library of Harvard University, is full of so many underlinings and marginalia that one can say with certainty that its owner read each volume carefully.

In the winter of 1836 Margaret's pressing need to earn money led her to take a position as a language teacher in the Temple School of Amos Bronson Alcott in Boston. This short-lived undertaking of Emerson's good friend, an autodidact who was sometimes called the "American Pestalozzi," was housed in the Masonic Temple. Like so many of Alcott's visionary experiments this too came to an early end.

Margaret Fuller's language instruction must have been awe-inspiring. She reported that after three months her German class could read very well and were able to prepare twenty pages per class. We even know the curriculum she taught. Her advanced students read the following works in fourteen weeks: Schiller's *Don Carlos,* and the long poems "Der Künstler" and "Das Lied von der Glocke;" Goethe's *Hermann und Dorothea, Götz von Berlichingen, Iphigenie,* and *Clavigo.* Furthermore, within three weeks the class also read *Faust I,* followed by Lessing's *Nathan der Weise, Minna von Barnhelm,* and *Emilia Galotti,* portions of Tieck's *Phantasus,* and almost the entire first volume of Jean Paul's *Titan.* One evening a week she translated Herder and Wilhelm de Wette for the eminent theologian William Ellery Channing. James Freeman Clarke (who returned to Boston in 1841) translated de Wette's novel *Theodor, oder die Bekehrung des Skeptikers* for George Ripley's series "Specimens of Foreign Standard Literature."

Ripley, who was a cousin of Ralph Waldo Emerson and a Boston minister as well, corresponded with Carlyle whom he admired greatly. He was also an enthusiastic reader of German philosophy and European literature. His fellow Harvard student Henry Hedge had tried to nurture Ripley's thirst for knowledge. Ripley wanted to spread his enthusiasm for European literature in America with a fourteen-volume series of translations, the first two volumes of which included works by Victor Cousin, Theodor

Jouffray, and Benjamin Constant, which he translated himself. Ten volumes of the series were devoted to German literature, and in 1838 he offered Margaret Fuller the chance to publish her "Life of Goethe" in this
series. In 1839 there appeared instead her translation of the *Conversations
with Eckermann*. This work dates from the time after her leaving Alcott's
school (where he was unable to pay her), and after spending another two
years at the progressive Green Street School in Providence, which was run
by another pupil of Alcott.

The *Conversations with Eckermann* was Margaret's real debut after
those first translations in *The Western Messenger*. The motto from Milton's
History of Britain (1670) at the beginning of the volume makes her am-
bitions clear. She wanted to enrich the young culture of America and
contribute to the country's emerging national literature. Milton's lines run
thus:

> As wine and oil are imported to us from abroad, so must ripe under-
> standing, and many civil virtues, be imported into our minds from for-
> eign writings; — we shall else miscarry still, and come short in the
> attempts of any great enterprise.[37]

Margaret Fuller's English version was an accomplished and precise
translation. It was obvious that the formal instruction in exact expression
that she had received as a child benefitted her as a translator. On the other
hand, even her admirers criticized her essays as poorly structured and dif-
fuse. But a text like the *Conversations* shows the full range of her expertise
and sensitivity to the English language. Eckermann's introduction, which
gives what he calls "some account of his parentage, his early life, and the
circumstances which led to his connection with Goethe," sounds in Margaret Fuller's version slightly more animated and elegant than in the
original.[38] It should be noted that she shortened the original somewhat by
omitting all references to Goethe's *Farbenlehre* (Theory of Colors). This
decision reflected not only the fact that the work was completely unknown to an English-reading public, but also Margaret's complete indif-
ference to the natural sciences. The omissions did not escape Emerson
who shook his head over Margaret's lack of interest — but then he had recently come under the spell of Goethe's scientific writings, especially the
phenomenon of the *Urpflanze*. The *Memoirs* record Emerson's reaction:
"She had never paid, — and it is a little remarkable, — any attention to
natural sciences. She neither botanized, nor geologized, nor dissected"
(*Memoirs*, 1:263). He also quotes her own words, "Only through emotion do we know thee, Nature!" (*Memoirs*, 1:265). In addition to elimin-
ating Goethe's color theory from her text, Margaret also omitted any reference to Eckermann's own journey to Italy.

But she handled the linguistic difficulties in the text well, despite the fact she was translating from a foreign culture as much as from a foreign language. Just rendering German titles into English was a task in itself. She wrote to Ripley:

> The title Counsellor is wrong; the word Justizbeamt I had confounded with Justizrath. It should be officer of justice, strictly; [. . .] I expect the chief trouble throughout will be with titles of men and books as, when I could not translate them to my mind, I have left them in German. Perhaps it would have been better not, but such combinations as Upper-forest-counsellor look very formidable in English. (*Letters,* 2:52)

In the preface to her translation Fuller describes Eckermann as the most reliable informant about Goethe's existence. "Never was satellite more completely in harmony with his ruling orb."[39] To be sure, the writer of these journals was not blinded by Goethe, as she observed. Her goal was to win new readers for Goethe and by doing so, to counter potential prejudice an American reading public might bring to the book:

> In these sober and enlightened days, we rebel against man-worship, even though it be hero-worship. But how could this person, so rich in natural gifts, so surrounded by what was bright, beautiful, and courtly, and at so high a point of culture, fail to be overpowering to an obscure youth, whose abilities he had been the chief means of unfolding? It could not be otherwise than that Eckermann should sit at his feet, and live on his bounty. [. . .] That Goethe also knew how to receive is evident from his correspondences with Zelter, Schiller, and Meyer — relations which show him in a better light than this with Eckermann, because the parties were on more equal terms. [. . .] [Eckermann's book] paints Goethe to us as he was in the midst of his family [. . .] his courteous grace, his calm wisdom and reliance on the harmony of his faith with his nature, must be felt by the unprejudiced reader, to be beautiful and rare.[40]

Margaret Fuller ultimately wanted to convey to her readers why Goethe was such an object of her own interest and edification. She did so by clearing away all prejudices that could oppose this interest. For example, her response to the opinion that it is too recent to judge objectively this "great movement in German literature," is to remind critics how much time it took for similar periods to be appreciated in France, Spain, and England: "they would not think fifty years' investigation too much for fifty years' growth, and would no longer provoke the ire of those who are lighting their tapers at the German torch."[41]

She continues with a systematic riposte against the main critical arguments levelled at Goethe by his detractors. She classifies them thus:

> He is not a Christian,
> He is not an idealist,
> He is not a democrat,
> He is not Schiller.[42]

Goethe was for Fuller by no means inured to "spiritual beauty in the human character." In his love of form he was surely a Greek, and his god was more an edifying than a patriarchal spirit. His religion taught that one must develop all one's powers; his faith was lodged in the truth that "'nature could not dispense with immortality.'" In the most trying of situations Goethe would refer to "'the great Idea of Duty which alone can hold us upright.'"[43] Renunciation — that power to sacrifice the momentary for the eternal — is a central idea in his great works. The Catholic philosophy of Dante permeates his *Faust;* the maid Ottilie in the much denigrated *Wahlverwandtschaften (Elective Affinities)* who sacrifices herself to avoid sullying her thoughts with passion, proclaims the poignant lesson of the Magdalene. Ottilie and Makarie in *Wilhelm Meisters Wanderjahre* represent two varieties of heavenly wisdom; Iphigenie disarms the powers of hell. With such examples Margaret wanted to show that Goethe was not a writer in the service of the church; rather, his readers had to draw the moral conclusions from his books themselves.

Goethe, Fuller claimed, was actually not an idealist. He thought less about the way things might be, than about the way things are. Otherwise he could never have produced such results with his research and experiments. Fuller writes: "I am well satisfied that 'he went the way that God and Nature called him.'"[44]

Margaret also noted the aristocrat in Goethe. But here the American also showed her tolerance: "My sympathies are with the great onward movement now obvious throughout the civilized world; [. . .] Yet a minority is needed to keep these liberals in check [. . .] for, as yet, the caldron of liberty has shown a constant disposition to overboil."[45] She counters those critics who compare Goethe unfavorably to Schiller with the reminder that Shakespeare was not Milton, Ariosto was not Tasso. It was not necessary to have two Schillers while one was enough. She cautioned, furthermore, that admirers of Schiller might learn from him a similar admiration for Goethe, his friend and helper. She recommends that modern readers might be enriched by Goethe as Schiller himself had been.

After showing what Goethe is not, Margaret briefly explicates his significance. He prefers, she claims, the perfection of the few to the insignificant progress of the many. He believes primarily in the individual rather than in humanity in general, more in striving than in success, more in thinking than in action, more in nature than in providence. Moreover, she recognized Goethe to be one of the greatest lyric poets of the modern age. "Bards are also prophets," she proclaims. Ultimately, she considers Goethe the best stylist who has done more to improve "the fantastic cumbrous, centipede style indigenous to Germany."[46] He is the most objective critic and the finest observer of human nature.

In her conclusion, however, Fuller performs an extraordinary about-face by taking issue with Thomas Carlyle, the only competent English judge of Goethe. Carlyle had called Goethe the "conqueror of his century" — an overstatement Fuller was not ready to share. She was put off by his "aversion to pain and isolation of the heart." In vain she sought heroic, saintly traits in the man. She did not praise his critical writings as masterful, feeling that they lacked a central point to orient the reader. She found in general that over the years he lost "his architectural vigor," finding in his works a growing resemblance to "Piranesi's *Visions* of galleries and balconies connected only by cobweb ladders."[47]

In Fuller's eyes Goethe had not yet found the critic worthy of him — a plight he shared with Shakespeare, Dante, and Calderon. For this reason one does better to doff one's hat and "shout vivat," rather than drag him through the mud. Margaret therefore pays homage to Goethe at the end of her preface with the lines from Hamlet:

> He was a man, *take him for all in all,*
> We shall not look upon his like again.[48]

Margaret Fuller remained on friendly terms with George Ripley after her translation work ended. When he founded his utopian community Brook Farm in 1841, he invited her to participate. Ripley undertook this communal agricultural experiment in the wake of a movement that gripped the United States in the years between 1825 and 1845. The first such social experiment was founded by the English Socialist Robert Owen in New Harmony, Indiana. He chose for his spot the site of a former settlement of a German Christian-communist sect called Harmonists, or Rappists after their founder, the Swabian farmer George Rapp. Following this settlement Owen established ten more, mostly short-lived communities in North America alone. Then in 1840 Albert Brisbane began to spread the ideas of the French socialist Charles Fourier through his book *The Social Destiny of Man*. Fourier asserted that a social order based on competition and individualism was ineffective and damaging for the common weal. He proposed instead a system whereby 1600 people lived communally in "phalanxes." Private property was allowed, but each member had to contribute agricultural and skilled labor toward the common income of the group. This model found immense popularity in America and more than forty phalanxes sprang up between Massachusetts and Wisconsin in three years.

This remarkable phenomenon occurred when America was in the throes of an economic depression beginning in 1837. So catastrophic were the effects, that the results have been compared to the stock market crash of 1929.[49] In July 1836 the federal government ended the overheated economic expansion by a draconian measure: purchases of land could henceforth be carried out only using metal currency, or currency backed by metal. Massachusetts was hard hit by this measure. Between 1830 and 1837, 76 banks had opened in that state alone and engaged in wild speculation, sometimes not having much more than 4% of their circulating money in reserve. As one after another of such banks closed, there followed widespread unemployment and poverty, especially in New York where the building industry was brought to a standstill. It was not until 1843 that the country began to recover from this crisis. It was no accident, then, that utopian communities such as these phalanxes sprang up during this period. Although Ripley's Brook Farm was neither a Harmonist community in the tradition of Owen, nor one of Fourier's phalanxes, the experiment owed much to the inspiration of the latter.

At the "Brook Farm Institute of Agriculture and Education," as Ripley's community was officially known, the deep interest many people had in German language and culture exerted a distinct influence upon life. Charles A. Dana taught Greek and German classes in the community school. John S. Dwight, who had given up theology for music and translating (especially from the German), was one of the members in longest standing. He later became the most prominent (if also the most conservative) music critic in America. Given this group of intellectuals, the level of conversation at Brook Farm was presumably very cultivated. It is reported that Isaak Hecker, later the founder of the Paulist Order, had Kant's *Critique of Pure Reason* open before him while kneading bread. The community newspaper *The Harbinger* was published between 1845 and 1847 to champion social and political progress. Although the paper was primarily promoting the teachings of Fourier and Swedenborg, its pages also printed reviews of such new publications as Goethe's *Essays on Art* and the *Correspondence between Goethe and Schiller*. Charles Dana translated Novalis and Rückert, and Dwight translated German love poetry.

Margaret Fuller spent two weeks at Brook Farm, after which she reported that in response to this social experiment she found herself in the amusing position of a conservative. She wrote in "Woman in the 19th Century" (1845):

> Fourier says, as the institutions, so the men! All follies are excusable and natural under bad institutions. Goethe thinks, as the man, so the institu-

tions! There is no excuse for ignorance and folly. A man can grow in any place, if he will. Aye! But, Goethe, bad institutions are prison-walls and impure air that make him stupid, so that he does not will. And thou, Fourier, do not expect to change mankind at once, or even "in three generations," by arrangement of groups and series or flourish of trumpets for attractive industry. If these attempts are made by unready men, they will fail. Yet we prize the theory of Fourier no less than the profound suggestions of Goethe. Both are educating the age to a clearer consciousness of what Man needs, what Man can be; and better life must ensue.[50]

Although Margaret Fuller never joined Brook Farm, she often visited her many friends at the idyllic community. It became a tradition for her to spend New Year's Eve there until 1847 when the most important buildings were destroyed by fire. By then, however, the economic recovery had stemmed the expansion of such communities and Brook Farm was not rebuilt.

It was in the building called the "Eyrie" at Brook Farm that Margaret Fuller also held two of her famous "Conversations," one on Goethe, another on mythology. She began these Conversations in Boston in 1836 as a source of income and an effort to liberate herself from school teaching. She held the first series in the winter of 1839–1840. They were conceived for the ladies of Boston who were seeking intellectual stimulation. She announced her program at the start of the first Conversation:

> Women are now taught, at school, all that men are; [...] But [...] men are called on, from a very early period, to reproduce all that they learn. Their college exercises, their political duties, their professional studies, the first actions of life in any direction, call on them to put to use what they have learned. But women learn without any attempt to reproduce. Their only reproduction is for purposes of display.
>
> (*Memoirs*, 1:329)[51]

It was her ambition to cover the most diverse areas of knowledge in these discussions, unifying their common connections. One has to imagine a seminar in which the instructor introduces a subject and then develops a discussion among the participants. If Margaret found the oral contributions by her participants unsatisfactory, she would sometimes require written versions. The first winter was spent on Greek mythology with a group of ten women who first met on November 6, 1839 at the home of Miss Elizabeth Peabody on West Street.

Elizabeth Palmer Peabody, whose sister Sophia married Nathaniel Hawthorne, and who was the governess of the Hawthorne children, studied Greek with Emerson and later founded a girls' school in Boston. As early as 1827 she had also held such conversations on the topic "The Historical Church." For a time she was an ardent admirer of Bronson Al-

cott's pedagogy and assisted him at the Temple School. But her importance for the Concord circle was in her function as bookseller and publisher. From 1839 she had a bookstore on West Street in which could
always be found copies of the latest European books as well as James
Freeman Clarke's *The Western Messenger*. She later published *The Dial*,
which failed, in part, because of her poor bookkeeping skills.

The first series of Margaret Fuller's thirteen, two-hour Conversations
were a success. She did not feel, she wrote, as she had feared, like "a paid
Corinne" (*Letters*, 2:97). Her group of participants subscribed to the entire course, and on November 25th she could boast 25 members. She
wrote to Emerson: "I assure you there is more Greek than Bostonian spoken at the meetings, and we may have pure honey of Hymettus to give
you yet" (*Letters*, 2:102). A course on the arts followed in the next winter.
In 1841 she took up such topics as ethics, the influence of women in the
church, literature, and in society. In 1842 she offered such favorite topics
as demonology and, in 1843, education.

For a few of these Conversations we have the notes of the participants
preserved. It is impossible to say how often German topics were discussed.
Probably the number was not great, for the discussions were meant to
give everyone a chance to participate and Margaret could not expect proficiency in German literature from many. She did, however, always offer
German examples to illustrate her points. Men also took part in these
"mythological evenings." In addition to whoever was the host or hostess
for the evening, Emerson, James Freeman Clarke, Henry Hedge, and
Bronson Alcott participated — all members of the "Transcendental
Club," which would soon give birth to *The Dial*. These evenings turned
out to be the only failures in five years. Emerson seems to have dominated, which annoyed Margaret who was prompted to make ironic comments. "She and Mr. Emerson met like Pyramus and Thisbe, a blank wall
between them," reported Caroline Healy in one of the few sets of notes
that survives of these meetings.[52] On one occasion the topic of discussion
was dance as the expression of national character. Margaret's ideas on the
subject give an impression of the enthusiastic tone typical of her Conversations:

> The German asks his *madchen [sic]* if she will, with him, for an hour for-
> get the cares and common-places of life in a tumult of rapturous sympa-
> thy, and she smiles with Saxon modesty her *Ja*. He sustains her in his
> arms; the music begins. At first, in willing mazes they calmly imitate the
> planetary orbs, but the melodies flow quicker, their accordant hearts beat
> higher, and they whirl at last into giddy raptures, and dizzy evolutions,
> which steal from life its free-will and self-collections, till nothing is left
> but mere sensation. (*Memoirs*, 1:335)

The Conversations enjoyed growing popularity. Subscribers paid six-teen dollars for 24 meetings, each lasting an hour and a quarter. In 1843, when she was fatigued and ailing, Margaret offered smaller classes of twice the length for 25 dollars. As her fame grew, she was invited to hold Conversations in Providence as well.

But between 1840 and 1844 Margaret Fuller was to make her most important contribution to the dissemination of German literature in America. This was, of course, in her capacity as contributor to and editor of *The Dial*.[53] A glance at the articles published in that journal shows that during the first two years under her editorship, many more translations and articles on German themes appeared than during the last two under Emerson. In the very first number there appeared Fuller's "Short Essay on Critics" in which she delineates three types of critic. The first type is the "subjective class (to make use of a convenient term, introduced by our German benefactors)," who never pass absolute judgment. The second group consist of "the apprehensive," those who simply describe a work lovingly, while "the comprehensive," the third type of critic, "enter[s] into the nature of another being and judge[s] his work by its own law" (*The Dial*, 1:6–7). It is significant that Fuller gave preeminence to the comprehensive critic, as those of the Romantic school were long considered. The critic, she believed, should have the role of "the younger brother of genius" (*The Dial*, 1:7) and be at once poet, philosopher, and observer — a far greater responsibility than showed by those "despotic" critics, "intrenched [sic] behind the infallible 'We,'" who dominate the English and American journals (*The Dial*, 1:8).

Among her own poems, which Margaret distributed throughout *The Dial*, were two about Jean Paul (referred to as "Richter"). The first of these praises him as a poet of nature, as the boldest satirist and artist who paints with Titian's colors, Raphael's dignity, and Hogarth's pencil. In a second poem she addresses readers who accuse Jean Paul of being unsystematic. He has a system, she asserts, "in its highest sense," for this free spirit is at home in the order of "Nature's wide temple" (*The Dial*, 1:135).

In her prose texts as well she displays her penchant for poetic expression on matters of literature. The third number of *The Dial* contained a short story about the wife of Klopstock, probably included for lack of other contributions. The predicament is a common one for editors, as the examples of Emerson's later experience with *The Dial*, or Schiller and his journal *Die Horen*, indicate. It was often the case that, shortly before going to press, Fuller either had to write long essays, or dig out one of her old manuscripts on any topic at all, just to fill pages. A case in point is the prose piece "Meta," which she had written seven years earlier, apparently inspired by Mrs. Jameson's *Loves of the Poets*, a collection of biographical sketches of women celebrated in ancient and modern literature. The roster of such famous and beloved figures stretches from Ovid's Corinna down to the modern day, with Mrs. Jameson placing special emphasis upon the beloved wife. She quotes "the very sweet line" by Lord Lyttelton: "How much the wife is dearer than the bride."[54]

This description applied to the angelic Meta Klopstock. After the disappointment of his unrequited love for Fanny Schmidt, Klopstock married Meta who was devoted to him and enjoyed four years of marital bliss until she died in childbirth with their first child. Mrs. Jameson gives a moving description of her death, but cannot resist quoting Klopstock's poem to Dona, written four years later:

> Du zweifelst, dass ich dich wie Meta liebe?
> Wie Meta lieb ich Done dich![55]

To this she appends the comment, "And such is *man's* fidelity!"[56]

In contrast to Mrs. Jameson's reliance on biographical material and the couple's correspondence, Margaret Fuller floats on the wings of poetry. Her rhapsodic prose describes a scene in which Meta appears to the recently widowed poet. In the afterlife she has met Petrarch's Laura who has urged her to await her husband in paradise, watching over him as a "Spirit of love" and bringing comfort and sympathy to other troubled souls. It is an episode of excruciating sentimentality, from which Margaret could often not free herself. Von Mehren calls "Meta and Klopstock" and "The Magnolia of Lake Pontchatrain," both of which appeared in the same issue of *The Dial*, "mystical contemplations."[57]

Her essays of literary criticism, on the other hand, are quite a different story. *The Dial* was Margaret's best platform for expressing herself on literary issues dear to her heart. Here she was assured of an informed readership that either knew what she was talking about, or educated and open-minded enough to be receptive to her message. The best example of Fuller's talents as a literary essayist is her furious review in the third number of *The Dial* of Wolfgang Menzel's German literary history. The work had just appeared in George Ripley's *Specimens of Foreign Standard Literature*, translated by the classicist (and later president of Harvard) Cornelius Felton with the assistance of Henry Wadsworth Longfellow. The title of the critique is "Menzel's View of Goethe" which is followed directly in the fist line of text, without so much as a comma, by "Is that of a Philistine, [. . .] who does not enter into Canaan, and read the prophet by the light of his own law." Whoever does so is led on and on by Goethe's works until "we live in them" — as Bettina Brentano answered Goethe's critics (*The Dial*, 1:341). Fuller views Goethe historically and decides

that he "needs no apology. His so called faults fitted him all the better for
the part he had to play" (*The Dial*, 1:341). Schiller was the moral enthusiast, Novalis possessed piety or "a pure mystic sweetness," while Richter
was full of feeling and the Schlegels had great critical talents. But the
American critic asks, "Who could fill Goethe's place to Germany, and to
the world, of which she is now the teacher?" (*The Dial*, 1:342). Her years
of Goethe study bear fruit in such essays; she is able to explain this unique
poet through his biography and his remarkable youth. "Never was a child
so carefully guarded by fate against prejudice, against undue bias, against
any engrossing sentiment" (*The Dial*, 1:342). Childhood anecdotes
gleaned from *Goethe's Correspondence with a Child* serve as illustrative
material for his character that was so often criticized for its self-control and
emotional distance, or for a preference for disguise and anonymity:

> In daily life many of these carefully recorded passages have an air of
> platitude, at which no wonder the Edinburgh Review laughed. Yet, on
> examination, they are full of meaning.[58]

One must measure Goethe with his own yardstick, she decides. She
quotes several strophes of her translation of Goethe's poem "The God-
like" to give an example of the standards he applied to himself and to others. Although Goethe may never have reached the highest heights of
human existence — "He might have been a priest; he was only a sage —
he was nonetheless neither the "Epicurean" nor the characterless talent
("debauchee") that Menzel's arrogance presents:[59]

> Here are sixty volumes, by himself and others, which contain sufficient
> evidence of a life of severe labor, steadfast forbearance, and an intellectual
> growth almost unparalleled.[60]

Since Fuller was not able to give an extensive characterization of Goethe in a review like this, there followed a forty-page article entitled "Goethe" in the July 1841 issue of *The Dial* (*The Dial*, 2:1–41). This essay,
which represented a critical encounter with the writer, shows the astonishing progress of Fuller's sophistication in her knowledge of Goethe.
Seven years had passed since the farmhouse days in Groton when she had
first wanted to be taken by the hand, so to speak, and led by Goethe
through the tribulations of life. By now she was herself in the position of
leading her readers through Goethe's work, life, and character, dis-
cerningly, and with an understanding for the critical attitudes of her New
England readers, as well as for the conditions that produced this literary
phenomenon.

To begin with, there was the man in whom "the intellect is too much
developed in proportion to the moral nature," a trait that made it impossible for him ever to succumb completely to feeling, leading Margaret

Fuller to the severe pronouncement, "of a deep mind and shallow heart" (*The Dial*, 2:2). She interprets this propensity of Goethe as a consequence of his upbringing, but exclaims in his defense, "Pardon him, World, that he was too worldly" (*The Dial*, 2:3). Goethe's life in Weimar, however, she judged as wasted time. The duties at court distanced Goethe from men of his own kind such as Herder and Wieland. Poets, she mused, are not always satisfied being merely poets: Petrarch was an ambassador, Cervantes a soldier. She then draws a connection between Goethe and his literary creations, Tasso and Werther, two characters imbued with much of his own nature, but whose weaknesses he himself was able to surmount. This section shows off some of Margaret's best formulations:

> In the calm air of the cultivated plain he attained, the remembrance of the miasma of sentimentality was odious to him. Yet sentimentality is but sentiment diseased, which to be cured must be patiently observed by the wise physician. (*The Dial*, 2:7)

Fuller and her friends saw in Werther primarily "morbid desire and despair[,] the sickness of a soul aspiring to a purer, freer state, but mistaking the way" (*The Dial*, 2:7). Like *Götz von Berlichingen,* this youthful work of Goethe's made little impression on New England readers around 1840. Similarly, nobody but Margaret Fuller showed much understanding, or even passable knowledge of *Faust.* The medieval aura surrounding *Götz* and the first part of *Faust* did not agree with these Americans, except when altered by the spirit of German Romanticism in *Des Knaben Wunderhorn* or in Tieck's stories.

Margaret therefore included the *Märchen* of the "New Paris" at this point in her essay in order to illustrate Goethe's genius. When he was only eight years old he told this tale to his playmates, which provides a glimpse of him "acting out the mystery of life" (*The Dial*, 2:17) as a controlled, unimpassioned observer. Particularly the conclusion of the tale, with "the ironical baffling at the end, and want of point to a tale got up with such an eye to effect as he goes along" (*The Dial*, 2:17), predicts the man he was to become.

Fuller's essay describes Goethe as a man who was serious when at play. He began friendships in a rush of passion, but ended them as a cool-headed observer, stripping them off "as a snake leaves its skin" (*The Dial*, 2:17). Fuller attributes significant influence to only two people: to Goethe's mother and the Grand Duke, whom Goethe describes as *"dämonisch,"* i.e., a gifted and spontaneous elemental force. To emphasize their importance she cites passages from *Dichtung und Wahrheit* and the *Conversations with Eckermann*. Goethe's misfortune, according to Fuller, was that he also wanted to become a man of the world. The first half of her essay explains why that had to be and the second half reveals the consequences for Goethe and his work. She is sympathetic to Goethe's assessment, which she translates and comments thus: "'Care is taken that the trees grow not up into the heavens.' Ay, Goethe, but in proportion to their force of aspiration is their height!" (*The Dial*, 2:20). According to Fuller Goethe never reached the height of a Shakespeare or Dante whose works were "instinct with the peculiar life of human resolve" (*The Dial*, 2:21).

Margaret Fuller also understood *Faust* and its status within Goethe's *oeuvre* better than anybody in the Concord circle. She said the drama contained "the great idea of his life" (*The Dial*, 2:21). If Goethe had ended the work in the same spirit in which he had begun it, then it would have become the *Divine Comedy* of its age. But, she felt, a comparison between the *Paradiso* and the second part of *Faust* shows the difference between a hard, earnest life, and a life that had at least adjusted to circumstances. In both works the soul was led back to God step by step. "But O the difference between the grandly humble reliance of old Catholicism, and the loop-hole redemption of modern sagacity" (*The Dial*, 2:21).

Fuller considered *Wilhelm Meister* the continuation of *Faust I*, for Wilhelm is no longer a seeker, but rather a "disciple of Circumstance" with a taste for virtue and knowledge (*The Dial*, 2:23). With this "negative character" Goethe wanted to paint a picture of true life and establish the ideal within the real world. The highest principle in this, as in all works by Goethe, always appears in female form, and Fuller finds the ideal women in the characters of *Wilhelm Meister* (as she had done in *Dichtung und Wahrheit*) whom she then presents as paragons. She gives sensitive characterizations of these figures: the delicate Philine, who embodies the disgrace that lies in the attempt to lead a poetic life; Mignon, the Goethe character who was probably the best loved in New England; the woman portrayed after a friend Goethe knew in his youth and called "Beautiful Soul;" Natalie; and "the celestial Macarie." To back up her judgment on *Wilhelm Meister* as a sober work, she invokes Rahel Varnhagen von Ense.

The one person who possessed all that Goethe lacked was, in her eyes, Beethoven. She quotes the often illustrated scene of Goethe, who with hat in hand, bows respectfully to the imperial family, while Beethoven responds to the greeting of the Archduke and Empress by pulling his hat tightly onto his head and hurries away through the crowd.

Margaret Fuller always regarded Goethe's works from the classical period as his best. She defended *Elective Affinities* against attacks from British and New England readers. The discriminating reader "will regard the *Elective Affinities* as a work especially that is called moral in its outward effect, and religious even to piety in its spirit" (*The Dial*, 2:32). This is, to be sure, a singular opinion for its time and place. Margaret's identification with Ottilie seems almost other worldly: "I see not only what she was, but what she might have been and live with her in yet untrodden realms" (*The Dial*, 2:33).

Iphigenie is, finally, "a work beyond the possibility of negation" (*The Dial*, 2:34). Fuller ends her long essay with translations of the opening monologue and portions of the second act. The author of this work, she concludes, was not the man of the world, the connoisseur, the friend of Mephistopheles, nor Wilhelm the Master, nor Egmont, "the generous free-liver" — it was Goethe in "his first-born glory," the poet who was destined to become the brightest star in a new constellation (*The Dial*, 2:41).

The Goethe essay is Margaret Fuller's most comprehensive statement about the writer. As she wrote to Emerson, she was not inclined to devote year after year to a single personality. German literature offered a field more rich, and furthermore, her interest in other European literatures had not waned. The musical life of Boston that was beginning to thrive spoke to her interest, for she also wanted to discover (and make known) the visual arts, especially Italian painting and sculpture.

After Goethe, the figure from German literature who captivated her most powerfully was Bettina Brentano. Margaret had discovered her during her biographical research on Goethe. She developed a love of reading Bettina that she shared both with Emerson and James Freeman Clarke, for whom "funny little Bettine" was a favorite.[61] As in the case of Goethe, Margaret was determined to publicize her appreciation of Bettina in reviews, essays, and translations. To this end she included the poem "Bettina" by her friend Caroline Sturgis (daughter of a wealthy Boston merchant) in the July number of *The Dial* in 1841. Using the image of an eagle, the text first depicts Bettina "proud and free" on the highest treetop; then, as a small, brown bird, fearless and happy upon a stone, singing all day and representing the two principle female characters of German Romanticism.

In the same number there appeared an announcement of the long-awaited reprint of the English translation of *Goethe's Correspondence with a Child*. The work had just been published in Lowell by O. Bixby along with the prose translation of *Faust* by A. Hayward. The eloquent notice in *The Dial* is surely Margaret's own: "We cannot but wonder that any one who aims at all at literary culture can remain ignorant of German, the acquisition of which language is not a year's labor with proper instruction, and would give them access to such wide domains of thought and knowledge" (*The Dial*, 2:134). The January number of *The Dial* then printed a long contribution by Fuller on "Bettine *[sic]* Brentano and her Friend Günderrode (*The Dial,* 2:313-357).

She chose Bettina's work *Die Günderode* as a subject because New England readers were already familiar with *Goethe's Correspondence with a Child;* she also considered *Die Günderode* to be Bettina's better work.[62] As she worked on the translation (which she was never able to finish), she expressed this opinion to Channing in a letter from February 19, 1841:

> I meant to have translated for you the best passages of "Die Gunderode" *[sic]* (which I prefer to the correspondence with Goethe. The two girls are equal natures, and *both* in earnest. Goethe made a puppet show for his private entertainment of Bettina's life, and we wonder she did not feel he was not worthy of her homage.) [. . .] The exquisite little poem of Gunderode read aloud two or three times that you may catch the music; it is of most sweet mystery. She is to me dear and admirable. Bettine *[sic]* only interesting[.] She is of religious grace. Bettina the fulness of nature.
> (*Letters,* 2:202–203)

Goethe's Correspondence with a Child was well received in New England, as Margaret wrote to Channing in October 1840:

> I am astonished to see how much Bettina's book is to all these people. This shows how little courage they have had to live out themselves. She really brings them a revelation. The men wish they had been loved by Bettina; the girls wish to write down the thoughts that come, and see if just such a book does not grow up. (*Letters,* 2:172)

She did, however, mention one female visitor who expressed the opinion that Bettina published what other writers burned.

> Would not genius be common as light, if men trusted their higher selves?
> (*Letters,* 2:172)

> Even those who are accustomed to measure the free movements of art by the conventions that hedge the path of daily life, who, in great original creations, seek only intimations of the moral character borne by the author in his private circle, [. . .] suffered themselves to be surprised in their intrenchments, by the exuberance and wild, youthful play of Bettina's genius. (*The Dial,* 2:313)

But Fuller also noted the less pleasant aspects in the relationship between Goethe and Bettina. She takes a monitory tone, for example, when warning against the dangers of the veneration in Bettina's letters. The dangers applied to both parties involved: infatuation on the one hand, and vanity on the other. Margaret Fuller herself possessed enough fervent sentimentality to be able to speak from experience. But she had also matured and gained the self-control to be able to make accurate observations about the dynamic of this incongruous couple. Bettina was no child when she wrote these letters — which Margaret naively thought were all genuine. For Margaret, Goethe did not seem to take a paternal attitude: "there is an air as of an elderly guardian flirting cautiously with a giddy, inexperienced ward" (*The Dial*, 2:316). It was not that he was toying with her affections, but that he used what she offered up to him from her whole soul for his art. This is the old reproach that Emerson levelled at Goethe. In regard to "the funny little Bettina" it was conduct that was doubly hard to accept and even spoiled the *Correspondence* somewhat for Margaret. Still, she compares Bettina's turbulent youth with the fate of Euphorion "in Goethe's great Rune" (a description she uses for *Faust*), with Tasso, Werther, Sappho, and Madame de l'Espinasse. While reading her, she hints, one also has the feeling that "It will not, nor it cannot come to good" (*The Dial*, 2:317). But, Fuller urges, we must be grateful to Bettina for her letters to Goethe, which she called "most delicate productions of literature" (*The Dial*, 2:317).

By contrast, Bettina's correspondence with the noblewoman Karoline von Günderrode is quite a different matter. These letters predate the *Correspondence with a Child*. Fuller sees the relationship between the two women as representing a state of innocence, as a harmonious balance between Nature (the bird-like Bettina) and the Ideal (the Canoness Günderrode). To Fuller the effect they had on one another seemed to be "of highest poetic significance." Whereas a similar friendship between two young men might have heroic aspects, between two young women it is seen as poetic. The reason for this interpretation can be traced to Fuller's understanding of Woman as poem, but of Man as poet — an utterance that clearly shows the contours of this Romantic woman's "feminism."

Fuller's depiction of the friendship between Bettina Brentano and Karoline von Günderrode is suffused with admiration. The discussions of these women about philosophy and literature, she noticed, were on the highest cultural plane, yet achieved with the ease young English and American women had when talking about their choice of dresses. Much of Günderrode's writing was possible only because she was a contemporary of Fichte and Schelling. "This transfusion of such energies as are manifested in Goethe, Kant, and Schelling into these private lives is a creation not less worthy our admiration, than the forms which the muse has given them" (*The Dial*, 2:320). A hint of envy sneaks into Margaret's descriptions of these women as they walk together along the Rhine or in Madame La Roche's garden, "where they 'founded a religion for a young prince'" (*The Dial*, 2:323). If she ever compared her friendship with Caroline Sturgis with that of the two ladies from Frankfurt, she must have

ascertained a marked difference in the educational level of the young German woman and her own partner.

To her own introduction Fuller added passages in English translation
from Bettina's *Goethe's Correspondence with a Child* as well as from her
Günderode. The first of these she quotes from Bettina's English with
which she does not find fault. On the contrary, "these inspired sayings
look almost as beautiful in the German-English of Bettine's translation as
in the original. I cannot hope for equal success in the following extracts
from 'Die Günderode'" (*The Dial*, 2:325). In her own version, Fuller
imitated Bettina's idiom as much as possible, even approximating her
"truly girlish punctuation. Commas and dashes are the only stops natural
to girls; their sentences flow on in little minim ripples, unbroken [...]
unless by some slight waterfall or jet of Ohs and Ahs" (*The Dial*, 2:325).

The English version of Bettina's text that flowed from this American's
pen is certainly a remarkable linguistic exhibit. She imitates German syntax
to the point where her English hardly communicates any more: "Long
followed me thy look, it was so still and so profound, and yet seemed to
pass away over me." In a sense, Margaret's English has out-Bettina-ed
Bettina, for her aim was to capture the cascade of feeling that the effusive
German poured into her letters. These overflow with feelings of heart-felt
friendship: "yes, a whole year have we been good friends to one another???!!!" Or, emotions that exclude the intellect: "we must go hand in
hand, and speak with one another not of things, but a great speech" (*The
Dial*, 2:326). This is a cult of friendship closely allied with religious ecstasy: "to-day have I seen Günderode, it was a gift from God" (*The Dial*,
2:326). Margaret is fascinated by Bettina's suggestion that they found a
new religion, and by her talent at formulating aphorisms. She loves to
translate sentences like "Man is nothing but the desire to feel himself in
another" (*The Dial*, 2:330).

She used the correspondence of the women as a source of information
about the daily lives of educated German contemporaries. She delights in
the humorous reports by Günderrode about a visit to the theater with
Goethe's mother in the summer, or her description of the chaos in Bettina's room. There she was amused to find copies of Homer, Ossian and
the *Frankfurter Chronik* lying on the floor (unspared by Bettina's canary),
the flageolet in a flower box, and the guitar strap fluttering out the window.

The suspicion also reached Margaret's ears that in the letters Bettina
may have interpolated portions from a later period. She attributes the possibility to Bettina's childlike nature, which made her such a fanciful
dreamer. A poetic eye cannot see the world as mere naked facts; reality
exists only to represent the ideal. She refers to Goethe who said of Jean

Paul's autobiography, to tell the truth about such a life could only show that he was a philistine. Bettina's flaws were character flaws, but "her book is true, a many-petalled flower on the bosom of nature, from which the dew shall never vanish" (*The Dial*, 2:353).

The excerpts from *Die Günderode* were Margaret Fuller's last great contribution to *The Dial* while she was editor. She never got to completing her translation of the entire work, which was done by Minna Wesselhoeft after Margaret's death. Minna's father, Robert Wesselhoeft, was the son of Johann Karl Wesselhoeft, who had run the Wesselhöft Printing Press in Jena since 1799. Robert studied medicine before falling in with the same radical student circle as Charles Follen, an association which forced him to emigrate. In New England he dedicated himself to innovative reforms such as his health spa in Brattleboro, Vermont, where he held his patients to strict diets and water cures. Thoreau was among those who made the pilgrimage to this fountain of health. After selling the family home in Groton and terminating her teaching career, Margaret Fuller moved back to the Boston area where for a time she rented near the Wesselhoefts in Cambridge. The completed translation of *Die Günderode* found readers in New England beyond Concord, among them Emily Dickinson who also owned a copy of *Goethe's Correspondence with a Child*.[63]

Margaret published two long articles in *The Dial* during the last two years that Emerson edited the journal. The first was a long synopsis of Karl Simrock's *Rheinsagen aus dem Munde des Volks und deutscher Dichter* (*Legends of the Rhine; A Poetical Guide to the Rhine* [1970]), which had appeared in Bonn in 1840.[64] She speaks of Simrock, as a "happy man [. . .], a 'Dr.' too, Doctor of Romance" (*The Dial*, 3:137), deriving from the work a picture of idealized, Romantic Germany. She envies the scholar lucky enough to grow up in this happy land and impart its traditions to others. She felt strongly that America was in need of the message of these traditions.

Fuller saw clearly (as did Emerson and Thoreau) that the constant development of the ever-expanding country was leading America in one direction, namely toward an all-embracing culture of materialism:

> It is good for us in this bustling, ambitious, superficial country, where every body is trying to do something new, where all the thought is for the future, and it is supposed the divine spirit has but just waked up, and that the blunders, committed on the earth during this long slumber, are now at once to be corrected [. . .]; it is good for us to look abroad and learn [. . .] that love and loyalty have bloomed and will bloom [. . .] and that hate and falsehood have been, as they will be, permitted conditions of man's willing choice of virtue. (*The Dial*, 3:138)

Margaret Fuller is also not shy about characterizing the Germans she was always reading about. They tend to two extremes, she concludes: the temperaments that are bubbling over become Phantasts; the strict and pious types become Pedants. They are good people, like the knights, monks, and monarchs who built the cathedrals. The modern German has, to be sure, lost the clear eye and practiced hand of his ancestors and today can only hold a pen. Still, Germans are the same human types about which the ballads sing.

It is to these that she then turns, she explains, translating and comparing the ancient tales. She emphasizes the similarities in the descriptions of the strengths and weaknesses of both men and women in the old tales. Sagas like *Lohengrin* are counterbalanced by tales of nixies or of Melusine with their weaker male characters. The pure emotions with which German men treat German women had been noticed first by the Romans, and Margaret discovers these traits in the ballads and sagas. "The ideal relation between them is constantly described with a delicacy of feeling, of which only the highest minds in other countries are susceptible" (*The Dial*, 3:143). Goethe's female characters had confirmed this for her. Margaret, it must be said, is one of the founders of the stereotype of the chivalrous German male, a figure who survived in American popular literature until the first world war.

The noble figures from these ballads reminded Margaret of classical precursors; Charlemagne loomed particularly large in these "national memories." The castles and cathedrals built by these men, the bells that ring forth from them (and whose voices echo more recently in Schiller's "The Song of the Bell") — all are particulars that convey Margaret's devout enthusiasm to her readers. She translates the ballad "The Death of Basle" as an example of "genuine German humor." The poem tells the story of a young man who marries an old wife, but then has Death fetch her after three days. He soon wishes her back, however, after taking a young wife who always beats him.

The Romantic Rhine is an aspect of German culture that still permeates the American image of Germany. The history and legends of the river certainly left a deep impression on Margaret Fuller, who wrote, "Rivers, like men, have their destiny" (*The Dial*, 3:139). The river's destiny, she goes on, determines its beauty and deeper meaning. The work of nature and the hand of man united to create of this river one continuous poem. Margaret discovered the special place of the swan in the poetry about the Rhine, be it in folksong, in the modern poem of Lohengrin — the knight of the swan — or in the phenomenon of the swan rings, which are engraved with images of swans and imbued with magical, other-worldly powers. The legends of the Loreley and the cliff of Drachenfels beguile their way into her private mythology: "I am on the Drachenfels and cannot get off," she writes to Emerson on December 26, 1839 to indicate that she is in one of her "naughtiest moods" (*Letters*, 2:104). She even writes a poem about this part of her fantasy, in which she speaks to the reader through "music and magnetism."

In Simrock's anthology she discovers the street songs *(Bänkellieder)* that embodied the popular loathing for Napoleon, as well as the ballads sung in honor of Charlemagne. The "Ballad of the Nibelungen" strikes her as extraordinary, with Siegfried representing the indigenous hero of the country: "unchristianized, unchristian, arrogant, noble, impetuous, sincere, overbearing, generous, no reflective wisdom, no side thoughts, no humility, no weakness" (*The Dial*, 3:152). One could almost think that Margaret Fuller had already read Nietzsche who would envision just such a liberated man of the future: "Of a stately native growth were the timbers from which this ship of Germany is built, all oak, proud, German oak" (*The Dial*, 3:153). Fuller's last important contribution to *The Dial* appeared in July 1843. It was called "The Great Lawsuit: Man versus Men. Woman versus Women," and is considered one of the earliest tracts of the American women's movement (*The Dial*, 4:1–47). It brought its author renown beyond the borders of New England and was actually the cause of her leaving the region — and ultimately America. The essay was to catch the eye of Horace Greeley who lured her away to New York City and subsequently sent her to Europe on assignment.

The idea for this work surely came to Margaret during those Conversations that she had started in order to promote the education of women. Wherever she looked she saw intelligent, open-minded young women, mothers or unmarried ladies like Elizabeth Peabody, who all had taste and intelligence. But she saw their possibilities restricted by social barriers and old prejudices, even in such a progressive man as Ralph Waldo Emerson who remarked at the birth of a friend's daughter, "Though no son, yet a sacred event." This provoked from her the response: "I do believe, O Waldo, most unteachable of men, that you are at heart a sinner on this point. I entreat you to seek light in prayer upon it" (*Letters*, 3:124).

In her "Great Lawsuit" Margaret is completely a child of her reformist era — and this in New England. "The time is come when Euridice is to call for an Orpheus, rather than Orpheus for Euridice" (*The Dial*, 4:7). The human image had up to that point been modelled after that of the male. Now, however, men also had begun to see that an improvement of the status of the daughters could most improve the sons of this era. She is concerned with true equality of women, which for Margaret meant the development of her talent, which was no less than a man's. All around her, however, she saw the powerless woman, a situation (hardly a progression) that she demonstrates with examples from Roman, English, and Russian history, and from Judaism, Christianity, and Islam, as well as from all literary traditions she knows.

In Schiller's "Würde der Frauen" ("Dignity of Women") there is no perfect man, but only a boy who must be "softened and restrained by the influence of girls. What can you expect of every-day men, if Schiller was not more prophetic as to what women must be?" (*The Dial*, 4:17). Even Jean Paul Richter requires no more from a woman than that she "cook him something good." And at the end of her essay, Fuller refers to Goethe: "I tire every one with my Goethean illustrations. But it cannot be helped" (*The Dial*, 4:46). Because Goethe was the intellectual prophet of his century, Fuller cannot spare her readers his attitudes toward women: "As his Wilhelm [Meister] grows in life and advances in wisdom, he becomes acquainted with women of more and more character, evolving from Mariana to Macaria" (*The Dial*, 4:46).

Makarie, the center of all planetary relationships, but herself free of all attachments, represents the side of Minerva. Mignon, on the other hand, is an expression of the energy of inspired lyrical nature. Practical Theresa, charitable Natalia, the fair Saint — all choose their paths without limiting their thinking. Everything is important to them, because they need nothing. Fuller especially admires the individuality of these characters, the freedom in which they live and can evolve. "Mignon and Theresa wear male attire when they like, and it is graceful for them to do so" (*The Dial*, 4:47). The harmony of this little world in which everything has its place, natural and free, is what Fuller wished for herself and her age. "New individualities shall be developed in the actual world," she prophesied, "which shall advance upon it as gently as the figures come out upon his [Goethe's] canvass" (*The Dial*, 4:47).

Fuller also sprinkled longer reviews in among the announcements of recent German literature. She herself was understandably interested in translations, as of *Egmont* (*The Dial*, 2:394ff) and works like *Conjectures and Researches Concerning the Love, Madness, and Imprisonment of Torquato Tasso*, by R. H. Wilde (New York, 1842). To her review of this work on the historical Tasso she appends her translation of the first scene of the second act of Goethe's *Tasso*. She wants to show this "as the best criticism" in which Goethe presents the sudden outbursts of blazing eloquence, the changing emotions, and the sensitivity of his Tasso — the qualities that comprise his strengths and weaknesses (*The Dial*, 2:399–407).

In January of 1843 Margaret Fuller reviewed a book on the life of Jean Paul Richter. The work was a compilation of several sources and of his autobiography, which had appeared pseudonymously in Boston the previ-

ous year (*The Dial*, 3:404–406). Fuller, however, must have known Eliza
Buckminster Lee who wrote the book. Her review chides the Germans for
their literary sins, particularly their weaknesses in the area of historiogra-
phy, which, she claims, are philosophies of history rather than history.
With the Germans' neglect of biographies and memoirs "the German histories [. . .] interest us rather by their speculations, than by their narra-
tive" (*The Dial*, 3:404). She wonders whether the cause can be traced to
the tendency to seek an inherent principle in all things, the "Noumen" in
all phenomena, the personified idea in all individuals. The Germans surround all great men with a mystery, which is unsatisfying to English readers who want to follow their subjects through the workroom, nursery, and
kitchen. German literature, as a result, has no Boswell and no Johnson to
show — a situation compensated for by Carlyle's biography of Schiller —
and "the author or authoress (if she will permit us so far to invade her pri-
vacy) of the work before us, has performed a similar office for the antipode
of Schiller, the rare, the *einziger* Jean Paul" (*The Dial*, 3:405).

The review of J. L. Weiss's translation of Schiller's letters (Boston
1841) from the period prior to his marriage, paints a picture that easily
arouses love and admiration. Fuller suggests that Schiller could even be
our neighbor. Yet, in analyzing Schiller, she finds him unable to interpret
his own early passions as transitions in his development; he thus writes
more nobly about friendship than about marriage (*The Dial*, 3:411–413).

Margaret Fuller did her best to inform readers of *The Dial* about all
aspects of art, and thereby educate their taste. She expressed such hopes to
William Channing when she was preparing the first number, clearly stating
that she expected *The Dial* to be an independent publication, written in a
"fair calm tone", free of dogma and compromise. The magazine, furthermore, was not to become a mouthpiece for public opinion, but one that
was supposed to make readers think for themselves (*Letters*, 2:126). Her
hopes for the enterprise were actually quite low, thanks in part to the
skepticism of her collaborators. But at least she could point to the higher
direction of the educational goals *The Dial* was aiming for.

More was needed than articles on German literature. In the first number of *The Dial* Margaret Fuller therefore included a report by John Sullivan Dwight on "The Concerts of the Past Winter." Dwight was a music-
loving theologian who had edited a volume in Ripley's series "Specimens
of Foreign Standard Literature," *Select Minor Poems of Goethe and Schiller*.
This volume contained pieces by the entire circle of friends, including
Fuller, Hedge, Channing, and Clarke. Among Dwight's own superb
translations is that of "Der Erlkönig." It seems that Margaret Fuller
wanted to do more for the project than she finally was able. Quoting from
Schiller's poem "Die Ideale" she writes to Dwight:

Wie wenig; ach! hat sich entfaltet,
Dies wenige, wie klein und karg.[65]

One can hear the complaint about flagging inspiration, indeed, she claims she would need the help of some good *daemon* to finish what she desperately desires to do. Her notebook of translations from this period is a sad sight:

> Goethe's unrhimed poems are entirely beyond me. When there is no metre to guide me I can bear no words but his own and could never get beyond the first verse of "Das Göttliche" — I have translated great parts of Das Ideal und das Leben, and about half of die Künstler, but I am altogether dispirited by the result and cannot, at present, summon courage to go on. (*Letters*, 1:281)

Before Dwight moved to Brook Farm he worked as music critic for *The Dial*. In a review essay in the first number, he emphasizes the importance of Beethoven, testimony to his personal taste that preferred a symphony by Beethoven to any other music except Handel's *Messiah*. Two Beethoven trios had been performed "in the best style of our young German professors, who always play as if they breathed an element which we do not" (*The Dial*, 1:131). But he also laments the uneducated musical audiences of Boston. "A magnificent Organ Fugue of Bach, performed by Mr. Müller, the most accomplished organist who has been among us, was thrown away upon a yawning, talking assembly" (*The Dial*, 1:131).

For the October 1841 number Margaret Fuller wrote a compilation of several musicians' biographies with the goal of improving the musicological level of her readers. The essay was called "Lives of the Great Composers: Haydn, Mozart, Handel, Bach, Beethoven," and contains several Goethe reminiscences in the introduction. "Like the hero, the statesman, the martyr, the artist differs from other men only in this, that the voice of the demon within the breast speaks louder" (*The Dial*, 2:149). She calls music the art in which "all is in each and each in all" (*The Dial*, 2:151). Her presentation of the five composers blends short biographical sketches with entertaining and characteristic anecdotes. But she also attempts to present the basic characteristics of the music. To do so she uses Bombet's *Vie de Haydn, de Mozart et de Metastas* (written pseudonymously by Henri Beyle, alias Stendhal), as well as the following: the Beethoven biography by Friedrich Ries and F. G. Wegeler (Koblenz, 1838); Anton Schindler's life of Beethoven; Schlichtegroll's book on Mozart; and J. F. Forkel's life of Johann Sebastian Bach, which she calls her best source.

Fuller's "Lives of the Great Composers" is a labor of love, while at the same time being a very personal statement. Three sonnets of hers are embedded in the body of the text. Their effect indicates the impact of these works on one listener whose only training was her profound love of music. This love, she asserts, gives her the ability to reject the modern counterfeits that are everywhere. The sonnets — entitled "Instrumental Music", "Beethoven", "Mozart" — are, she notes "the merit of being a pure New England growth" (*The Dial*, 2:172).

The sequence of the five composer portraits is a clue to Fuller's personal taste. Her Handel overshadows Haydn; Bach she finds to be "the towering, snowy mountain" (*The Dial*, 2:179); and Beethoven is not just the absolute pinnacle of music, but of art *per se*. This portion of her account also gives Margaret an opportunity to break a lance for Bettina Brentano. Schindler's life of Beethoven had been very critical both of Bettina and of Ries. But Fuller states: "Let only the reader read poetically, and Germany *by* Madame de Staël, Wallenstein *by* Schiller, Beethoven *by* Ries, are not the less true for being inaccurate. It is the same as with the Madonna *by* Guido, or *by* Murillo" (*The Dial*, 2:186). It ought to be clear, she maintains, that the great man never spoke such words:

> the whole narration is overflowed with Bettina rose-color. [. . .] Yet "the good Bettina" gives us the soul of the matter. Her description of his manner of seizing a melody and then gathering together from every side all that belonged to it, and the saying, "other men are touched by something good. Artists are fiery; they do not weep," are Beethoven's, whether he really said them or not. (*The Dial*, 2:186)

The reason Beethoven touched Margaret Fuller so deeply lies in these lines. The American applauded, of course, his "uncompromising democracy." Then, there is her ability to empathize with this giant and to make his unhappiness hers. This establishes the bond that leads her to him — a case of identification that was not possible with Goethe who in life had never felt as rudely rejected and isolated. Nor did Goethe have comparable financial struggles; he was spared physical infirmities and, when he loved, he was loved in return. Fuller, by contrast, identified personally with Beethoven's suffering. When she reads that ignorant critics had declared the composer ripe for the madhouse, she cries out: "Ah men! almost your ingratitude doth at times convince that you are wholly unworthy the visitations of the Divine!" (*The Dial*, 2:188). Of course she includes Beethoven's "Heiligenstadt Testament" in her essay, but she comes to the conclusion that Beethoven's life was destined to run the course it did, and no good fortune and no woman could have made him happy.

John Sullivan Dwight left Boston in 1840 and, after an unsuccessful stint as a pastor, joined Brook Farm. As a consequence, in July 1842 Margaret Fuller had to provide her own report on "Entertainments of the Past

Winter" (*The Dial,* 3:46–72), which included the musical offerings. The success of the city's cultural life leads her to muse, "What would our Puritan fathers say, if they could see our bill of fare here in Boston for this winter? The concerts, the opera dancing, which have taken place of their hundred-headed sermons, how would they endure?" (*The Dial,* 3:46). She argues that the noble deeds of the Pilgrim fathers represent but one side of human nature, and that the desire for entertainment and instruction are as irrepressible as the force within the earth to bring forth spring flowers.

Fuller regrets that the greater part of the populace of Boston was cool to the theater. Shakespeare could not have succeeded with Boston audiences, although lower forms of entertainment were unfortunately popular with the youth of the city. Fuller also perceives the reasons for the stark contrasts between European and American theater life, noting that the European theater was supported privately by the most cultivated classes. She finds some comfort, however, in the conclusion that the sun has set on the age of the drama. It had flourished in Germany where Don Carlos could meet a Marquis Posa on stage, as in Schiller's drama *Don Carlos,* or where Götz could accept the hand of the modern Arminius, as in Goethe's drama. Her awareness of censorship in contemporary Germany, however, prompts the sad note: "the black eagles have shrieked into silence these great voices, for the drama cannot live where man cannot walk in the freedom of a hero" (*The Dial,* 3:46).

For Fuller art — European art, that is — was currently alive in opera and ballet. Through her stays in Providence and Boston, she became more and more receptive to the arts:

> The Ton-Kunst, the Ton-Welt, give me now more stimulus than the written Word; for music seems to contain everything in nature, unfolded into perfect harmony. In it the *all* and *each* are manifested in most rapid transition. (*Memoirs,* 1:186)

America, she observes, still stands as a beggar before the great riches of the world of music. Here she points to the future in which Handel's *Messiah* will remain America's favorite oratorio, followed by Haydn's *Creation.* She provides detailed descriptions of both works, but accords the laurel to Handel, calling him "a primitive Christian" (*The Dial,* 3:55).

In Margaret's opinion Ludwig Spohr's oratorio *The Last Judgment* paled beside Handel, despite Madame Spohr-Zahn's superb singing in the Boston performance. The winter of 1841–1842 saw so many musical performances that the season seemed like one continuous concert. Of the performers, who came almost exclusively from Europe, Margaret could not relate to the pianists, but did find rapport with the violinists and cel-

lists. Her descriptions of these musical experiences use a style as emotional
as ever, as when she hears in the sounds of cellos, "the farewell of a disem-
bodied spirit [. . .] both male and female" (*The Dial,* 3:59). Above all,
Margaret desired orchestral music, and here she was overcome by Beethoven's Fifth and Sixth symphonies. She compares Beethoven's art with
that of two other titans when she says that Beethoven possesses the
strength of Michelangelo's sibyls and prophets, and within him Dante's
heaven is opened above us (*The Dial,* 3:62).

After a concert on November 25, 1843, she actually wrote a letter to
Beethoven (who had died in 1827). It begins as follows:

> My only friend,
>
> > How shall I thank thee for once more breaking the chains of my sor-
> > rowful slumber? My heart beats. I live again for I feel that I am worthy
> > audience for thee, and that my being would be reason enough for thine.
> > (Memoirs, 1:232–233)

The letter presents her as a kindred spirit, who lacks the advantage of art
to express the agitation of her soul. She feels certain that he would have
welcomed her as no other person on earth. Finally, she asks the master
why genius has been denied her: "Is it because, as a woman, I am bound
by a physical law, which prevents the soul from manifesting itself?" (*Memoirs,* 1:233). Nowhere else in her writings does Margaret Fuller ever ask
this question, but when confronted with the example of Beethoven, she
forgets all ambition. The presence of Beethoven diminishes all other gi-
ants: Raphael, Plato, Shakespeare, even Michelangelo and Dante. She begs
Beethoven to accept and inspire her: "If thou wouldst take me wholly to
thyself — ! I am lost in this world, where I sometimes meet angels, but of
a different star from mine" (*Memoirs,* 1:234).

During the 1840s the art of the dance was gaining popularity in America. Among the European dancers to perform in Boston, Fanny Ellsler deserves special mention. Margaret once went to the theater with Emerson
to see her perform. Whereas his reaction was disapproval (as it had been
earlier in Italy), Margaret found Ellsler's magic "of a naive sportive character, it is as the young girl, sparkling with life and joy" (*The Dial,* 3:65).

The final group of articles that Margaret wrote for *The Dial* examined
fine arts, particularly painting, which had a richer tradition in New England than literature and music. John Singleton Copely, for example, who
had been born in Boston, was one of the great painters of portraits and
historical scenes of his age. He settled in London in 1775 and became a
member of the Royal Academy in 1779. Washington Allston (born in
South Carolina in 1799) had a career with a similar path. But after several
years in Italy he returned to Boston where he had a number of exhibi-

tions. Margaret Fuller spent many an hour admiring his pictures of heroic scenes and landscapes in the grand style of Copely and Benjamin West. Fuller recorded her impressions of an Allston show in Boston in 1839 for a *Dial* article that appeared the following year. Her later reports about art are mostly of European painting on display in Boston. The Boston Athenaeum was one venue for many such important exhibitions of Italian art where viewers could enjoy a broad fare that encompassed painting from Raphael to contemporary artists. The Athenaeum purchased several portrait busts by Thorwaldsen who was highly regarded in America; Emerson even visited him in his studio in Rome. These busts depicted "representative men" as described in Emerson's essays: Byron, Napoleon. In a *Dial* article of 1843 Fuller wrote critically about Antonio Canova as the prince of modern Italian art. *The Dial* contained no reports on German art, an omission explainable by the fact that American painters of a later generation first visited the German academies such as the one in Düsseldorf. Before American collectors could turn to German artists, American taste had to be exposed to French impressionism. Consequently, American reception of German art actually begins in the following century.

In her capacity as editor and writer at *The Dial,* Margaret Fuller was responsible for more than German culture. But such substantial articles as Emerson's "Thoughts on Modern Literature," which contained a long discussion of German writers and was printed in the second number of *The Dial,* were absent from later volumes of the journal. Margaret Fuller had subjected the manuscript to a critical reading and sent the corrected galleys with comments by her and George Ripley back to Emerson. Ripley, she wrote:

> is much distressed at what he thinks a falling off in the end of your paragraph about the majestic Artist, and I think when you look again you will think you have not said what you meant to say. The "eloquence" and "wealth", thus grouped, have rather l'air bourgeoise — [. . .] Mr. R. hates prettinesses, as the mistress of a boarding house hates flower vases.
>
> "Dreadful melody" does not suit me. The dreadful has become vulgarized since its natal day.
>
> So much for impertinence! I am very glad I am to own these remarks about the Meister. As to the genius of Goethe the statement, though so much better than others, is too imperfect to be true. He requires to be minutely painted in his own style of hard finish. As he never gave his soul in a glance, so he cannot be painted at a glance. I wish this "Kosmos Beauty" was not here ever again, [. . .] And is this *costly* true to the sense of kostiliche *[sic];* that means worthy a high price, the other obtained at a high price, n'est ce pas? [. . .] I wish the word *whipped* was never used at all and here it is twice in nearest neighborhood. (*Letters,* 2:152)

The passage is a good example of Fuller in the role of the demanding editor. As a result, Emerson acceded partly to her evaluation, at least omitting the phrase "Kosmos Beauty" from the final version of the text.

When Theodore Parker's essay "German Literature" appeared in the January 1841 number it caused quite a stir (*The Dial*, 1:315–339). Parker, born the same year as Fuller, was a farmer's son from Lexington who had been able to afford his education by living literally on bread and water. He did his studying at home on the family farm, appearing at Harvard College to take his final examinations at the end of each semester because he could not afford the fees. He was later able to finance his theology studies through scholarships and by working as a translator and teacher of Hebrew.

Thanks to his omnivorous reading habits and retentive memory, Parker's knowledge of German literature was immense. As a child he was able to recite a thousand-line poem after one reading. This enthusiast, who later saw Bettina von Arnim with his own eyes, wrote one of his breath-taking articles for *The Dial* that typically was dense with factual material. The opening contains a wonderfully ironic depiction of his Germanophile circle of friends:

> Opinions are divided respecting German literature. If we are to believe what is currently reported, [. . .] there is, somewhere in New England, a faction of discontented men and maidens, who have conspired to love everything Teutonic, from Dutch skates to German infidelity. It is supposed, at least asserted, that these misguided persons would fain banish all other literature clean out of space; [. . .] Whatever is German, they admire; philosophy, dramas, theology, novels, old ballads, and modern sonnets, histories, and dissertations, and sermons; but above all, the immoral and irreligious writings, with the generous intention of corrupting the youth of the world, restoring the worship of Priapus, or Pan, or the Pope, — it is not decided which is to receive the honor of universal homage, — and thus gradually preparing for the Kingdom of Misrule, and the dominion of Chaos, and "most ancient Night." (*The Dial*, 1:315)

Parker noted in his article that lovers of German philosophy and art were sometimes accused of being moved by "a disinterested love of evil," as if the devil himself had inspired this German epidemic spreading through "the boarding-schools for young misses," and had wrought damage to colleges and universities, in comparison to which fever, jaundice, and catarrh were nothing. Intelligent men with umbrellas and overshoes, wrapped to the teeth in scarves, were not safe from the evil that, like cholera, lurked in books of German history. The recommended countermeasures included quarantine and arming the sufferers with copies of the *Westminster Catechism*, Confessions of Faith adopted by the Council of

Trent, and the Athanasian Creed worn around their necks. Little children might still be saved, suggests Parker, by fasting and reading these texts. But the best antidote proves to be a strong dose of Dulness — an excellent medicine, that, when consistently applied, can save anybody from the mildest attack.

The parody goes on to say that the author and his friends are free of this contagion, for although they read the horrible German literature, their cool heads do no succumb to it. On the other hand there is a group of more sober and respectable people who hate German literature, but their judgment is mostly prejudice. They condemn Goethe, Schleiermacher, Schiller, Arndt, Kant and Leibnitz, Heine and Jakob Böhme, Schlegel, Pückler-Muskau, Hegel and Strauss as mystics, as unbelievers, pantheists, in short, as Germans. These judges treat German writers the way the Middle Ages treated the classics: as though it were dangerous to read the Latin, Greek, and Hebrew writers who contained all the heresies. Thus, suggests Parker, certain people ask today:

> Shall we Americans, excellent Christians as we are, who live in a land of education, of righteousness, of religion, and know how to reconcile it all with our three millions of slaves; in the land of steamboats and railroads, we Americans, possessed of all needed intelligence and culture, shall we read the books of the Germans, infidels as they are? Germans, who dwell in the clouds, and are only fitted by divine grace to smoke tobacco and make dictionaries! (*The Dial,* 1:319)

These modern haters of Germans, Parker continues, would like to see an embargo against the importation of words from Germany, such as the one against crackers from India. Of course, one can read the 98 volumes of Walter Scott faster than the one obstinate book by Kant, *The Critique of Pure Reason.* English writers tend to be better for the digestion. "Why should America's youth in Colleges and block houses sit bent over Leibnitz and Hegel until the bloom of their cheek fades?" (*The Dial,* 1:320).

After playing devil's advocate for so long, Parker changes his tone and prints a fiery defense of German literature, which he finds the most beautiful and original, the richest, and most religious of the modern age — and this despite the fact that Germany had not produced the greatest poetic genius of the modern age. There was, after all, only one Shakespeare.

Parker then turns to German scholarship. Although England boasts of a classical culture, the best editions of the classics come from Germany, while those produced in England are the work of Germans. Parker then lists 28 German scholars who have no equal in England. The same is true of English historians and theologians, while the Germans in this century have founded a new discipline, bible criticism. And, thanks to German philosophy, four names must be mentioned along with Plato, Aristotle,

Bacon, and Descartes: Kant, Fichte, Schelling, and Hegel. On literary matters, German literature, according to Parker, has found no equal since the English literature of Shakespeare's time. In comparison to this abundance, America is still too "young and raw to carry out the great American idea, either in literature or society. At present both are imitations. [. . .] No doubt the time will come, when [. . .] like all other nations, we have begun with imitations, and shall come to originals, doubtless, before we end" (*The Dial*, 1:327).

If German literature has one foremost charm for Parker, it is its religious character. Indeed, he finds this body of works to be the most religious literature since the Greeks, works that testify to the deep piety of the German heart: "We say it advisedly, that this is, in our opinion, the most religious literature the world has seen" (*The Dial*, 1:327).

At the end of his Germanophile essay Parker discusses Menzel's literary history that had come under such harsh criticism from Margaret Fuller for its Goethe interpretation. Similarly, he finds nothing good to say about the work by such a "Berserker of modern critics." Parker also sees through Menzel's ideological position, which he describes as one of a nationalist with the judgment of an amateur incapable of objectivity. Especially his "unmanly hostility" to Goethe grows to an "absolute hatred" of not only the works but of their creator as a man. Like Margaret Fuller, Parker insists that one judge a work by the standards inherent in it. "We would not censure the Laocoon, because it did not teach us agriculture, nor the Iliad, because it was not republican enough for our tastes" (*The Dial*, 1:332). Menzel, by contrast, is capable of writing only as a patriot. Fichte's "egoism" was tolerable because Fichte was a liberal, but in the case of Hegel, Menzel's mistreatment of the "Young German" movement beggars description in its disregard for all laws of literary combat, its blows below the belt, and downright lies. Menzel's deficient knowledge is even apparent to this American, as when Parker points out the errors in his presentation of Kant, Leibnitz, Fichte, and Schelling. Parker obviously knew their works better than Menzel. The chapter on religion, furthermore, is an outrage for Parker. Whereas it was supposed to describe the contributions of Catholics and Protestants to the four great divisions of exegesis, history, systematic theology, and practical theology, the author apparently had no idea of these concepts. Parker called the book a compilation of newspaper clippings, anecdotes, and gossip — qualities that made it appealing to a broad public, but dangerous as scholarship.

Three years later, thanks to the generous aid of a friend, Parker was able to take his wife to Europe for a year. The materialism of England horrified him: "was it to be the destiny of America, too, to pay so great a price for wealth and power?"[66] The light-hearted spirit of France amused him and the poverty of Italy filled him with sadness. But Germany, as his biographer writes, "was his spiritual home."[67] There he met extraordinary characters such as the tailor's assistant who, on the way to Tübingen, introduced himself as "Bekleidungs-Kunstassessor" who was travelling "to give his heart aesthetic advantages."[68] In Germany Parker threw himself into the academic life. Behind every hill and around every corner there was a university and Berlin was so full of great men that nobody paid them any more attention than the Parisians would to a giraffe.[69]

The great men he was referring to spent their days sitting in studies writing thick tomes, all of which Parker had read. He went to these scholars' lectures and introduced himself personally with, "I am an American, I have read your books," whereupon he was greeted cordially.[70] Nobody, to be sure, asked him about his own writing, for nobody in German academic circles read American sources. It was remarkable enough to find an American who spoke German, not to mention a young man who had all the *Theologische Jahrbücher* in his head.

Parker's letters home to his friend, the theologian Francis Converse, are filled with the atmosphere of Berlin. "It will take you a day to imagine them all,"[71] he reported of the hubbub of Berlin with its 1000 hackney coaches, 400 horse-drawn beer carts, 30,000 soldiers, 180 professors, 1600 students, and 270,000 other smoking, walking, weaving, pipe-making, cooking and eating inhabitants. Among the most interesting accounts of his stay in Berlin are Parker's stories of specific lectures and professors, notably Schelling. A Young Hegelian named Werder filled him with amazement during a lecture devoted to "Bestimmtheit" (certainty). The professor achieved a state of high passion and found himself in a distressing predicament trying

> as I dimly gathered, to discover the "Ur-Bestimmung." He said, in "Bestimmung" there was "Daseyn" (being) "and Realite." Hereupon a fat, chubby student, with cheeks like one of your classmates, evidently his Ma's darling, tried hard to conceive the difference; but after numerous ineffectual attempts gave up in despair. Then said the professor, "In 'Daseyn' there is 'Etwas real und Anders'" (something real and something else); now, "Etwas ist durch und durch Etwas und nicht Anders; Anders ist durch und durch Anders und nicht Etwas."[72]

Before Parker hurried on to visit universities in Halle, Heidelberg, Bonn, Leipzig, Stuttgart, Freiburg, Tübingen, and in Switzerland, he paid a visit to Bettina von Arnim, which must have been more or less a transcendental summit. He had already reported to Converse Francis of Bettina's recent book publication:

[the book] was "verboten" and "confiscirt" years ago. Then she wrote another, drove up to the King and asked, "May it be published?" "Yes," said the King. So it appeared with the title "Dies Buch gehört dem König." [This book belongs to the King]. It was worse than the first; the ministers "kicked," it would not do. Now she prints another, "Clemens Brentanos Laubenkrantz," Charlottenburg 1844, [Clemens Brentano's Wreath], and will carry it to the King for his "privilege." She is writing another on the sufferings in Silesia; a terrible book it is, too, to judge from the pages of the manuscript she read me. She showed me a letter from your sister, and sends thanks.[73]

By 1844 at the latest, then, Bettina was aware of the body of readers and admirers she had in America. Despite his somewhat distanced remark in his letter to Francis, Parker was certainly among them. His journal records the conversation he had with Bettina on May 23, 1844:

I told her that, if the men lack courage [as she complained] she had enough; that she had the courage of a Jewish prophet and the inspiration of a Christian apostle. She said she was not Christian, but heathen, — she prayed to Jupiter. I told her that was nothing; there was but one God, whose name was neither Jupiter nor Jehovah, and he took each *true* prayer. Then she said again she was no Christian. I asked, "Have you no respect for Christ?" "None for the *person,* for he had done more harm to the world than any other man." I found, however, that for the man Jesus of Nazareth, and for all the great doctrines of religion, she had the pro-foundest respect. I told her there was, to my thinking, but one relig-ion, — that was *being good and doing good.*[74]

In a letter probably written five years later, Bettina complained to the bookseller Barthold that "she was inundated with letters from America which cost her a more or less monstrously high postage."[75] She had also had to have her portrait drawn again to satisfy the throngs of her admirers. Parker later gained a reputation in Germany through the translation of his work *The Discourses of Religion.* Many emigrants turned to him for help after 1848 and he lent his support to the best of his ability.

None of the other contributors to *The Dial* reached this level of ex-pertise in the field of German literature, theology, and philosophy, not even James Freeman Clarke who also published in the magazine. Among Clarke's publications was the poem "The Real and the Ideal: On the Marble Bust of Schiller" (*The Dial,* 1:468–469), which appeared in a group of "Poems on Art" and was introduced by a motto from an essay by Karl Philipp Moritz, "Über die bildende Nachahmung des Schönen." The poem is a dialogue in which one viewer of the bust notes the lack of the man's individualized facial features, and the other explains that this is not a depiction of Schiller as friend and companion, but rather an expression of the poet, the luminary and genius of his country.

Finally, Christopher Pearse Cranch must be mentioned among the contributors to *The Dial* devoted to German literature. Cranch had also studied divinity and was the only friend of the Concord circle from the South. Born in 1813 in Alexandria, Virginia, he found his way via Clarke's *Western Messenger* to the Transcendentalists, a group he was to memorialize in his whimsical cartoon drawings. He took Clarke's place both in the pulpit and in the editor's office, but preferred to give *The Dial* poems and prose pieces rather than critical essays. The second number printed his "Musings of a Recluse," in which he shows himself to be one who reveres Bettina's correspondence with Goethe (*The Dial*, 1:182–194). Tired of his daily toil, he seeks pleasure in reading her journal:

> For hours I bathed and floated in the sea of her beautiful thoughts; [. . .] one who was born to tell us the secrets of nature, and reveal to us what she may become to every child-like, loving soul. Bettina grew up in her lap like a pet infant, kept apart from every other influence, that we might see how wise are the teachings of our mother. [. . .] This little heroine is the first I have ever known, who thoroughly understood, and used what we all enjoy. [. . .] Goethe was to her the expression of the divine soul in humanity. It might have been another, perhaps Novalis.
> (*The Dial*, 1:189–190)

Cranch's assessment of the relationship between Goethe and Bettina was vastly more positive than Fuller's:

> With a little more of trust and kindness there would be something almost as beautiful in Goethe's calm way of encouraging Bettina's passion, as in the passion itself. He met it in the only way it could be met, and most gently breathed upon it. (*The Dial*, 1:192)

Bettina, he goes on, had only profited from her association with Goethe, and Cranch thus finds nothing eccentric about her, describing her "extravagance" as the healthiest kind. On the other hand, this reader of *Goethe's Correspondence with a Child*, has difficulty accepting the idea that years later Bettina translated the story of her love into a foreign language and circulated it throughout the world. "Yet when we have learned to love her, this thought becomes less revolting" (*The Dial*, 1:192).

Margaret Fuller's last long contribution to *The Dial*, "The Great Lawsuit: Man vs. Men. Woman vs. Women," caught the attention of Horace Greeley, the editor of the *New York Daily Tribune*. Greeley, born in 1811, had grown up in poverty on a farm in Vermont. After learning the printing trade he went to New York and in 1841 founded the *Tribune*. This family newspaper, which was aimed at a wide public, had such influence in the United States that for 35 years Greeley was called the biggest political power since Thomas Jefferson. He was a progressive man, committed to social issues. He spread the ideas of Fourier, supported the equal education of women, but opposed women's suffrage and liberal divorce laws; he polemicized against alcohol, tobacco, against the theater, slavery, and the Mexican War; he was active in the founding of the Republican Party and the nomination of Lincoln. In 1872 he was himself a candidate of that party, but exhausted by the rigors of the campaign, he died in the same year after losing the election against Grant.

It was Greeley who in 1844 prevailed upon Fuller to move to New York. Until 1846, the summer she left for Europe, she lived in that city in a remote house belonging to the Greeleys. She was one of Greeley's colleagues and contributors at the *Tribune*. Margaret's good friend from *The Dial* and Brook Farm days, George Ripley, was in this circle, as were the young Henry James and Carl Schurz. Karl Marx reported to the newspaper from London. Fuller's job was to take over literary topics, but she also wrote on music, art, and the social institutions of New York. She visited poorhouses, prisons, and insane asylums and showed special interest in the rehabilitation of the female inmates. Her efforts to promote the cultural life of New York can be seen in her concert reviews. Here, of course, German music had a prominent role, although her visits to the theater were sometimes under less than ideal circumstances. She reported of a production of *Der Freischütz* at Palmo's Opera House that the audience was nearly choked by the sulphurous smoke used in the sorcery scenes. In raising her voice for the improvement of standards of the city's musical life, she proposed that concerts should avoid mixing of good and bad works on one program. Furthermore, they should play entire pieces, not just excerpts.[76]

Margaret also worked tirelessly to spread the German language. She was a strong supporter of Moritz Ertheiler who published textbooks and taught German in New York. In her review of Ertheiler's handbook of German idioms she regrets the intolerance that German is subjected to. She claimed that a knowledge of German was a healthy antidote to the defects to which America tends: "hasty observation, shallow judgment, self-complacent ignorance, and a devotion to the merely temporal uses of life.[77] Only through the acquaintance with its language

> can the German mind in its purity, in its piety, its homely tenderness, its boundless aspiration, and its unwearied diligence (Reader, this last is climax, not bathos) be brought home to *us*.[78]

In her literary essays Margaret Fuller directs her attention toward Europe as well as America. It is significant that the recently named editor should begin her series of almost 300 articles for the *New York Tribune* with a piece on Emerson's *Essays*. But she did not lose her particular interest in German literature. She informed *Tribune* readers on new publications coming out of Germany, as well as of the translation of Ida Hahn-Hahn's *Gräfin Faustina* (Countess Faustina), the first novel in a whole series by this writer announced by the New York firm, New World Press. The author of *Woman in the Nineteenth Century* understandably finds the most valuable aspect of this book in the depiction of the female figures, figures such as only a woman could describe. The style of Countess Hahn-Hahn, which for modern readers is almost unbearably bombastic, even annoyed Margaret. "The dialogue is often heavy; the speakers making long orations upon art, literature, and the conduct of life, not only longer than any real talker ever made, but in a style such as not good talker ever used.[79]

The English translation of Jean Paul's humorous novel *Siebenkäs* received a mixed review in the same number of the *Tribune*. Fuller predicts that many a reader will skip portions of the work because they will tire of the often tasteless meanderings and intricate whims of the author.

Her longest and most thorough articles on German literature are devoted to Goethe. On March 14, 1845 she reviews George Calvert's translation of the *Correspondence Between Schiller and Goethe,* calling it "one of the most valuable records in the history of literature."[80] Her years of study were now serving the broad American public well. Fuller tried to swim against the current of American letters that consistently tried to elevate Schiller at the price of denigrating Goethe. She emphasized Schiller's reliance on, and respect for, Goethe who in turn had such warm feelings for Schiller. Margaret describes the relationship metaphorically when she says, "Friendly, as the oak grows up beside the pine, they addressed their heads to the same heavens and gladdened by their beauty the same field of earth."[81] She takes the opportunity to put in a word for Goethe's correspondence with Zelter, the only work, in her mind, that equalled the correspondence with Schiller. She suggests, however, that these letters would never find an English translator, despite the fact that "they would put an end at once to the absurd supposition that a man of genius can fail to have a heart."[82] George Henry Calvert, who studied in Göttingen after graduating from Harvard, met Goethe and was introduced at court. In her preface to his translation Fuller describes his experience as having seen "with his own unprejudiced eyes the modern Jupiter." She could thus understand his "just contempt for the assumption of ordinary minds" who wanted to displace Goethe from his eminent position.[83] As one example of such an attitude, she recalled an example of a Mr. Putnam who in the previous spring had delivered the inaugural Phi Beta Kappa address to Harvard students. Much to Fuller's distress, the students had applauded. Seizing the next opportunity to set Mr. Putnam straight, on May 29, 1845, she filled four columns with a review of Goethe's *Essays on Art,* a work that had just appeared in Boston in Samuel Gray Ward's translation. Putnam's abuse of Goethe even eclipsed the bitter disappointment Margaret had felt six years earlier when the same Samuel Ward had married the lovely Anna Barker from New Orleans and become a banker. She would have preferred he devote his life to art and scholarship, which would have been easy for the heir to a Boston fortune. Ward, who was talented and good-looking, was probably Margaret's greatest love before she moved to New York.

In her review of the *Essays,* which she called "a precious gift" to the American public made by the "most accomplished observer the world has ever known,"[84] she quotes an unnamed friend at length who had responded to Putnam's lecture with an unpublished manuscript. Using all the rules of rhetoric, this anonymous writer counters the criticism that Goethe's morals would prevent his works from standing the test of time. Rather than engaging in a defense of Goethe, the opponent cleverly presents the reader with the means to reach a different conclusion. This is achieved in a fictional dispute between Putnam and his opponent who at first falls for Putnam's arguments. In the course of the dialogues, however, he strikes back when, for example, Putnam tries to restrict the poet with his preconceived moral concepts. Morality, says the voice of the opposition, is not inherent in man from birth, being unknown in savages and children. On the other hand, the love of truth, which Putnam declares to be the goal of all intellectual activity, is the basis for artistic creativity. Thus, it is the poet's highest goal to write good poetry.

This long discussion reveals the beginning of a social process of liberation that leads in two directions. To begin with, traditional Puritan values that viewed art in the service of morality have been transcended. Furthermore, the writer has glimpsed the future and seen an America possessing an independent culture in the years to come. When compared to other nations, America is unique, for it was neither a savage nation, nor a cradle of art:

> Our elder brothers across the water retained everything except the unretainable, poetry. [. . .] We are not destined to have an American Art. But higher destiny: World Art. We are citizens of the world. At home under every sun, delight in every literature."[85]

On the path to this goal Goethe represents the great example. For the artist of world rank must study and know all art, he must penetrate the scholarship of art. Goethe was just such a student of art, whereby Margaret defines student as "he who masters."

It is significant that when Margaret Fuller wants to describe an exemplary literary culture for readers of the *Tribune,* she always comes back to the German literature of the previous epoch. Contemporary writers were for her simply not comparable with their forebears. On this theme she writes in a short review of Longfellow's anthology *The Poets and Poetry of Europe* that

> it is obvious enough that the great time of literature is past in Germany
> and that the national Genius turns now more to action. And it is well
> that it should be so. Enough has been done by them in the way of study
> and with the pen.[86]

Current news of Germany could be found in the New York biweekly newspaper, *Deutsche Schnellpost,* a consistent source of material that Fuller translated for the *Tribune.* Her first of these articles on December 16, 1844 seems to register a feeling of fatigue in Germany. It describes the dedication of a Goethe monument by Ludwig von Schwanthaler in Frankfurt and the general lack of interest on the part of the public. On the other hand, the *Tribune* reported on September 3rd that preparations for the unveiling of the Beethoven monument in Bonn were proceeding better. Whereas the "cold ceremony" of Frankfurt had indicated that Goethe was no longer dear to the Germans' hearts, Beethoven represented a different emotion. It was an honor to be invited to the ceremonies where the Queen of England and the King of Prussia were to receive all the great musicians. Fuller includes an indignant reaction to the rumor that Beethoven was an illegitimate son of a different King of Prussia. She notes that although intellectual lights were to be found in the royal family of King Friedrich (himself a student of Leibnitz), they amounted to little in comparison with Beethoven. The *Schnellpost* had carried the report from the *Nürnberger Kurier* that described the Bonn monument in its immense proportions for American readers.

Margaret Fuller gradually turned her attention more and more to the political situation in Germany. In an article on March 25, 1845 she took the emigration from Prussia to Brussels of the poet Freiligrath as an occasion for sharp criticism: "It is melancholy to see the youth of Germany wandering about in exile, because the petty princes are startled by the mighty call for Liberty."[87] She reports that Arnold Ruge and Karl Marx, who had been co-editors of the *Rheinische Zeitung,* had been despotically silenced by the Prussian king. Bernays, the editor of the German newspaper in Paris, had been forced to leave the city within 24 hours because the Prussian ambassador was indignant about his efforts to eliminate the chains of feudalism from the fatherland, home of Kant, Luther, and Schiller. But the freedom that had nonetheless grown strong and fled to England and America, assures Fuller, would someday return to Germany.

The Parisian correspondent of the *Schnellpost* had reported on a book by "our excellent friend Engels," a report that Fuller used in the *Tribune* on August 5, 1845. She even included the remark that in his work *The Situation of the Laboring Class in England,* Engels could just have easily written about Germany, especially the worsening conditions in the Harz region, Wuppertal, the Mosel, Thüringen, the Odenwald, Silesia, and the Riesengebirge.

Whenever Fuller came upon radical reformers who wanted to spread their ideas in America, she sharply distanced herself from them. Just as she had earlier said no to Fourierism, she also rejected the German newspaper, *Der Volks-Tribun* (January 17, 1846). She explains her position, acknowledging that the publication expressed the feelings of many German-born American workers, but noting that the spirit of defiance and the haste of the *Volks-Tribun* was not in the spirit of a young nation like America. "She needs it not," Fuller affirms. Instead, America needed great intelligence and serious convictions rather than such "heat and abuse."[88]

Among Margaret Fuller's contributions to the *New York Tribune* there is one from April 21, 1845 on "The Modern Jews." The topic, unusual for her, is a summary of a longer article in *The North American Review,* which provides an explanation. Before Margaret Fuller came to New York City, she had never known Jews who seemed an exotic minority in distant lands. But it is clear from the essay in the *North American Review,* and from Marggraff's *Deutschlands jüngste Literatur- und Culturepoche,* (Leipzig, 1839), that there was a remarkable change occurring within German Jewry who were emancipating themselves from rabbinical instruction and tradition. Mendelssohn, Heine, Börne, Rahel Varnhagen ("the intellectual Queen of Berlin") were proof of this change.

Fuller quotes Marggraff and Wolfgang Menzel who agree that the Jewish element in German literature is too great — a fact that is to the detriment of the Jews! Although this phenomenon could be viewed as an expression of revenge for earlier suffering, it simply hinders them in winning and exercising their rights. For similar reasons, the kind of partisan Jewish support that proclaims Bendemann the greatest painter and Meyerbeer the greatest composer ought be condemned. Fuller relates these arguments without comment, which suggests she perhaps agreed with these views.

Her attention turned to these issues after making friends with a German Jew (thus doubly exotic), for before this friendship she had little contact with native Germans. James Nathan was born in Eutin in 1811 and had lived as a banker in New York since 1830. In 1855 he changed his family name to Gotendorf and returned to Germany in 1862, dying in Hamburg in 1888. But for four months in 1845 James Nathan and Margaret Fuller were together in New York almost daily. They visited concerts, took walks along the East River, and James sang her German songs accompanying himself on the guitar. Despite their frequent private contact, Margaret often wrote him letters that were full of feeling. These were almost without literary allusions, except when she once sent Nathan the epic poem *Festus* of more than 40,000 verses, a work that was a new rendering of *Faust* by the ardent Goethe admirer, Philip Bailey.[89] *Faust,* of course, was a work of Goethe's she identified with more than any except *Wilhelm Meister*. Another time she quotes Novalis,[90] or copies from the folksong collection *Des Knaben Wunderhorn* the text "Mutter, ach Mutter," calling it "a folksong of your [Nathan's] adopted nation, and deeply expressive of that deepest sadness in life, that, though blessings come, they so often come too late."[91]

James Nathan probably misunderstood Margaret's passionate outpourings of feeling, for he precipitated a crisis when once he did not behave like a gentleman. But Margaret kept writing to him, spicing her letters with countless German expressions like "Seligkeit" (bliss), "Sehnsucht" (longing), "Wehmut" (sorrow), "Grossmut" (magnanimity), "Sanftmut" (gentle nature). At one point she writes, "I was *überspannt*" (wild, eccentric),[92] which must have summarized the effect she had on James Nathan, for in 1845 he set off on an extended European journey, armed with letters of introduction from very reputable personalities (such as George Bancroft) that Margaret had helped him secure. He also had her to thank for his correspondent's assignment with the *Tribune*.[93]

Nathan's trip to Europe motivated Margaret to consider a journey again herself. At last the *Tribune* was able to make possible what had been prevented by the death of her father ten years before. So, in the summer of 1846 Horace Greeley sent Margaret to Europe as an American foreign correspondent. In the meantime she had continued to write to Nathan in the hope of meeting him, perhaps even in Germany. On August 1 she set sail on the *Cambria;* on that day the *Tribune* printed her "Farewell to New York," in which she thanked the city for the experiences of the last 20 months, experiences she could never have had in any other city in 20 years.

Margaret Fuller doubtless planned to visit Germany. To this end her friend Robert Wesselhoeft had given her letters of introduction. They were addressed to his cousin, the bookseller Friedrich Johann Fromann in Jena; to Carl Grosch, the mayor of Gotha; an engineer in Eisenach named Sältzer; and even to Johann Peter Eckermann in Weimar. They identified her as the translator of Goethe's *Conversations with Eckermann*. As Wesselhoeft wrote to Fromann, Fuller had shown him the greatest kindness in America and now needed the hand of a friend herself. The letter to Eckermann runs as follows:

> Hochgeehrtester Freund
>
> Vor etwa zwei Jahren sendete ich Ihnen die Übersetzung Ihrer Gespräche mit Goethe von Miss Fuller von Boston, einer unserer literarischen Nobilitäten; jetzt kommt diese Dame selbst mit einem Brief von mir und bittet Sie, ihr einige Augenblicke zu schenken und tiefer in Ihre Heiligthümer der Erinnerung einzuweisen.
>
> (Most esteemed Friend,
>
> Approximately two years ago I sent you the translation of your conversations with Goethe by Miss Fuller of Boston, one of our literary aristocracy. Now this lady is herself coming with a letter from me, and requests that you might grant her a few moments and introduce her more deeply to your shrines of memory.)[94]

But events never reached this point. Margaret's ship sailed first to England where she immediately began her work as foreign correspondent, reporting (as she had in New York) on social themes like working-class poverty. In Newcastle she was lowered by basket into a mine and groped her way through the shafts lighted only by a candle. She naturally kept up her literary interests and visited the aged Wordsworth, though the meeting was as unrewarding as Emerson's had been thirteen years earlier. She visited Harriet Martineau and met Carlyle and his wife more than once. In one of her reports to the *Tribune* she mentioned the house where the exile Ferdinand Freiligrath lived temporarily while in London:

> England houses the exile, but not without house-tax, window-tax, and head-tax. Where is the Arcadia that does invite all genius to her arms, and change her golden wheat for their green laurels and immortal flowers? Arcadia — would thy name were America! [95]

There are two reasons why Margaret Fuller never visited Germany. While in Edinburgh, she received a letter from James Nathan saying that he was to be married in Hamburg. Her reaction to this profound and bitter disappointment was dramatic. She rode atop an open coach during a rainstorm and wandered for an entire night on a mountain in the Scottish highlands, actions which led the editor of her letters to suspect suicidal intentions (*Letters*, 4:10). Nathan's rejection prompted the journal entry of September 8, 1846, which Julia Ward Howe cited in her edition of Fuller's love letters: "From 1st June, 1845, to 1st Sept., 1846, a mighty change has taken place, I ween. I understand more and more the character of the *tribes*. I shall write a sketch of it and turn the whole to account in a literary way, since the affections and ideal hopes are so unproductive."[96]

The second reason for Fuller's avoidance of Germany was her friendship with Giuseppe Mazzini, whom she had met at the house of Carlyle. Margaret expressed her unreserved sympathy for this exiled fighter for the cause of Italy's unification. In mourning for his country, he always wore black and was constantly being shadowed by agents. She submitted a fervent and compassionate report on Mazzini for the *Tribune,* and her wish to travel to Italy as soon as possible was born.

She took the route via Paris where she met another democrat, the Polish poet Adam Mickiewicz, who was living in exile for his anti-Czarist activity in his own homeland. Mickiewicz became her best friend and advisor in Europe. While in Paris she visited George Sand, whose books she had reviewed in the *Tribune;* Chopin played the piano for her in his rooms.

Then Italy took hold of her, never again to let go its grip. The country was on the threshold of freedom, a state that was obvious to the young New Englander whose own nation had won its independence 60 years earlier. During her years in Italy Margaret did not remain the distanced observer she had been when she arrived, but got caught up in the turbulent events of the struggle.

Shortly after her arrival in Rome, Margaret met Giovanni Angelo Ossoli. Eleven years her junior, and from an impoverished noble family in papal service, he quickly won her heart. However, the young Marchese could not propose marriage to the Protestant American as long as his father was still living. Their son Angelo Eugenio Filippo was born out of wedlock in Rieti on September 5, 1848. The baby's existence had to be kept secret from Ossoli's family, as well as from the American colony in Rome, which would have quickly broadcast the news back home. Margaret was still dependent upon the United States, for her work as a *Tribune* correspondent was their only source of income.

Rome of 1848–1849 was indeed a place where one could stand at the center of historical events. Here the people were struggling to cast off the rule of papal authority — a revolution that was quelled by a prolonged French siege during which the people of Rome, volunteers from all parts of Italy, and Garibaldi's red-shirts, defended the city heroically. There is no doubt that Margaret's reports to the *Tribune* influenced American opinion, but as soon as Washington's representative in Rome received permission to recognize the Roman republic, the struggle was decided in favor of the French troops and of Pope Pius IX who had fled the city. Giovanni Ossoli participated in the toughest fighting, but escaped miracu-

lously unhurt. Margaret, meanwhile, worked for weeks to the point of ex-
haustion nursing the sick and wounded in the hospital of the Fate Bene
Fratelli on the Tiber Island and at the Quirinal, which had been transformed into a military infirmary.

Ossoli did not dare remain in Rome after the capitulation to the
French. He presumably took Margaret to Florence where they perhaps
were married formally, although no documentation of the ceremony survives. In Florence Margaret wrote her "History of the Italian Republic." It
was a comprehensive work, impressive to anyone who saw it in manuscript
form, that drew on her close connections with Mazzini and other Italian
republicans such as the Marchesa Costanza Arconati Visconti who had
spent 26 years in Austrian exile. As a result of these associations, the work
contained considerable first-hand information about the republican
movement. When English publishers turned down the manuscript, Margaret decided to return to America with her family. Relatives and friends
were informed after the fact about her marriage and the birth of their son.
The Ossolis left Italy in an American freighter on May 17, 1850; it ran
aground off the American coast in sight of Long Island on July 17. A
sailor tried to swim ashore with the baby Angelo, but all three tragically
lost their lives in the shipwreck. Waldo Emerson sent Henry David Thoreau to the spot with the assignment of finding baggage and manuscripts
that might have been saved, but to no avail.

The monument placed to Margaret Fuller Ossoli by her distressed
friends, the two volumes of *Memoirs,* naturally emphasizes the woman
they knew: the New England Corinna, a poetic, a Romantic, a cultural
mediator. Emerson invoked characters from Goethe's *Wilhelm Meister*
when he wrote that to the younger generation she would be remembered
as Makarie; to the older, as Euphorion.

This noble metaphorical stylization, however, overlooks the fact that
Margaret Fuller's literary phase lay four years behind her. After 1847 the
New York Tribune did not carry a single review by her, nor does her stay
in Italy provide many literary reminiscences. It had not been Margaret's
intention to undertake an educational journey in Goethe's footsteps as
had her friend Ralph Waldo Emerson. Italy was for her a political experience that she invited her compatriots at home to participate in through
her impassioned reports. "O men and women of America, spared these
frightful sights, these sudden wrecks of every hope, what angel of heaven
do you suppose has time to listen to your tales of morbid woe? If any find
leisure to work for men to-day, think you not they have enought to do to
care for the victims here?"[97] Margaret Fuller naturally followed her cultural
interests while in Italy, especially before the political unrest began. She
paid a visit to the painter Friedrich Overbeck, noting, "it is well known in

the U.S. what his pictures are. […] He himself looks as if he had just stepped out of one of them, — a lay monk, with a pious eye and habitual morality of thought which limits every gesture."[98]

During the Roman carnival she even attended the German artists' ball, about which she reported to Emerson:

> I forgot to mention one little thing rather interesting. At the *Miserere* of the Sistine chapel, I sat beside Goethe's favorite daughter-in-law, Ottilia [Pogwisch, wife of Julius August], to whom I was introduced by Mrs. Jameson.[99]

It is inconceivable that at every turn Margaret Fuller was not reminded of her intellectual ideal, Goethe, although at the moment she felt she had more important things to report to her American readers from Italy. Her goal was no longer the transmission of literature, for she had taken the step from literature to history. Perhaps it could be said that, more than any other member of the Concord circle, she made history.

Notes

[1]   The German original text is as follows: "Durch Brüder, durch! Dies werde/Das Wort im Kampf und Schmerz./Gemeines will zur Erde./Edles will himmelwärts!"

[2]   *The Works of Charles Follen with a Memoir of his Life*, 5 vols. ed. Eliza Follen (Boston: Hilliard, Gray & Co, 1841–1842).

[3]   "Young Frederic Hedge," *Unitarian Review*, 34 (October 1890), 288.

[4]   Germaine de Staël, *Germany*, 2 vols., ed. Orlando W. Wight (New York: Derby & Jackson, 1859), 1:37.

[5]   Germaine de Staël, *Germany*, 95.

[6]   Germaine de Staël, *Germany*, 232.

[7]   James Freeman Clarke, "Thomas Carlyle, The German Scholar." *The Western Messenger* (June 1838), 4,6: 418.

[8]   *The Letters of James Freeman Clarke to Margaret Fuller*, ed. John Wesley Thomas; Britannica et America, vol. 2 (Hamburg: Cram, de Gruyter, 1957), 28. Clarke is here referring to an aphorism by Goethe that was often quoted in New England: Was ist deine Pflicht? Die Forderung des Tages." (What is your duty? The demand of the day.) from his *Sprüche in Prosa*, no. 3.

[9]   *The Letters of James Freeman Clarke to Margaret Fuller*, 36.

[10]   *The Letters of James Freeman Clarke to Margaret Fuller*, 38.

[11]   The following excerpts are from Clarke's unpublished, handwritten diary in the archives of the Perry-Clarke Collection at the Massachusetts Historical Society, Boston.

[12]   James Freeman Clarke, "Journal to Margaret Fuller," Perry-Clarke Collection, n. p.

[13]   James Freeman Clarke, "Journal to Myself," (February 13, 1832), Perry-Clarke Collection, 31.

[14]   *Ibid.*

[15]   James Freeman Clarke, "Journal to Myself," *ibid.*

[16]   *The Letters of James Freeman Clarke to Margaret Fuller,* 57–58.

[17]   *The Letters of James Freeman Clarke to Margaret Fuller,* 85.

[18]   *The Letters of James Freeman Clarke to Margaret Fuller,* 89. The journal is described in detail in Robert D. Habich, *Transcendentalism and the Western Messenger; a History of the Magazine and its Contributors, 1835–1841* (London & Cranbury, NJ: Fairleigh-Dickinson UP, 1985).

[19]   *The Western Messenger* (January, 1836), 2:1, 59–62.

[20]   Margaret Fuller, *The Western Messenger* (January 1838), 3,1: 306.

[21]   Margaret Fuller, *The Western Messenger* (February 1838), 3,2: 369.

[22]   *The Western Messenger,* (January 1837), 3,1: 306. Fuller did not read Heine in the original, but quotes from a translation.

[23]   *The Letters of James Freeman Clarke to Margaret Fuller,* 99–101.

[24]   The first analysis of Margaret Fuller's translations was made by Renate Delphendahl: "Margaret Fuller: Interpreter and Translator," *in Margaret Fuller: Visonary of the New Age,* ed. Marie Olesen Urbanski (Orono: Northern Lights Press, 1994), 54–100. It was followed by an imaginative discussion of Fuller's translations by Christina Zwarg, *Feminist Conversations: Fuller, Emerson, and the Play of Reading.* (Ithaca, London: Cornell UP, 1995).

[25]   *The Letters of James Freeman Clarke to Margaret Fuller,* 245.

[26]   John Sullivan Dwight, not Margaret Fuller, translated these lines by Goethe. See *Memoirs,* 1:254, note 1.

[27]   'Whoever surrenders to the highest love, never recovers from its wounds.' See *Memoirs,* 1:254, note 2 for John Weiss's translation of Novalis, which Fuller slightly misquotes.

[28]   Excerpts of Fuller's notes are to be found in Hertha Marquardt, "Die erste Biographin in Amerika: Margaret Fullers geplantes *Life of Goethe,*" in *Festschrift für Theodor Spira,* ed. Willi Erzgräber, (Heidelberg: Carl Winter, 1961), 313.

[29]   Hertha Marquardt, "Die erste Biographin in Amerika," 314.

[30]   *Ibid.*

[31]   Compare Judith Mattson Bean, "Texts from Conversation: Fuller's Influence on Emerson," in *Studies in the American Renaissance 1994,* ed. Joel Myerson (Charlottesville: The University Press of Virginia, 1994), 227–244.

[32] Johann Peter Eckermann, *Gespräche mit Goethe in den letzten Jahren seines Lebens* (Frankfurt am Main: Insel, 1984), 163.

[33] *The Correspondence of Emerson and Carlyle,* ed. Joseph Slater (New York and London: Columbia UP, 1964), 150.

[34] *The Correspondence of Emerson and Carlyle,* 154–155.

[35] *The Correspondence of Emerson and Carlyle,* 155.

[36] On Margaret Fuller's teaching duties in Providence, see Loraine Ferguson, "Margaret Fuller as a Teacher in Providence: The School Journal of Ann Brown," in *Studies in the American Renaissance 1991,* ed. Joel Myerson (Charlottesville: The University Press of Virginia, 1991), 59–118; Daniel Shealy, "Margaret Fuller and her Maiden: Evelyn Metcalf's 1838 School Journal," in *Studies in the American Renaissance 1996,* ed. Joel Myerson (Charlottesville: The University Press of Virginia, 1996), 41–67; Paula Kopack, "The School Journal of Humah (Anna) Gab, *Studies in the American Renaissance 1996, op. cit.,* 67–113.

[37] *Specimens of Foreign Standard Literature,* ed. George Ripley. 1839, 2:n.p.

[38] Margaret Fuller, *Conversations with Goethe: From the German of Eckermann; Specimens of Foreign Standard Literature,* vol. 4, ed. George Ripley. (Boston: Hilliard, Gray, and Co., 1839), 8.

[39] Margaret Fuller, "Translator's Preface to Eckermann's *Conversations with Goethe,*" in *The Writings of Margaret Fuller,* ed. Mason Wade (New York: Viking Press, 1941), 232.

[40] "Translator's Preface," 233.

[41] "Translator's Preface," 234.

[42] "Translator's Preface," 234–235.

[43] "Translator's Preface," 235.

[44] "Translator's Preface," 236.

[45] *Ibid.*

[46] "Translator's Preface," 238.

[47] "Translator's Preface," 239.

[48] "Translator's Preface," 240.

[49] Zoltan Haraszti, *The Idyll of Brook Farm: as Revealed by Unpublished Letters in the Boston Public Library* (Boston: Trustees of the Public Library, n. d. [1937], 9–12.

[50] "Woman in the 19th Century," in *The Writings of Margaret Fuller,* ed. Mason Wade (New York: Viking Press, 1941), 182. For more on the influence of Fuller's interpretation of Fourier for Emerson, see Zwarg, *Feminist Conversations,* 221–237.

[51] A transcript of the notes taken during 12 Boston Conversations, probably by Elizabeth Peabody have been published. See Nancy Craig Simmons: "Margaret Fuller's Boston Conversations: The 1839–1840 Series," in *Studies in the American Renaissance 1994*, ed. Joel Myerson (Charlottesville: The University of Virginia Press, 1994), 195–226.

[52] *Margaret and her Friends, or Ten Conversations with Margaret Fuller upon the Mythology of the Greeks and its Expression in Art*. Held at the House of Rev. George Ripley, Bedford Place, Boston. beginning March 1, 1841. Reported by Caroline W. Healy (Boston: Roberts Bros., 1895), 13.

[53] Fuller's contributions and her editorial work for *The Dial* are described in detail by Joan Von Mehren, *Minerva and the Muse: A Life of Magratet Fuller* (Amherst: U of Massachuetts P, 1994), 120–125; 144–146.

[54] Mrs. Jameson (Anna Brownell Murphy Jameson), *Memoirs of the Loves of the Poets* (Boston: Houghton, Mifflin and Co., n.d.), 358.

[55] You doubt I love you as I loved Meta?/Done, I love you as I did Meta!

[56] *Memoirs of the Loves of the Poets*, 357.

[57] Von Mehren, *Minerva and the Muse*, 146.

[58] *The Dial* (1841), 1:343.

[59] *The Dial* (1841) 1: 345–346.

[60] *The Dial* (1841) 1: 345–346.

[61] *The Letters of James Freeman Clarke to Margaret Fuller*, 119.

[62] Fuller's decision to translate *Die Günderode* is evidence of the increased production of literary texts by women and constitutes the first stage of her argument (later developed *in Woman in the Nineteenth Century*) that women, not men, would lead the way in developing new critical thought. See Zwarg, *Feminist Conversations*, 86.

[63] For more on Dickinson's putative knowledge of German literature, especially German romantic works, see Barton Levi St. Armand, "Veiled Ladies: Dickinson, Bettine, and Transcendental Mediumship," in *Studies in the American Renaissance 1989*, ed. Joel Meyerson (Charlottesville: The U of Virginia P, 1987), 1–51.

[64] Margaret Fuller, "Romaic and Rhine Ballads," *The Dial* (1842), 3:137–180. The first edition of Simrock's popular *Rheinsagen* appeared in 1836.

[65] "Ah, how little has unfolded itself,/that little, how small and mean." Fuller quoted the original in German; the translation is in *Letters*, 1:281–282, note 1.

[66] Henry Steele Commager, *Theodore Parker* (Boston: Little, Brown, and Co., 1936), 94.

[67] *Ibid.*

[68] John Weiss, *Life and Correspondence of Theodore Parker*, 2 vols. (New York: Appleton, 1864), 1:218.

[69] *Letter to Converse Francis,* in Weiss, 1:235.

[70] Commager, *Theodore Parker,* 95.

[71] *Ibid.*

[72] "Something is thoroughly Something and not something else; something else is thoroughly something else and not Something." *Life and Correspondence of Theodore Parker,* 1:237–238.

[73] *Life and Correspondence of Theodore Parker,* 1:238.

[74] John White Chadwick, *Theodore Parker: Preacher and Reformer* (Boston: Houghton, Mifflin and Company, 1900), 137. On this subject, compare: Konstanze Bäumer, *"Bettine, Psyche, Mignon"* — *Bettina von Arnim and Goethe* (Stuttgart: Akademischer Verlag, 1986), 248–251.

[75] Bettina von Arnim, *Werke und Briefe,* 5 vols., eds. Gustav Konrad, Joachim Muller (Frechen: Bartmann-Verlag, 1959–1963), 5:448.

[76] *New York Tribune: Daily,* (Dec. 11, 1845).

[77] Margaret Fuller, "Ertheiler's Phrase Book," *New York Tribune: Daily,* May 1, 1845.

[78] *Ibid.*

[79] Wilma Robb Ebbit, *The Critical Essays of Margaret Fuller from the "New York Tribune,"* Edited with Introduction and Notes (Dissertation Brown University, 1943), 107.

[80] Ebbit, *The Critical Essays of Margaret Fuller,* 108.

[81] *Ibid.*

[82] *The Critical Essays of Margaret Fuller,* 109.

[83] *The Critical Essays of Margaret Fuller,* 110.

[84] Margaret Fuller, "Essays on Art by Goethe, Translated by S. G. Ward," *New York Tribune: Daily* (May 29 1845).

[85] *Ibid.*

[86] Margaret Fuller, "The Poets and Poetry of Europe by H. W. Longfellow," *New York Tribune: Daily* (June 17 1845).

[87] Margaret Fuller, "Frederick Von Raumer upon the Slavery Question," *New York Tribune: Daily,* (March 29, 1845).

[88] Margaret Fuller, "Der Volks-Tribun: Organ der Deutschen Sozial Reform Association in New York," *New York Tribune: Daily* (January 17, 1846).

[89] *The Love Letters of Margaret Fuller 1845–1846.* With an Introduction by Julia Ward Howe (New York: D. Appleton & Co., 1903), 61.

[90] "No angel can ascend to heaven/Till the whole heart has fallen to the earth in ashes." *The Love Letters of Margaret Fuller,* 83.

[91] *The Love Letters of Margaret Fuller,* 117.

[92] *The Love Letters of Margaret Fuller,* 53.

[93] In her detailed account of Margaret Fuller's and James Nathan's relationship, Joan Von Mehren emphasizes that without Nathan's letters to Fuller, which have never been discovered, the story of this relationship is "one-sided and perhaps totally deceptive." See Von Mehren, *Minerva and the Muse,* 208.

[94] The Papers of Margaret Fuller, vol. 16, Houghton Library (Harvard University).

[95] Margaret Fuller Ossoli, *At Home and Abroad; or Things and Thoughts in America and Europe.* Edited by her Brother Arthur B. Fuller, 1856; Kennikat Scholarly Reprints, (Port Washington, NY: Kennikat Press, 1971), 180.

[96] *The Love Letters of Margaret Fuller,* 187.

[97] *At Home and Abroad, or Things and Thoughts in America and Europe,* 420–421.

[98] *At Home and Abroad,* 222.

[99] *Letters,* 4:276. For further information on Margaret Fuller's Italian sojourn, see Joseph Jay Deiss, *The Roman Years of Margaret Fuller* (New York: Thomas Y. Crowell Co., 1969).

Henry David Thoreau
Courtesy of Concord Free Public Library

3: Pan: Henry David Thoreau

HENRY DAVID THOREAU, WHO WAS BORN in his grandmother's house on Virginia Road on July 12, 1817, was the only member of Waldo Emerson's circle who was a native of Concord. The family, however, lived in nearby Chelmsford where Thoreau's father had a grocery store before getting a position as schoolmaster in Boston. The following year he gave up the job in order to take up residence in Concord and enter the small pencil factory of his brother-in-law. It was this modest family business that guaranteed Henry and his siblings a secure childhood.

The Thoreaus were ardent naturalists whose great love was to take far-ranging walks and boat trips on the Concord, Sudbury, and Assabet rivers, or on nearby Walden Pond. It is said that one of the Thoreau children was almost born on Lee's Hill during such an outing. Henry and his brother John roamed the region's alluvial terrain, fished in the well-stocked waters populated by beavers and turtles, and floated down the rivers on home-made rafts and boats. Thoreau was interested in the traditions and customs of the native Indians, who he always represented to his contemporaries as ideal figures. When he was twenty years old he wrote a letter to his brother in the character of Chief Tahatawan of the Musketaquid tribe:

> Musketaquid two hundred and two summers — two moons — eleven suns since the coming of the Pale Faces. Tahatawan — Sachimausan — to his brother sachem — Hopeful — of Hopewell — hoping that he is well.

> Brother, it is many suns that I have not seen the print of thy moccasins by our council fire [. . .] — the earth has become hard like a frozen buffalo skin, [. . .] I have been thinking how the Pale Faces have taken away our lands — and was a woman. You are fortunate to have pitched your wigwam nearer to the great salt lake, where the pale-Face can never plant corn.[1]

Concord also provided Thoreau with the foundation of his education. At age six he entered Phoebe Wheeler's school, and at eleven Concord Academy, which gave him a thorough grounding in Latin and Greek. Music lessons made him accomplished on the flute — an instrument he would henceforth carry when he roamed the woods. He also attended lectures in the Concord Lyceum.

Thoreau was the only son in the family to attend Harvard College, entering at age sixteen. His entire family all pooled their resources to pay his fees. Henry was thus able to continue his studies in Greek and Latin at an advanced level and also make his first acquaintance with modern languages like French, Spanish, Italian, and German. In his third year at Harvard he began German with Charles Follen's successor, Hermann Bokum, a native speaker who was entrusted with the teaching of German at Harvard between 1835–1838. Bokum used Follen's grammar and reader and published his own introduction to German literature (Philadelphia, 1832), which contained excerpts from the best German authors, an English interlinear translation and explanation, as well as a treatise on the pronunciation. Bokum was a great admirer of Jean Paul and held public lectures on that German writer in Boston. His anthology used in German classes has as its opening texts Jean Paul's poem "Der Mond" ("The Moon"), as well as to "Die Neujahrsnacht eines Unglücklichen" ("An Unhappy Man's New Year's Eve"). Like Follen's *German Reader for Beginners* (Boston, 1826), Bokum's book introduced readers to Wieland with excerpts from *Die Abderiten,* Goethe (*Egmont,* "Zum Shakespeare-Tag"), Winckelmann, Schiller, Wackenroder, Tieck, Lessing, Fichte, etc. — all authors who enthralled Henry Thoreau. In any case, he also read Goethe's *Tasso* and *Iphigenia* and owned a copy of Schiller's *Geschichte des Dreissigjährigen Krieges* [History of the Thirty-Years War], which was also a textbook at Harvard.

In 1836 Thoreau took part in the "round table course" offered by Longfellow, in which the professor (just returned from his second European trip) lectured on European literature and translated ballads with his students. Longfellow seemed too bohemian for Thoreau's taste and he left the course, probably before encountering German literary texts.[2]

Nonetheless, Thoreau's interest in German literature had been awakened — although, like many a college student of his generation, he had to interrupt his studies for a period while he earned money as a school teacher. This interlude brought him together in 1835 with a man who was to promote his penchant for German letters even more. Orestes Augustus Brownson — who at the time was in his third stage of a long series of religious conversions — had settled in Canton, Massachusetts as a Unitarian pastor. Like the journalist Horace Greeley, Brownson was from Vermont where he had been born in abject poverty in 1803, the same year as Emerson. In the course of his life he acquired an impressive body of knowledge with only a minimum of schooling. Being interested at first in religion, he joined the Presbyterian church and became a minister; this he then exchanged for Universalism, before becoming finally a Unitarian. He taught himself German and French, read Heine, Kant, Saint-Simon, Jouffroy, and Victor Cousin, with whom he also corresponded. Brownson's efforts were focused on justifying the well-being of the laboring classes through Christianity. "If I repeated the words of Jesus in the marketplaces of this city," he proclaimed in a sermon in Boston that Harriet Martineau heard with fascination and recorded in her book on America, "you would call me a 'radical,' an 'agrarian,' a 'trades-unionist,' a 'leveller.'"[3] Brownson, writes his biographer Arthur Schlesinger, "was [Karl Marx's] nearest forerunner in America."[4] The essay on "The Laboring Classes," published in 1840 in his own publication *Boston Quarterly Review,* excited great controversy and not a little fear. Only James Freeman Clarke in his *Western Messenger,* defended the courageous loner, whose social position was somewhere between the utopian socialists Owen, Saint-Simon, and Fourier on the one hand, and Karl Marx on the other.[5]

The eighteen-year old Thoreau arrived at Brownson's home in the summer of 1835 to interview for the position of assistant teacher of the town of Canton. His conversation with Brownson lasted until midnight, after which Thoreau not only got the job, but also an invitation to live in Brownson's house as tutor of the preacher's children.

The six summer weeks in Canton must have been a happy time. Thoreau and Brownson took long walks together and in the evenings delved into German literature. In a letter to Brownson from December 30, 1837, Thoreau writes:

> I have never ceased to look back with interest, not to say satisfaction, upon the short six weeks which I passed with you. They were an era in my life — the morning of a new *Lebenstag.* They are to me as a dream that is dreamt, but which returns from time to time in all its original freshness. Such a one as I would dream a second and a third time, and then tell before breakfast. [. . .] Thank heaven, the toothache occurs often enough to remind me that I must be out patching the roof occasionally, and not be always keeping up a blaze upon the hearth within, with my German and metaphysical cat-sticks.[6]

We do not know which books Brownson read with the young instructor he employed. The twenty volumes of Brownson's own collected works contain only a few essays devoted specifically to German themes (such as Schiller's "Aesthetic Theory"), which appeared later in the journals he published. It is certain, however, that his primary interest was in philosophy. In the journal titled *Brownson's Quarterly Review,* which he published between 1844 and 1875, he printed an 84-page introduction to Kant's *Critique of Pure Reason.* According to Brownson's son Henry, Kant provided much conversational material for the family circle, and even the children spoke of the "Ding-an-sich."[7] In 1846 Brownson took issue with Schiller's "Aesthetic Theory," criticizing it from a Christian position. Nonetheless, he could still come to a judgment somewhat surprising for a

New Englander: "There is more perfect art in the *Elective Affinities* than in the *Wilhelm Tell* or the *Wallenstein*.[8]

Brownson proved to be a staunch supporter of the Transcendentalists in the pages of his *Quarterly Review*. He even proposed making the magazine the mouthpiece for the movement. But Alcott and Emerson preferred to found *The Dial*, which they entrusted to Margaret Fuller rather than the dominating Brownson who could never stop talking and who was never invited back to the Transcendental Club after his first visit.

Brownson's life was to take a course that was highly unusual in New England. In 1844 he and his family converted to Roman Catholicism, a move that elicited groans of resignation from his friends. He was prepared for this conversion by Isaak Hecker, the former baker from Brook Farm (where Brownson's son Henry was schooled for two years), the same who later founded the Paulist order. Hecker even tried to win Thoreau for the Catholic faith. Estranged from the Concord circle after his conversion, Brownson moved to New York in 1855. There he devoted himself to opposing the anti-Catholic sentiments of the day, trying to correct the image of the "purple lady," as the Roman church was sometimes called in New England. He promoted progressive Catholic writers in his magazine such as the Munich philosopher Jakob Frohschammer, who was a man after his own heart. Nonetheless, Brownson in many ways remained hopelessly behind the modern temperament of Emerson and his colleagues. There is, for example, a huge discrepancy between Brownson's and Theodore Parker's ideals of modern woman. As late as 1873, three years before his death in Detroit, Brownson issued a negative judgment on the emancipation of women. The title of his essay, "Religious Novels, and Woman versus Woman," is clearly in reference to Margaret Fuller's work, "The Great Lawsuit: Man versus Men. Woman versus Women" (1843).

Henry Thoreau finished college in 1837 to return to Concord where he took a post teaching in the grammar school. He simultaneously continued studying German with Sarah Ripley who some thought the most learned woman in New England. She had married the Reverend Samuel Ripley, an uncle of Emerson's, and with her husband ran a school in nearby Waltham that prepared generations of pupils for Harvard College. She owned a large library and was a participant at the meetings of the Transcendental Club. Emerson always held her in the highest regard, as shown by his many diary entries where she turns up as a beloved and open-minded conversational partner whom not even Margaret Fuller could match.

In the same year Thoreau began to keep a journal, an activity he was to continue for the rest of his life. A considerable component of his literary output is to be found in these nineteen volumes. It can be said that all the works of this great namer of phenomena and observer of American nature are derived from these entries. It is therefore quite significant how often the young diarist quotes one particular German writer in these first months, namely Goethe. As early as the first entry from October 22, 1837, one hears what was to be the main theme of Thoreau's life — supported by a fragment of German wisdom:

> To be alone I find it necessary to escape the present — I avoid myself. [. . .] I seek a garret. The spiders must not be disturbed, nor the floor swept, nor the lumber arranged. — The Germans say — Es ist alles wahr wodurch du besser wirst. (*Journal,* 1:5)

Three days later he ventured a brief description of spring as only a lad trained in Latin and Elizabethan epigrams could appreciate:

> Spring. She appears and we are once more children; [. . .] we yield to the advances of poetic frenzy. "The flowers look kindly at us from the beds with their child eyes — and in the horizon, the snow of the far mountains dissolves into light vapor." Goethe. Torq. Tasso.
>
> (*Journal,* 1:6)

More translations from *Tasso* follow, from which Thoreau formulated his own epigrams such as one entitled "The Poet." On the following day one finds an entry under the heading "How Man Grows." It is a prose translation from the same play by Goethe, this time of the words of Alfons: "A noble man has not to thank a private circle for his culture. Fatherland and world must work upon him." The following lines are, significantly, also included: "A talent is builded in solitude,/A character in the stream of the world." And we also read: "He only fears man who knows him not, and he who avoids him will soonest misapprehend him" (*Journal,* 1:7) — quotations that are revealing for the future solitary dweller of Walden Pond.

Thoreau also translates the final passage of Antonio's hymn of praise to the poet Ariosto:

> As nature decks her inward rich breast in a green variegated dress, so clothes he all that can make men honorable in the blooming garb of the fable. — The well of superfluity bubbles near, and lets us see variegated wonder-fishes. The air is filled with rare birds, the meads and copses with strange herds, wit lurks half concealed in the verdure, and wisdom from time to time lets sound from a golden cloud sustained words, while frenzy wildly seems to sweep the well-toned lute, yet holds itself measured in perfect time. (*Journal,* 1:7)

Thoreau completes a total of thirty lines, closing with the epigram, "That beauty is transitory which alone you seem to honor" (*Journal,* 1:7).

It is possible that Thoreau may have translated these German selections while he was still a student, but the fact that he begins his new journal with this material is significant. In the process he is not interested solely in the figure of Tasso, but equally in Goethe's description of nature in all her glory, which culminates in the paean to Ariosto as a pure rococo apotheosis.

At the same time that this young translator was engrossing himself in Goethe's texts, he was also reading *Nature,* the first book written by his Concord neighbor. He had heard Emerson speak in lyceum lectures and met him personally during his last year at Harvard. Emerson later recounted to Thoreau's biographer F. B. Sanborn how Mrs. Lucy Jackson Brown (the sister of his second wife) had lived with the Thoreaus in Concord in a guest house they kept near the pencil factory. From there she would bring him young Henry's poems, one of which he had wrapped around a posy of violets tossed through her window; another time it was a passage from Thoreau's diary in which Mrs. Brown and Henry's aunt Sophia were struck by thoughts similar to those in one of Emerson's lyceum lectures.[9]

The thoughts that Thoreau committed to his diary centered on man in nature. He was particularly fascinated by the problem of how one defines and perfects oneself in and through nature. To reach this goal his task was first to observe and comprehend nature through description. The descriptions in Thoreau's journal, which follow the translated passages from Goethe's *Tasso,* have such titles as "The Fog," "Ducks At Goose-Pond," or "The Arrowhead." None of these conjures up the sublime natural description of the Ariosto passage in *Tasso.* Rather, Thoreau seems to be describing elements of the New England landscape using a technique he had observed in a work by Goethe, namely the *Italian Journey,* which he read in the original German. He borrowed this volume from Emerson's library and entered his own translation from it into his journal.

Thoreau was struck by the description in Goethe's travel account of the evening in the section "From the Brenner to Verona":

> And now that it is evening, in the mild air a few clouds rest upon the mountains, in the heavens more stand still than move, and immediately after sunset the chirping of crickets begins to grow more loud; then one feels for once at home in the world, and not as concealed or in exile."[10]

Similar nature descriptions by Goethe of northern Italy alternate in Thoreau's journal with his own renderings of New England's late autumn mood: "The snow gives the landscape a washing day appearance — here a streak of white, there a streak of dark — it is spread like a napkin over the hills and meadows. This must be a rare drying day; to judge from the vapor that floats over the 'vast clothes' yard" (*Journal*, 1:12).

After this passage there follows an entry from the *Italian Journey* in which Goethe describes to the people of the town of Malesine the cliffs, tower, and the walls of their own ruined castle with such enthusiasm that they look at these familiar details with renewed curiosity.[11] It is not important that a translation error creeps into Thoreau's English to distort the original meaning or that (like Margaret Fuller's translation of Bettina von Arnim's *Günderode)*, his close adherence to German syntax resists natural English style. This does not obscure his objective to understand this narrator, which he does soon thereafter when his journal entry of December 8, 1837 contains the following comment on Goethe:

> He is generally satisfied with giving an exact description of objects as they appear to him, and his genius is exhibited in the points he seizes upon and illustrates. His description of Venice and her environs as seen from Saint Mark's is that of an unconcerned spectator, whose object is to describe faithfully what he sees, and what is more, in the order in which he sees it. It is this trait that is chiefly to be prized in the book — even the reflections of the author do not interfere with his descriptions. It would thus be possible for inferior minds to produce invaluable books.
>
> (*Journal*, 1:16)

The precision of Goethe's prose — his "snails pace," — safeguarded him in Thoreau's eyes from superficiality. "His Italy is not merely the fatherland of lazzaroni and macaroni, but a solid turf-clad soil — daily illumined by moonshine — to say nothing of the frequent showers which are so faithfully recorded" (*Journal*, 1:30). Goethe's "hearty good will to all men" ultimately made him very likeable in Thoreau's eyes. "Not one cross word has he spoken," except once when he chided a boy on the back of the wagon who had broken into a horrible shriek of joy at the magnificent sight of the city of Naples. The boy responded to Goethe's annoyed reproach with, "Signor, perdonate! questa è la mia patria!" Goethe had to admit, "to me poor northerner came something tear-like into the eyes," which Thoreau quotes and translates as well (*Journal*, 1:30).[12]

The influence of this sympathy with Goethe is evident in Thoreau's first book publication eleven years later. *A Week on the Concord and Merrimack Rivers* tells of a journey that Henry took with his brother John in the summer of 1838. Three years later John died suddenly of tetanus, making the account a monument to a dead brother who is never mentioned by name in the text. For the writing of *A Week on the Concord and Merrimack Rivers* Thoreau left himself ample time. He put it together from journal entries when he was living in his cabin on Walden Pond between July 1845 to October 1847 and also, in part, from pieces he had

published in *The Dial.* When he had no luck finding a publisher, he had
the work printed in 1849 at his own expense. Barely 300 of the 1000
copies sold, which forced Thoreau to buy back the rest himself, making
the wry comment that he possessed a library of nearly 900 volumes, 700
of which he had written himself.

The travel account describes the brothers' one-week river journey in
their fisherman's dory. They begin on a Saturday; by Monday the wayfar-
ers progress through the early mists of the Merrimack and imagine themselves on the upper Nile, convinced that here they can lead a similar oriental existence. While long passages are devoted to depictions of orient
and occident, Thoreau regrets the western ignorance of asiatic cultures.
Even Germany, where the energies of philology indirectly serve philosophy and poetry, is no exception. He writes that Goethe "wanted that universality of genius which could have appreciated the philosophy of India, if
he had more nearly approached it. His genius was more practical, dwelling
much more in the regions of the understanding, and was less native to
contemplation than the genius of those sages."[13] But he paid no attention
to Goethe's *West-östlicher Diwan,* which Emerson had known prior to
1840, nor of Hammer-Purgstall's translations from the Persian, a book
that Emerson acquired when Thoreau was living on Walden Pond.

Goethe remained Thoreau's model of the quintessential writer. This is
evident in the Thursday chapter of the river journal: "We can never safely
exceed the actual facts in our narratives. Of pure invention, such as some
suppose, there is no instance. To write a true work of fiction even is only
to take leisure and liberty to describe some things more exactly as they are.
A true account of the actual is the rarest poetry."[14]

To cite an example, Thoreau quotes a slight variation of his journal
entry from December 8, 1837, which contains Goethe's description of
Venice as seen from the campanile on St. Mark's Square. However, he
admits to a certain unfamiliarity with the whole of Goethe's *oeuvre.* Yet he
does claim enough knowledge to be able to say that most travellers lack
the self-respect to see things around them from their own perspective.
Their reports are usually worthless because they invent points of view and
perspectives that are superior to reality. The quality of moderation that
Goethe practiced in such matters was for Thoreau the proof of his preeminence among writers.

Thoreau also discovered why Goethe had mastered the art of description; he explains the phenomenon in *A Week on the Concord and Merrimack Rivers.* Thoreau argues that Goethe's education — like his life —
was that of an artist. He lacks the unconsciousness of the poet. This is an
insight Thoreau derived from Goethe's autobiography, in which he found
wondrous and solemn truths combined with triviality and petty exagger-

ations. Wisdom, he felt, was too often applied in order to produce a partial, merely well-bred man, "a magnifying of the theatre till life itself is
turned into a stage, for which it is our duty to study our parts well, and
conduct with propriety and precision."[15] The only fault in Goethe's education is, so to speak, its artistic perfection. What this education lacks could
only be recognized by someone like Thoreau who had grown up in and
with nature, and consequently found the influence of nature on Goethe's
childhood limited, "though she prevails at last in making an unusually
catholic impression on the boy. It is the life of a city boy, whose toys are
pictures and works of art, whose wonders are the theatre and kingly pro-
cessions and crownings. [. . .] He was defrauded of much which the savage boy enjoys."[16] Thoreau quotes from Goethe's memoirs the passage
where Goethe finally escapes to the woods, yet still misses a more primitive wildness: "Thus much is certain, that only the undefinable, wide-
expanding feelings of youth and of uncultivated nations are adapted to the
sublime, which, whenever it may be excited in us through external objects, since it is either formless, or else moulded into forms which are incomprehensible, must surround us with a grandeur which we find above
our reach."[17]

This is a case in which Thoreau is in agreement with Emerson who
also found fault with Goethe's striving for education. Goethe was "too
well-bred to be thoroughly bred," says Thoreau, for he lacked not only a
life amidst nature, but also contact with children of the lowest social
classes. The pedagogue Thoreau has this to say: "The child should have
the advantage of ignorance as well as of knowledge, and is fortunate if he
gets his share of neglect and exposure."[18] In support of this point he cites
the Elizabethan poet Francis Quarles: "The laws of Nature break the rules
of Art."[19]

Goethe speaks one more time during Thoreau's trip down the New
England rivers, this time from his *Italian Journey*. Thoreau appends a
Goethean description of the route along the river Etsch to his own observations about the man of genius. Goethe's character he judged to belong
to a demonic creator of original works, for he was an artist who produces
a perfect work of art in obedience to laws yet unexplained. It is a longer
passage than the one in the journal from 1837 and includes idyllic reminiscences of "the most precious images of art,"[20] as though to prove that
the German measures nature against art, while the best American reader
thinks, "nature is prepared to welcome into her scenery the finest work of
human art, for she is herself an art so cunning that the artist never appears
in his work."[21]

By the time Henry David Thoreau finished his book *A Week on the
Concord and Merrimack Rivers,* eight years had passed since he had

graduated from Harvard College. These were passed in the shadow of Emerson who, for one, had not been satisfied with reading the journal and the poems of this young teacher. Yet, from the first meeting of the two men sprang one of the greatest literary friendships in American letters and — as in the case of Orestes Brownson — a close family accord. In collaboration with his brother John, Henry founded a progressive private school in Concord where the brothers put the spirit of Pestalozzi into practice. In this atmosphere juvenile activity was permitted to emerge and develop in the absence of any corporal punishment; Henry also took his pupils regularly on long nature walks. When John's poor health finally forced the school to close in 1841, Henry moved in with the Emerson household where he performed divers tasks from splitting wood to working as tutor and private secretary.

In November 1838 Emerson was still pencilling short messages to Thoreau in which a certain "My dear Sir" was invited to take part in an afternoon walk in the woods (and to bring his flute to amuse the ladies). But by the summer of 1841 Emerson's journal entries show how the relationship between both men was no longer simply the influence of the older upon the younger, the master and the pupil, but rather was mutual: "Then the good river-god has taken the form of my valiant Henry Thoreau here & introduced me to the riches of his shadowy starlit, moonlit stream, a lovely new world lying as close & yet as unknown to this vulgar trite one of streets & shops as death to life or poetry to prose."[22]

When *The Dial* was in its second year Thoreau began working closely with Emerson; soon he was attending meetings of the Transcendental Club. Margaret Fuller, who was editor at the time, printed a poem by Thoreau, "Sympathy," but rejected his essay entitled "Service," on the grounds that it was too unpolished. As soon as Emerson took over the editorship of the magazine in July 1842, Thoreau's "Natural History of Massachusetts" appeared, as well as several poems. Thoreau himself even edited the April 1843 number while Emerson was away on a long lecture tour.

In 1844 Thoreau took a post as tutor with Emerson's brother William on Staten Island. During this period he met Horace Greeley and Walt Whitman, the only American poet he regarded highly, one who was also esteemed and supported by Emerson. At this time he also reviewed a book by a German that was widely circulated in England and America, *The Paradise Within the Reach of All Men Without Labor, by Powers of Nature and Machinery* (1833)[23] by John Adolphus Etzler. The book had appeared in London and seen a second edition in Pittsburgh in 1842 before appearing in Ulm in 1844. In that book, and in the second part entitled *The New World* (Philadelphia 1841), Etzler proposed harnessing the energy of wind, water, sun, and tides in great cooperative ventures for the welfare of all. He envisaged the manufacture of synthetic fabrics and tractors, of prefabricated houses with thousands of rooms and communal kitchens. He saw individual man as helpless, but when functioning as a collective, as powerful.[24] These were ideas that had slight appeal to Thoreau, the solitary individualist. He found the greatest error in the work, however, to be its goal of greatest comfort and pleasure in life, at the expense of attending to the reform of the inner human being.

Thoreau also had his reasons for not joining Brook Farm, despite the emphasis placed on the inner life there. He had put his mind to quite a different experiment, which was diametrically opposed to the spirit of the collective. For this undertaking he also drew his inspiration from a German author. Johann Georg Zimmermann (1728–1795), one of the best-known physicians of the time, wrote a book *Über die Einsamkeit* (1777), the American translation of which, *Solitude Considered,* appeared in Albany in 1796 and was in Thoreau's library.[25] It is the work of a man with an enlightened mind who associates the most beautiful memories of his youth with solitary experiences in nature, with old castles, and with hermits' cells. But Zimmermann did not necessarily regard the condition of solitude as one of seclusion, for one can be solitary in a cloister, in a small town, as well as in one's study. He analyzes the reasons that draw men together into society: boredom and disgust with one's own person; and the reasons to flee society: desire for peace, independence, and the company of the best brains. He weighs the advantages and disadvantages of solitude, with the result that the advantages dominate."[26]

Zimmermann enjoyed success not only in Germany. The cult of solitude was prevalent in early nineteenth century America where Thoreau was its most prominent spokesman. When he was a student he spent six weeks in 1836 with his classmate Charles Wheeler (who would later file reports from Germany for *The Dial*). The two lads lived in a cabin they built on Flint's Pond in Lincoln, a town adjacent to Concord. When Thoreau later made his famous move on July 4, 1845, to Emerson's wooded plot a few miles outside of Concord, built himself a cabin from a former shed, and set out his bean patch, he by no means became the hermit as he has been stylized by popular legend. He paid regular visits to Concord and had regular visitors from town (Bronson Alcott came to call every Sunday evening in the last year). Emerson, Margaret Fuller, and many friends and relatives also called on him, which made it possible to realize a radical variation of Emerson's theme of "Society and Solitude."

Walden, or Life in the Woods (1854) is, of course, a very different book from that by the German doctor, for it is simultaneously cultural criticism, natural description, and literature. It is a celebration of a quality of freedom attainable only by frugality. All property, says Thoreau, is a kind of servitude, as his very first chapter "Economy" demonstrates. Every young farmer who inherits his father's farm is to be pitied as much as the man who works half his life to possess a house he will use for only one third of it. Clothing is nothing more than "false skin" or "true bark"; to subject this skin to the vagaries of fashion seemed to Thoreau absurd.[27] One needs even less for sustenance, and in the manner of an "agricola laboriosus" he plants his beans and wages a "Trojan War" against the weeds. He gathers wild grapes, apples, chestnuts, proclaiming as his motto: "simplicity, simplicity, simplicity." He needs no postal address, for to the philosopher all news is merely gossip.

The time that Thoreau gained by his retreat from the world he put to use reading Homer, Plato, and the Indian *Vedas*. In his vision of a new New England, the American village acquires the role of the European aristocratic patron that invites the artists and the great minds of the world in order to learn from them. Most of all, however, Thoreau had time for his natural observations, documented so well in *Walden*. He describes bird song, animals in winter, two ants locked in deadly historical combat. He measures the snowfall and the thickness of the ice, and recounts the people who had once lived in the woods as well as those one encounters now. In addition to such meticulous nature description, his account also includes praise for modern developments in technology, especially the railroad. In fact, Thoreau had all the sensibilities of a modern man stirred by the exciting potential of technological progress.

Thoreau never mentions German literature in *Walden*, in his journals after 1838, or in his later lectures and essays. The name of Goethe does not appear. It is as though Thoreau were recalling an essay he had written as a college student, "Advantages and Disadvantages of Foreign Influence on American Literature." There the nineteen year old student grappled with the issue of American dependence on the culture of the mother country: "though we have rejected her tea she still supplies us with food for the mind."[28] He criticizes his countrymen with authority saying, "we are a nation of speculators, stock-holders, and money-changers,"[29] used to judging everything, even books, for their utility. Now that political independence from England had been won, it was time, Thoreau stated, to gain intellectual independence as well, which meant most immediately ceasing the blind admiration for imported genius. In contemporary America,

> the aspirant for fame must breathe the atmosphere of foreign parts, and learn to talk about things which the homebred student never dreamed of, [...] Then will they dwell on every word he utters, watch the cut of his coat, the cock of his hat, — ape his pronunciation and manners, and per-

haps honor him with a public dinner. [. . .] How much ink has been shed, how much paper wasted, in imitations of Ossian, [. . .] [Even those who celebrate the New England nature] are prone to sing of sky-larks and nightingales, perched on hedges, to the neglect of the homely robin-red-breast, and the straggling rail-fence of their own native land.[30]

Thoreau, more than Emerson, directed his vision more decisively westward. In 1841 in the pages of *The Dial* Emerson had predicted the abatement of European influence on America. He foresaw the core of the English race located in America, which would give rise to the "great Yankee." With Henry David Thoreau he had indeed been born. Thoreau looked upon Europe as a finishing school for privileged daughters: "they went away squashes, and they return gourds," he wrote in his journal July 30, 1853. For this reason he rejected the notion of travelling to Europe himself, making him — arch-Yankee that he was — the only member of the Concord circle who never made the journey. He wrote, "I must walk toward Oregon, and not toward Europe. And that way the nation is moving, and I may say that mankind progresses from east to west."[31]

Thoreau as a walker is a figure who has entered American literature. He scouted the area around Concord on foot in his capacity of surveyor, and more far-flung territory as botanist and geologist. He hiked along the coast of Cape Cod, through the state of Maine, getting as far as Canada. He would walk day and night in any weather. While counting the rings of a tree stump in 1860 he got a chill that developed into tuberculosis, from which he died two years later. A last trip to Minnesota, taken as a health cure, brought no relief.

We must not underestimate the influence Thoreau's early reading of German literature had upon him. Although it was not as wide as some other of his contemporaries, his knowledge of German texts was nonetheless representative of the reception of all German literature in New England. Whether we look at Emerson or Margaret Fuller, Amos Bronson Alcott or James Freeman Clarke, Theodore Parker or Orestes Brownson, or even such authors like Nathaniel Hawthorne who did not belong to the circle of Transcendentalists — all these in their youth were exposed to Goethe, Bettina, Schiller, Tieck, Kant, Schleiermacher, August Wilhelm Schlegel, Fichte, and Hegel. For a period during their personal and intellectual development, they were all enthralled by the experience. For each and every one of these Americans, this German phase was an important step in their intellectual education. Perhaps it was most important for someone who outgrew and concealed that phase most completely, namely Thoreau, for whom German literature was a more formative influence than for anybody else.

All these American readers of German literature had other commitments than the dissemination and promotion of German authors in the United States — Margaret Fuller's energy devoted to that task notwithstanding. But even she later realized her mission to be advancing European (particularly Italian) political developments. It was Thoreau's ambition to hold up before his increasingly materialistic country the ideal of the individual. This ideal was to be unencumbered by property, by the state, or by the institution of slavery, which he saw as enslaving the whole nation. His famous tract "On the Duty of Civil Disobedience" (1849), as well as his speeches and essays, bear witness to his fervor.

Thoreau doubtless knew more of German literature than we can surmise. Harvard first drew his attention to the rich tradition, where as a student he read English translations of Friedrich Schlegel's lectures.[32] Besides the German texts from his college days, his library contained Carlyle's *Life of Schiller,* as well as his translation of *Wilhelm Meister.* In addition, he owned Bettina von Arnim's *Günderode* in the translation begun by Margaret Fuller and finished by Minna Wesselhoeft. In Emerson's library he would have found an extensive collection of German books, but it is significant that as the traveller that he was, he borrowed the volume of the *Italian Journey* from the German Goethe edition. Goethe and Thoreau were similar travellers, each outfitted with their telescopes and botanical guides as collectors of rocks and plants.[33]

The discovery of nature's energy during the period of German literature known as *Storm and Stress* has been compared to Thoreau's later discovery of the American wilderness. Moreover, one scholar has emphasized that, in contrast to the European Romantics, Thoreau had no fear of the threatening dangers of anarchy and chaos inherent in these energies.[34] Thoreau had given himself up to nature and tried to become one with its forces. All his senses focused on perception, the colors and forms of the autumn leaves, the taste of wild berries, and the smell of honeysuckle and wild mint, the whirring of the summer heat over the meadows and the tinkling of the frost around Walden Pond. His descriptions frequently reveal traces of earlier impressions gained from his reading that were absorbed into his personal observations. In the chapter in *Walden* entitled "Sounds" one reader has even tried to discern an explicit knowledge of Novalis, which was probably not that precise.[35] In the final chapter about spring, however, Thoreau describes the form of the leaf as the basic underlying form in nature. In such a form, which is modelled in the sand as the ground thaws, it is hard to miss the echo of Goethe's *Metamorphoses of Plants,* or at least his remarks on the *"Urpflanze"* in the *Italian Journey.* Thoreau also sees the form of the leaf in the lung, liver, and fat layers of the animal and human body. Feathers and the wings of birds, ice crystals, the entire tree, as well as river beds are, in his eyes, variations of the leaf form — even the human hand is seen as an imitation of the palm leaf. By trying to reconcile the derivation of botanical and philological forms, Thoreau combines biological observations with extremely modern linguistic ones.

For Thoreau nature could truly harbor no terrors. He saw in it not chaos, but rather an order structured on its own principles. This was proof to Thoreau of the inner truth and necessity that Goethe had attributed to the *Urpflanze*. "The same law will be applicable to all other living organisms," Goethe maintained.[36] Nearly a half century later Thoreau pursued this idea in the American wild to its logical end.

Notes

[1]   *The Correspondence of Henry David Thoreau,* ed. Walter Harding and Carl Bode (New York: New York UP, 1958), 16.

[2]   See Anton Huffert, *Thoreau as a Teacher, Lecturer and Educational Thinker* (Diss. New York University 1951), 176–200. Also Robert D. Richardson Jr., *Henry Thoreau: A Life of the Mind* (Berkeley: U of California P, 1986), 27–31.

[3]   Arthur M. Schlesinger, *Orestes A. Brownson: A Pilgrim's Progress* (Boston: Little Brown, 1939) 53–54. "Agrarians" demanded the equal division of property, "levelers" the elimination of social differences.

[4]   Schlesinger, *Orestes A. Brownson,* 100.

[5]   Schlesinger, *Orestes A. Brownson,* 95–99.

[6]   *The Correspondence of Henry David Thoreau,* 19.

[7]   Schlesinger, *Orestes A. Brownson,* 178.

[8]   Orestes A. Brownson, *Works,* Collected and arranged by Henry F. Brownson (Detroit: Thorndike Nourse, 1882–1887), 19:127.

[9]   Franklin Benjamin Sanborn, *The Life of Henry David Thoreau, Including Many Essays hitherto unpublished and Some Account of His Family and Friends.* (Boston, New York: Houghton Mifflin, 1917), 128ff.

[10]   *Hamburger Ausgabe,* 11: 26; Henry David Thoreau, *The Writings of Henry David Thoreau,* vol. 1: *A Week on the Concord and Merrimack Rivers* (Boston and New York: Houghton Mifflin Co., 1906); Rpt: New York: AMS Press, 1982; 2nd. ed., 1:352.

[11]   *Hamburger Ausgabe,* 11:33.

[12]   *Hamburger Ausgabe,* 11:220.

[13]   Henry David Thoreau, *A Week on the Concord and Merrimack Rivers,* 149.

[14]   *A Week on the Concord and Merrimack Rivers,* 347.

[15]   *A Week on the Concord and Merrimack Rivers,* 349.

[16]   *Ibid.*

[17]   *A Week on the Concord and Merrimack Rivers,* 349; *Hamburger Ausgabe,* 9:223.

[18]   *A Week on the Concord and Merrimack Rivers,* 349–350.

[19]   Francis Quarles, "To my Booke," In *Divine Fancies,* Lib. Iv, piece 117, 1.36.

[20]   *Hamburger Ausgabe,* 11:26.

[21]   *A Week on the Concord and Merrimack Rivers,* 337.

[22]   Emerson, *Journals,* 7:454.

[23]   *The Paradise Within the Reach of All Men Without Labor, by Powers of Nature and Machinery. An Address to All Intelligent Men,* 2 vols. (Pittsburgh, PA: Etzler and Reinhold, 1833).

[24]   Thoreau's review of the 1842 London edition is entitled "Paradise (to be) Regained" and appeared in *The Democratic Review.* See *The Writings of Henry David Thoreau,* 20 vols. (Boston & New York: Houghton Mifflin, 1906), 4:280–305.

[25]   *Solitude Considered with Respect to its Influence Upon the Mind and the Heart* (New York: Mott & Lyon for E. Duyckinck & Co., 1796).

[26]   Johann Georg Zimmermann, *Über die Einsamkeit,* 4 vols. (Leipzig: Weidmans Erben u. Reich, 1784–1785), In: Deutsche National-Literatur, ed. Joseph Kürschner, vol. 73. (Stuttgart: W. Spemann, n.d.), 359. For a detailed study of the parallels between Thoreau and Zimmermann, see Grant Loomis, "Thoreau and Zimmermann," *New England Quarterly* (1937), vol. 4, 789–792.

[27]   Henry David Thoreau, *The Writings of Henry David Thoreau,* vol. 2: *Walden* (Boston and New York: Houghton Mifflin Co., 1906). Rpt: New York: AMS Press, 1968, 2:26.

[28]   Sanborn, *The Life of Henry David Thoreau,* 132.

[29]   *The Life of Henry David Thoreau,* 131.

[30]   *The Life of Henry David Thoreau,* 133–134.

[31]   Henry David Thoreau, *The Writings of Henry David Thoreau,* vol. 5: *Excursions and Poems,* "Walking" (Boston and New York: Houghton Mifflin Co., 1906); Rpt: New York: AMS Press, 1968, 5:218.

[32]   Cf. Sherman Paul, *The Shores of America: Thoreau's Inward Exploration* (Urbana: U of Illinois P, 1958), chapter 1.

[33]   John Aldrich Christie, *Thoreau as World Traveler* (New York: Columbia UP, 1965), 64–70.

[34]   Frederick Garbow, *Thoreau's Redemptive Imagination* (New York: New York UP, 1977), 73–74.

[35]   Garbow, *Thoreau's Redemptive Imagination*, 90.

[36]   *Hamburger Ausgabe,* 11:375; Cf. Richardson, *Henry Thoreau: A Life of the Mind,* 157.

Amos Bronson Alcott
Courtesy of Concord Free Public Library

4: Orpheus: Amos Bronson Alcott

A MOS BRONSON ALCOTT WAS IN MANY respects an exception among Emerson's circle of friends. In addition to being a pure autodidact, he was eccentric, penniless, and enthusiastic. He was also known as a tireless teacher, writer, speaker, and especially as a "conversationalist." Alcott spent years of his long life travelling to the West spreading ideas born in New England. He was four years older than Emerson and outlived him by another six. Margaret Fuller, Henry David Thoreau, and many other friends from the Transcendental Club and *The Dial* predeceased him by decades. His life thus spans the whole era during which open-minded New Englanders turned to contemporary European culture and responded to it by applying its ideas to the basis of their new culture.

Alcott was born on November 29, 1799, in the tiny town of Wolcott, Connecticut. He was the eldest of ten children whose father, a farmer, augmented his meager income by producing ploughs, rakes, and brooms. The descendants of English Puritans in the Connecticut villages were strict Congregationalists, with neither time nor money enough to afford a basic education for their children. When the school budget ran dry, they simply closed the town schools. Between the age of six and ten, young Bronson Alcott received very uneven training in reading and writing; he subsequently attended two other village schools for a couple of months, which was an experience that depressed him profoundly.[1] Yet, it is hard to imagine a child who enjoyed learning more than Alcott, practicing his penmanship in the snow or or the floor — a child who, despite backward rural schools, felt impelled to become a teacher himself. This role as educational reformer was ultimately to earn him the epithet of "the American Pestalozzi."

Before reaching this stage, however, Alcott endured difficult times. The strength of his indefatigable optimism helped him survive periods of deep depression. At the age of fifteen he began to work as a peddlar in Massachusetts, expanding his travels to the South until he could finally fulfill his dream of becoming a teacher. In 1823 he passed his qualifying examination and took a post as teacher at a rural Connecticut school.

The changes he introduced in his school room there were revolutionary. They ranged from the elimination of corporal punishment and the arrangement of desks in a circle, to the purchase of a school library out of his own pocket. Pictures decorated the walls of his school room and the instruction was interspersed with dancing and games. The young teacher, who was reading *The American Journal of Education,* discovered to his surprise that his methods corresponded to those of the Swiss reformer Johann Heinrich Pestalozzi. He consequently called his own enterprise "The Cheshire Pestalozzian School."

These innovations met with such suspicion from the local populace that in 1828 Alcott was forced to begin his long odyssey as an educator. Leaving Connecticut for Boston, he opened a school for children in that city. Fearing opposition there as well, Alcott wrote an essay for the *United States Gazette,* which was printed in Philadelphia, thereby smoothing his path to that city. He lived in Philadelphia for three years and founded a school in nearby Germantown.

Alcott's Philadelphia years can actually be viewed as the equivalent of his college education. Running his school in quiet Germantown left enough free time both for his family and for reading in the Philadelphia library. After the birth of the first daughter he started keeping a journal, "Observations of a Child During her First Year," in which he made extensive daily entries. For two weeks after the birth he rarely left the room occupied by mother and infant. The observations Alcott made about infant development supported the educational ideals he had cherished for years and had also been the source of conflict in every conservative community where he had taught. These ideas, on the other hand, also won him new adherents, among them Ralph Waldo Emerson who was ultimately instrumental in bringing him to Concord.

Like Pestalozzi, Alcott believed that man was by nature good and only succumbed to evil through external influences. Education alone, he believed, could protect from evil. In practice, this meant a child's judgment and decision-making energies had to be trained to resist evil. It is not hard to imagine the horror with which the Calvinists reacted to such notions, which even excluded the concept of original sin. On the other hand, one can also understand Alcott's response to the modern authors who believed in the perfectibility of human nature, an idea he had also come to hold during his years in Philadelphia. They were primarily German writers he was reading in translation when he was turning away from English literature and philosophy. English culture he found to be dominated by John Locke's empiricism, a school of thought that interpreted reality as only that which could be perceived by the sense perceptions, simultaneously disavowing the existence of any innate human ideas. On April 22, 1832, Alcott noted in his journal:

> The endeavor to nurse my mind on the literature of England has
> been a great drawback to my spiritual and intellectual growth. Ignorant
> until quite lately of the treasures which lie in Germany, and, from the

want of scholastic education but little acquainted with the lore of the ancients, I have been from infancy plodding my way onward to life and
light, shrouded in the darkened atmosphere of self-ignorance and feeding
my yearning spirit with the godless nutriment of a literature spawned
from the heart of moral disease. I have fed, over-fed, and at last found
that the food cannot fill; it cannot supply the deeper wants of my nature;
it is but children's pap — [. . .], not for the spiritual sustenance; for
body, not for the soul.

Of this truth I am conscious from the perusal of Goethe, Schiller,
Richter, and whatever comes from the higher order of mind in Germany.
All that I have read teems with the spirit of a new life; it comes from the
heart; it does justice to the spirit of man. Far removed is it from the dust
of the earth, from the plodding business of sublunary life; or if it descend
to these it throws around them its own divine light. [. . .] Imagination
and Reason blend in one whole, and the human spirit is led onward by
their mutual aid.[2]

Long complaints follow this declaration as he bemoans the fact that he has
spent years of his life in darkest ignorance. Finding no solace in English
literature, he turned to nature:

at last came the era of meditation, [. . .] Coleridge assisted me in the
beginning, Wordsworth too exerted a genial influence, and by these and
my own innate tendency to pure ideality and a life of intellectual pursuits,
I was led to the full view of things. Herder, Schiller, Richter, Goethe —
and even Bulwer and Carlyle, though Englishmen yet German in education and in spirit — were understood and believed. Before this, however,
[. . .] I had sympathized with the spirit of Plato, perused Plotinus, and
found the depths of Aristotle, Bacon, Locke, and Kant. With these last I
was dissatisfied. They narrowed the range of the human faculties, re-
tarded the progress of discovery by insisting on the supremacy of the
senses, and shut the soul up in the cave of the Understanding.

(*Journals*, 39)

This style shows Bronson Alcott's true intellectual colors, as well as the
sorts of errors he committed when reading. The association of Kant and
Locke was, in fact, a considerable misunderstanding that was unavoidable
for a solitary reader who did not even have an English translation of Kant
at his disposal. His tone is spontaneous, enthusiastic, and stubborn as he
pours a wild stream of metaphors over the page. This was a style that
caused his critics to break into scorn and contempt and even embarrassed
his friends, especially when he gave them copies of his manuscripts to
proofread. "I have read Psyche twice through some pages thrice," Emerson wrote Alcott in June 1838 after being presented with a revised version
of the observations on the development of his baby daughter Ann. Emerson had made extensive comments on this sheaf of pages when he read

them two years earlier. He now adds the comment: "yet [I] am scarcely able to make up my mind on the main question submitted to me — Shall it be published?"[3]

During the years in Philadelphia Alcott read Carlyle's translation of *Wilhelm Meister*. The lack of an English Kant edition necessitated his use of F. A. Nitsch's overview of Kant's philosophy. He also read Herder's *Ideen zur Philosophie der Geschichte der Menscheit* (1799), which had already appeared in English (*Outlines of a Philosophy of the History of Man* [London, 1800]), but Alcott's understanding of the transcendental nature of man was especially reinforced by the utterance in *Wilhelm Meister* about man's capacity to educate himself. Alcott's commonplace book for the period contains extensive notes on his reading, thereby providing a glimpse of his intellectual interests. The neat chapter divisions divide the fruits of his labor into selections of Plato, Dante, Bacon, Berkeley, Shaftesbury, Lamb, Kant, Prince Pückler, Krummacher, and Goethe.[4] Chapter 15 consists of excerpts of *Wilhelm Meister's Apprenticeship* that Alcott compiled as general guidelines for life and human character. The first passage is drawn from the conversation in the first book between Wilhelm and the unnamed man about necessity and freedom:

> The fabric of this world is made of necessity and chance. The *reason* of
> *man* takes its place between them, and may rule them both. Reason
> treats necessity as the reason for its existence; the accidental it can direct,
> guide, and employ for its own purposes. And only while the principle of
> reason stands firm and unshakable, does man deserve to be called a god
> of the earth.[5]

To some extent Alcott notes the same passages that would also strike Emerson who at the time was on his first trip to Europe. A case in point is the passage where Goethe writes "Man is properly the *only* object that interests man."[6] Alcott also copies out the fable of the wanderer who falls into the water not far from his inn, but because he receives no help, struggles to the far side and must make a arduous detour to reach his goal. Goethe recounts this anecdote after Jarno has taken his leave of Wilhelm who would "gladly have spoken at length with him, who (despite his unfriendly manner) gave him new ideas, ideas he needed."[7] Because Alcott lacked such a friend in Germantown and Philadelphia, books had to take his place. His commonplace book also contains passages from Hermann von Pückler-Muskau's *Letters of a German Prince,* a work containing progressive ideas that interested Alcott, such as the opinion that preachers ought to take their sermon texts from other sources than the bible. By far the most complete excerpts in Alcott's commonplace book come from Nitsch's introduction to Kant. Alcott seems to have copied the entire chapter on "Kant's Theoretical Principles," which he then annotated with countless diagrams.

He begins another commonplace book the following year entitled *Aids to Thoughts.* It contains long quotations from the recently published *Characteristics of Goethe,* by Sarah Austin, a work that was shortly thereafter to have a great impact on Margaret Fuller. In the meantime a dearth of students forced Alcott to close his school in Germantown. Undeterred, he soon after opened a second one in Philadelphia. A second daughter, Louisa, was born, and her father devoted a journal to her development.

While Philadelphia offered no permanence, Boston beckoned with prospects of a better teaching position. During a trip to that city Alcott had tried to publish a new edition of Pestalozzi's *Leonhard and Gertrude* in English translation, as well as publish an anthology to include fables by Lessing and Friedrich Adolf Krummacher — texts also available in readers edited by Follen and Bokum. The title was to be "Pictures of Thought" and the introduction was to describe allegories and emblems as spiritual food for the soul. He found no publisher for this project. Instead, in 1836 Alcott was able to acquaint the American reading public with the Heidelberg jurist Friedrich Wilhelm Carové whose tale, *The Story Without an End,* Sarah Austin had translated into English. Carové had written a constitution for the Heidelberg fraternities and had been one of the speakers at the Wartburg, where 500 students from 12 German universities gathered in 1817 to demand reforms and German unification. His short story tells of a child who speaks to flowers, animals, and drops of water and learns from them the secrets of nature. Echoes of Goethe's *Märchen* are unmistakable even before two will-o-the-wisps impart their moral lesson to the child. Alcott's foreword promises that the little work will be especially stimulating for children, its strength being the use of nature imagery as an emblem of their spiritual lives:

> Under the Type of a Child, the Soul communes with the Beautiful in the visible World, quickening whatever it beholds from its own Ideal, thus apprehending its latent faculties, their resurrection from the senses, and final ascension into the Spiritual. It is a revival, in a new form, of the beautiful fable of Psyche.[8]

Alcott's table of contents divides the book into fourteen chapters, each entitled after human characteristics or attributes: "Appetite," "Passion," "Fancy," "Love," "Dislike," "Faith."

Carové's story and Krummacher's fables served Alcott as teaching material in the progressive Temple School that he opened in Boston in 1834. Margaret Fuller contributed her extraordinary foreign language instruction to the undertaking for more than a year. The school even received a visit from Dr. Nikolaus Heinrich Julius who was travelling for the Prussian crown to collect information on America's education systems. Nonetheless, Alcott had to close the Temple School after three years. He published his Socratic dialogues with his pupils under the title *Conversations with Children on the Gospels* (Boston, 1836–1837), a work that was chastised by orthodox educators as pure blasphemy and the work of a madman. It is easy to see how some might take offense at the subject matter of the *Conversations*. Alcott discussed subjects like birth and life after death, and encouraged the children (many of whom were under ten years old) to find symbolic representations of these phenomena in accordance with his precept of "the child as book." After he admitted a black child to his school, enrollment dwindled and Alcott's debts continued to rise. The pupils in the Temple School had come from Boston's best and most enlightened families. A few months after it closed, he founded another, this time a paupers' school, that soon had only five pupils, three of whom were his own daughters.

During the years when Alcott was enduring public derision and personal enmity, his friends in Emerson's Concord circle did not abandon him. Emerson, who not only published open letters in defense of Alcott, frequently also offered financial assistance. James Freeman Clarke raised his voice of support in the pages of *The Western Messenger;* George Ripley and Elizabeth Peabody (Alcott's assistant in the first year of the Temple School) also offered their help.

Alcott found friends in Concord and soon became an important figure among their circle. Although he lacked formal schooling, had not attended Harvard College, had no training in theology, lived with his family of five mostly in rooming houses, and always was in financial difficulty, hardly anyone was able to resist the appeal of his dynamic personality. These Unitarians, the same who had rejected New England Congregationalism and rebelled against Unitarianism itself, admired in Alcott a radical dissident who had turned his back upon all religious affiliation. He did not seek revelation in the writings of Christianity alone, he attended no services, but rather prayed in his own temple of the soul (Dahlstrand, 89). That the soul formed the basis for the entire man, for all his virtues and potential, was an idea that emerged during his years in Philadelphia. Although he had not studied divinity and was not a minister, he was in Emerson's words "a prophet"[9] and was invited to attend the first meeting of the Transcendental Club. Alcott was also an important catalyst for founding *The Dial* and actually is responsible for naming the journal: the sundial signified for him the soul that was an index to the spirit.

Both of Alcott's contributions to *The Dial* were overly rich in enigmatic, symbolic imagery and mystical concepts. These pieces are two groups of fifty "Orphic Sayings," as they were called, published by Margaret Fuller in the first year of the journal's life. The "Orphic Sayings" met, as usual, with rejection, a reaction Emerson had anticipated. He wrote to Margaret Fuller in May 1840:

> One grave thing I have to say, this, namely, that you will not like Alcott's papers; that I do not like them; that Mr. Ripley will not; & yet I think, on the whole, they ought to be printed pretty much as they stand, with his name in full.[10]

The editor followed this advice, finding that Alcott's "'Sayings' are quite grand, though ofttimes too grandiloquent."[11]

In these often puzzling texts Alcott's soul speaks, as it were, in concentrated form. The most important themes of his transcendental message are stated: the heart, i.e., the soul, is the seat of all human energy, while man's likeness is a semblance of the divine. All this is rendered in a language fraught with enthusiasm and pathos. The first "Orphic Saying" begins: "Thou art, my heart, a soul-flower, facing ever and following the motions of thy sun."[12] Enthusiasm itself is extolled as the glory and hope of the world. Man, who is made divine through hope, experiences his own divinity by standing above the senses, the mores and customs. "Men shall become Gods," Alcott declares apodictically. A sampling of his declarations includes: "All life is eternal"; "God, man, nature, are a divine synthesis"; "Man is a rudiment and embryon of God: eternity shall develop in him the divine image." Alcott, the individualist, condemns the rule of the majority:

> In the theocracy of the soul majorities do not rule. God and the saints; against them the rabble of sinners, with clamorous voices and uplifted hand, striving to silence the oracle of the private heart. Beelzebub marshals majorities, [. . .] Multitudes ever lie. [. . .] The voice of the private, not popular heart, is alone authentic.

He continues in the same vein in the 68th saying entitled "Diabolus":

> Seek God in the seclusion of your own soul; the prince of devils in the midst of multitudes. Beelzebub rules masses, God individuals. *Vox populi vox dei,* — never, (save where passion and interest are silent), but *vox populi vox diaboli.*

The following words introduce Alcott's second group of "Orphic Sayings": "The trump of reform *[sic]* is sounding throughout the world for a revolution of all human affairs." It was a revolution the born reformer wanted to be a part of, for his goals were not exclusively for school reform but primarily reform of the entire human being — something he was having difficulty introducing to New Englanders. After the sharp attacks on his *Conversations with Children on the Gospels* and such parodies of his "Orphic Sayings" as "Gastric Sayings" (in the pages of the *Knickerbocker)*, the indefatigable Alcott became an itinerant preacher. The failure was depressing. In one crowd an old man demanded that Alcott be nailed to a cross, whereupon the reformer replied that he was ready any time (Dahlstrand, 186). While such episodes contributed to Alcott's gradually growing sense of hopelessness, the completely impoverished family sought refuge in Concord where Alcott found work as a common laborer. Emerson reported to Carlyle:

> A. Bronson Alcott who is a great man if he cannot write well, has come to Concord with his wife & three children & taken a cottage & an acre of ground to get his living by the help of God & his own spade. I see that some of the Education people in England have a school called "Alcott House," after my friend. At home here, he is despised & rejected of men as much as was ever Pestalozzi.[13]

Progressive educators who were spreading the methods of Pestalozzi in England were actually familiar with the *Records from a School* (1833), which comprised the daily notes Elizabeth Peabody took when she was Alcott's assistant at the Temple School. They invited the American Pestalozzi to their communal school, Concordum, in Ham Common near Richmond (Surrey). Thanks to Emerson's assistance, he was able to make the journey and even able to meet Carlyle while abroad, although this visit, like that of Margaret Fuller's to Carlyle, was destined to fail. For years Emerson had praised Alcott to Carlyle as "a great & one of the jewels we have to show you," as "a majestic soul with whom conversation is possible," and says of him that "since Plato and Plotinus we have not had his like."[14] To Carlyle he seemed more like "a kind of venerable Don Quixote, whom nobody can even laugh at without loving! ," someone who wanted to save the world "by a return to acorns and the golden age."[15] Alcott apparently had no more important topic to discuss with the translator of *Wilhelm Meister* and the biographer of Schiller than the benefits of vegetarianism.[16] For Alcott the reformer, Carlyle the man of letters was dead, for he seemed incapable of believing in the renewal of the world.

Alcott came to see that a renewal, as he envisioned it, was only possible in the new world. Two teachers at Alcott House in England were equally fervent about creating a new social model and joined Alcott on his return trip to Concord in October 1842. They were Charles Lane (who brought his young son), and Henry Gardner Wright. Their baggage contained a library of a thousand books, the property of the founder of Alcott House, James Pierpoint Greaves, a former merchant and adherent of Pestalozzi. These books included almost all the German literature in translation then available to an English-reading public, among them Jakob Böhme, Schlegel's history of philosophy, a selection of Herder, the works of Kant in eight volumes (London, 1836), the letters of Pestalozzi to Greaves, and even a book about Kaspar Hauser.

Yet, the newly-arrived innovators had no time to immerse themselves in German works. A place had to be found for their new life. Once in Concord Alcott introduced his new rules of conduct, which included a vegetarian diet and cold baths. In fact, the regulations were so strict that Wright left the group after a few months. In the spring of 1843 Alcott and Lane found a farmhouse with land in the nearby town of Harvard, and on July 1st a heavily loaded horse cart bearing the Alcotts and the two Lanes made its way toward the most radical communal experiment America had ever known.

From the pen of Louisa May Alcott we have a parodistic treatment of life at "Fruitlands," as her father called the property. She entitled her per-siflage "Transcendental Wild Oats," which echoed the English translation of Jean Paul's novel *Flegeljahre* (Wild Oats). Jean Paul's spirit, and natu-rally that of his English mediator Carlyle in *Sartor Resartus* informs the little tract, which the author (whose fame would ultimately outstrip and outlast her father's) wrote thirty years later. At the time of the Fruitlands experience she was only ten years old.

A. Bronson Alcott, of course, was not the first to experiment with communal living. He could look back on the utopian societies of Robert Owen and on George Ripley's Brook Farm. Alcott's organization of his so-called "Consociate Family" differed in its strict rules of conduct that governed all. As the name Fruitlands suggests, one goal of the farm was to bring forth the fruit of the land; Alcott's extreme vegetarianism forbade the keeping of cattle and even regarded the milking of cows a form of animal exploitation. For similar reasons the members of the community wore no clothing made of leather, wool, or cotton. The stricture against cotton was justified by the argument that it was a crop harvested by slaves. Instead, the inhabitants of Fruitlands wore linen smocks and trousers, straw hats and sandals, with little differentiation in the dress of men and women. Alcott writes "The divine man dwells amidst gardens and or-chards, a grower of plants and fruits; a handler of spades and pruning knives; not a goader nor throttler of oxen, nor strippers of udders nor scavenger of cattle, nor feeder of swine" (Dahlstrand, 196). Alcott's model for this existence was, of course, the biblical image of paradise that he hoped to recreate in New England.

In Louisa's disguised depiction of life in her father's commune, she clearly allies her sympathies with the character of Hope Lamb. Hope is the wife of Abel Lamb who "with the devoutest faith in the high ideal, which was to him a living truth, desired to plant a Paradise, where Beauty, Virtue, Justice, and Love might live happily together, without the possibility of a serpent entering in."[17] Behind the figure of Hope is Alcott's wife Abby, a woman who called herself "ballast for his balloon."[18] She supported all the high-flown plans Bronson Alcott conceived. In the course of her marriage she had to organize fifty moves for her itinerant family, sometimes keeping them financially above water with the meager income from her sewing, or by working as a menial servant at a health spa in Maine. Indeed, she seems to be the only practical member of her family. In Louisa's account Abel Lamb goes forth with Timon Lion (Charles Lane) preaching to attract new converts just at the time when the harvest work fell upon Hope's shoulders:

> About the time the grain was ready to house, some call of the Oversoul wafted all the men away. An easterly storm was coming up and the yellow stacks were sure to be ruined. Then Sister Hope gathered her forces. Three little girls, one boy (Timon's son), and herself, harnessed to clothes-baskets and Russia-linen sheets, were the only teams she could command; but with these poor appliances the indomitable woman got in the grain and saved food for her young, with the instinct and energy of a mother-bird with a brood of hungry nestlings to feed.[19]

The diary entries of ten-year-old Louisa also describe happy times spent with her tutor Lane, reading authors from Plato to Luther and Byron. She also recalled housework, playing in the woods, and the many cold baths that her father espoused in accordance with the German therapist Vincent Priessnitz's cold water cures. The lives of the imaginative and resourceful Alcott children (with the Fruitlands experiment omitted) would later become a classic of juvenile fiction, Louisa's *Little Women* (1868).

Emerson's summer visit to Fruitlands produced a skeptical journal entry: "They look well in July. We will see them in December."[20] And December was in fact the last entire month in the life of the small colony, for Charles Lane left the farmhouse in January to join the Shaker community in Harvard. Alcott, however, could not accept the rule of celibacy that the Shakers observed. The only female member of the community (other than Alcott's wife and daughters) had departed earlier because she had been taken to task for eating a piece of fish as a guest at another house. By the time the Alcotts finally returned to Concord where Emerson helped them to find lodgings, the other members of Fruitlands had scattered. Two of these were Isaac Hecker and Joseph Palmer who had been members of Brook Farm. The Kantian Hecker later became a monk; Palmer, often ridiculed for his long beard, attacked a man with a knife and served a year-long prison term. Then there was Samuel Larned who had lived for a whole year entirely on crackers and another year on apples; and Samuel Bower who used to take moonlight baths walking naked through the nocturnal woods.

This somewhat more detailed summary of a period from the life of members of the Concord circle should serve to illustrate the intellectual and social climate in which German literature found reception in New England — and why this reception could not be anything but limited. A reformer like Bronson Alcott, whose primary goal was at first progress in the field of education, and later the reform of all society, was in no position to devote himself to literary studies, much less to a specialization in German literature. Nonetheless, he was consistently motivated by German writers, although their influence was sometimes second-hand. So it came that in 1848, as he was leading a retired life in Concord cultivating his fruit and vegetable garden, he read *The General Principles of the Philosophy of Nature* by Johann Stallo, a German immigrant who also wrote about Hegel's and Schelling's philosophies of nature.

When Alcott published excerpts of his journals, *Concord Days* (1872), he included a chapter on Goethe, a writer he always returned to. In this piece he calls the poet an observer and master of "this fine law" wherein an author makes suggestions to his readers, leaving them the pleasures and benefits of their own exploration and conclusions. Alcott found in Goethe a mind with the power to read the mysteries of nature. Alcott's enthusiasm carries him and his subject as if on wings:

> Writing faithfully to the form of things, he yet had a finer moral than these could deliver; the vein of quiet mysticism in which he delighted, giving a graceful charm to the writing. How finely his senses symbolized his thought, and his eye how Olympian! He has treated the strife of the Worst for the Best, the problem of evil, more cunningly than any; than Moses; than the author of Job of Uz; than Milton, the Puritan, fitted as he was alike by birth and culture to deal with this world fable, — his faith in nature being so entire, his rare gifts at instant command for rendering perfect copies of what he saw, and loved to represent in its truthfulness to sense and soul alike.[21]

The reference is to the legend of Faust, a figure in whom Alcott sees Goethe personified in all his greatness and faults: his ability to be simultaneously present in the multiplicity of things, but never identifying himself with the whole. "Cunning he was, not wise in the simplicity of wisdom. [. . .] All he was, his Faust celebrates — admitted to heaven, as Goethe to glory, without the fee that opens honestly its gates."[22]

Alcott had even greater difficulty than Margaret Fuller expressing himself clearly in writing and, like her, he balanced this flaw with his talent for intelligent conversation. Encouraged by Emerson, he began to hold his cherished "conversations" in the neighboring towns around Concord and eventually around the state, and finally in other states. All this activity improved his financial position, and in 1857 he received an invitation to St. Louis where the so-called "Hegel School of St. Louis" had formed around the figure of William Torrey Harris. The organization, officially called "The Philosophical Society," drew its members mostly from the ranks of teachers and professors. The most prominent member besides Harris was the Prussian exile and Hegel translator, Henry C. Brokmeyer. This group in St. Louis is a significant barometer for the influence on American intellectual life that emanated from Emerson and his circle. Harris wrote Alcott in his first letter that he had been converted to Idealism by Emerson and also owed both to him and to Thoreau his eternal gratitude. Furthermore, Brokmeyer's first encounter with Hegel had not been in Prussia, but in Henry Hedge's collection, *Prose Writers of Germany* (Philadelphia, 1847).

This comprehensive anthology represented a more ambitious project than the readers compiled by Follen and Bokum for their students. Hedge wanted to collect the highest intellectual achievements of a nation. He chose as his epigraph a quotation by Friedrich H. Jacobi: "The German nation may not be the best educated, nor the richest in terms of its intellectual and artistic production, but it is the most enlightened for it is the most thorough; it is a philosophical nation." For this reason Kant's texts take up the greatest space in the 567-page anthology. Otherwise, a broad spectrum is represented, from Luther to Jakob Böhme to Justus Möser, Lessing, Mendelssohn, Claudius, and Schleiermacher. Hegel's "Introduction to the Philosophy of History" and "Who thinks Abstractly?" were included, as well as excerpts from Goethe's *Elective Affinities,* the chapter "Mignon's Death" from *Wilhelm Meister's Apprenticeship,* and his "Novelle" and "Märchen." There is only one piece by Schiller, "On Naive and Sentimental Poetry," while the Romantics are represented by E. T. A. Hoffmann's "The Golden Pot" and Chamisso's "The Wonderful History of Peter Schlemihl."

Hegel's optimistic philosophy — according to which America represented the next stage in the development of civilization — was eagerly received by the Philosophical Society of Philadelphia. Furthermore, a group of German Hegelians had formed in Cincinnati, among them John Stallo, whose above-mentioned book on natural philosophy certainly influenced Alcott.

When Alcott went to St. Louis in 1858 he was greeted by Harris as the greatest conversationalist since Socrates. But when his conversations sparked little interaction with his audience, he had to resort mostly to monologue. Still, the New England Orpheus later returned to the Hegelians in the Midwest, although he remained troubled by Brokmeyer's faith in reason. "I defend the Heart," said Alcott, "and marry the head and heart in my philosophy" (Dahlstrand, 309).

This philosophy took him across the land, as far west as Iowa, on journeys that sometimes lasted months. The longest of these was a seven-month, 35-city tour, which he undertook at age 81. He would proclaim the transcendental message of Idealism as he spoke of his friends in Concord, of other New England writers, and of his own goals for school reform. He even lectured on the notion of a "new church" in which spontaneity was to replace ritual, conversations sermons, and religious scriptures of all world faiths would be read.

As a result of Alcott's trips west, his connections with the St. Louis group remained the closest. In 1879 the midwest Hegelians and the New England Transcendentalists announced a summer meeting, and with careful planning, the first Concord Summer School for Philosophy and Literature was launched. For a month the price of three dollars per week bought one admission to Orchard House (where the Alcott's had once lived) for the lectures by Alcott, Harris and others. Emerson lectured on "Memory," although his own had become very unreliable during his last years. Nonetheless, he was popular enough to warrant the use of the largest church in Concord for an auditorium.

The topics of the lectures at the first Summer School were quite varied. They included issues like education, public welfare, the art of Albrecht Dürer, and American literature. Harris tried to mediate between religious faith and Hegelian logic; Alcott spoke on personal theism. The 400 participants came from as far away as San Francisco and, all in all, the project was a success. Louisa May Alcott, who always maintained a critical distance from her father's enterprises, wrote in her journal: "The town swarms with budding philosophers, and they roost on our steps like hens waiting for corn. [. . .] If they were philanthropists, I should enjoy it; but speculation seems a waste of time when there is so much real work crying to be done. Why discuss the 'unknowable' till our poor are fed and the wicked saved?"[23]

The Summer School continued the following year. A female patron contributed one thousand dollars for the building of a wooden structure called the "chapel" behind Orchard House that served as a lecture hall. Professors, students, teachers, and ministers used the summer weeks for these intellectual activities. To Alcott's dismay, there was a preponderance of philosophy in the presentations, which he tried to counterbalance with his own talks on the mystics Tauler, Meister Eckart, Jakob Böhme, and Swedenborg. But in the following year Harris gave five lectures on the speculative philosophy of Kant, Fichte, and Hegel. In 1881 and 1882

Kant was the center of the discussion as Concord also celebrated the one-hundredth anniversary of the first publication of "The Critique of Pure Reason." Similarly, Amalia Hathaway gave an introduction to Schopen-hauer. It was the last summer school in which Alcott could actively participate. As always, he held the opening and closing speeches in addition to his own four conversations. In October 1882 he suffered a stroke, and although he lived six more years, he was no longer able to write or engage in public speaking.

The fifth Summer School was devoted completely to "The Genius and Character of Emerson," who had died the previous year. For the first time, this year's lectures were published, preserving several important contributions, among them Harris's essay on the relationship between Emerson, Goethe, and Carlyle. Fifty years had passed since Carlyle had persuaded Emerson to read Goethe, and now Harris's lecture showed that Goethe, as well as Emerson and Carlyle (whose correspondence had just been published) was being read in a very different light. As was to be expected, Harris views Goethe from the Hegelian perspective as a herald of a new stage of human existence in which the individual is seen less as an agent than a product of the institutions he has created. Man may not negate institutions like church and state as does Goethe's Faust, Harris states, nor may he see in them his highest goals, which happens in the second part of *Faust*. Rather, he must finally find his paradise — as does Faust — in selflessness:

> Goethe is the world-poet of this movement. He shows in the Faust that if the individual would find a permanent state of blessedness, and be able to say the happy moment, "Stay, for thou art fair," he must energize not against the institutions of the world, as he does in the first part of the drama. he must find the paradise in altruism.[24]

The age of science had not only dawned, but had brought with it technological progress, which (like Goethe) the Transcendentalists welcomed. One only need recall the paean to the railroad in Thoreau's *Walden*. At the same time the new age brought with it the negative specter of materialism. As if materialism were not all, the newest diabolical manifestation of the scientific age was Darwinism. Alcott crusaded against this scientific movement while Harris used a Goethean metaphor to do the same:

> Refined selfishness, enlightened self-interest, cold, calculating understanding, supreme individualism, is the dry-rot of character; and it is the special form in which the diabolic makes its appearance in the age of science. This is the meaning of Mephistopheles, whose spiritual import is so well expressed by Emerson in his "Representative Men" [. . .] Mephistopheles is the devil that tempts men of culture. Not merely nor chiefly in

sensuous things, but rather in skeptical coldness towards one's fellow-men.[25]

Harris also recognizes what Emerson could not see, namely that Goethe's ideal of education was always subordinate to the ideal of selflessness. If that were not the case, he argues, one could not count him among the four great poets of the world, as Emerson had done. He cites Emerson's poem "Test and Solution" as proof. In "The Test (Musa loquitur)" (referred to in chapter one of this study), the muse asks the reader to find the five poets that have survived five hundred others. "Solution" gives the answer: Homer, Dante, Shakespeare, "the Swede EMANUEL [Swedenborg]," and

> When France, where poet never grew,
> Halved and dealt the globe anew
> GOETHE, raised o'er joy and strife,
> Drew the firm lines of Fate and Life
> And brought Olympian wisdom down
> To court and mart, to gown and town,
> Stooping, his finger wrote in clay,
> The open secret of to-day.[26]

Harris's lecture amplifies themes that were present in the first Summer School five years earlier: Concord showed its colors as a bastion of German-American philosophical Idealism. This was the sentiment that determined the subject for the following year when the eighth Concord Summer School took up the theme "Goethe's Life and Genius." Thirteen of the seventeen lectures were published the following year, again by Franklin Sanborn, under the title *Goethe's Life and Genius*. An impressive group of Goethe authorities assembled in Concord. Among them were contemporaries of Emerson like the eighty-year old Frederick Henry Hedge, as well as a twenty-four year old representative of the next generation, the New York aesthete dilettante William Partridge; the poet John Albee from New Hampshire; the Boston activist Julia Ward Howe; and divers professors, ministers, women as well as men, as they had attended meetings of the Transcendental Club fifty years earlier.

One message that emerges from their lectures is that Europe, Germany, and Weimar had moved closer to these Americans. They were able to inform themselves about the latest publications and other events pertaining to Goethe. Professor W. T. Hewett of Cornell University lectured on "Goethe in Weimar," which, instead of appearing in Sanborn's collection, was printed in a series in *Harpers Magazine* called "Homes of the German Poets." He reported on the founding of the Goethe Society and the Goethe Archive in Weimar and included a useful bibliography of works by and about Goethe. The latter begins with Madame de Staël's *Germany* and includes among the latest publications *Alide: an Episode of Goethe's Life* by Emma Lazarus, as well as Correspondence with Goethe by Catherine E. Goethe, the poet's mother; and Herman Grimm's *Life and Times of Goethe* (1880). From the time of its inception, Hewett reports, *The Journal of Speculative Philosophy,* published thirteen contributions on Goethe.

Although the collection of lectures from this Goethe convention was supposed to focus on Goethe's genius and life, there was only one purely biographical piece, "Goethe's Youth."[27] This lecture by Horatio White, also from Cornell, provided a sympathetic account of his subject. For this critic, Goethe (especially the young Goethe) appears as the forerunner of forces stirring in New England of the 19th century: "Goethe feels the far-reaching, penetrating agitation, and through his soul quiver and thrill the subtle and potent forces which are at work to fashion the coming era."[28] The young Goethe as prophet of the new, is nowhere more clearly indicated than in his language. With the exception of *Werther* — more the character than the entire work — whose "unhealthy sentimentality in place of healthy sentiment is specially repugnant to the present age," White praises all that the young Goethe wrote, quoting letters of the Leipzig student, his essays and reviews in the *Frankfurter Gelehrten Anzeiger,* poems from his Sesenheim period, in order to demonstrate that all that the older poet created was predicted by his youthful writings.

Goethe's genius was treated in lectures about his ideal of self-culture, his titanism, his friendship with Schiller, and relationship to English literature. His thoughts on culture had always interested New Englanders, although this was an aspect of Goethe that was a stumbling block for Emerson who failed to understand it. Margaret Fuller, on the other hand, became New England's authority on Goethe, precisely because she grasped this ideal of education. In 1885 John Albee (previously known only for a volume of poetry) opened the Summer School with a lecture on "Goethe's Self-culture," which explored this aspect of education.[29] He regretted that the ideal of self-culture had been lost in the wake of a misguided drive for innovation. Pragmatic thought of the present demands of man especially that he be useful to others and this can be achieved "only by devotion to one single department." Goethe's strength, on the other hand, lay therein that in his special studies he "stopped at the point where it would be necessary for going on with one to give up all the others." True self-culture, according to Albee's definition, is "all that which cannot be taught, but which every earnest, striving spirit wishes to know and succeeds in knowing through his own power and will and in his own way, — that is, as his genius guides him." One mustn't compare such a person with the autodidact, of these we already have enough and have heard enough. Because Goethe was continually attempting to teach himself, he made such an excellent teacher. "For poets and writers especially, [Goethe was] the most helpful master that has ever lived" because he led his students there where they could continue on their own, until finally having achieved self-reliance, the great ideal of Emerson. Moreover, for this Goethe critic, a new epoch had also begun with the great German poet. In contrast to Shakespeare and the Greek poets, Goethe found his material, his ideas, and poetic impulses in his own experiences, which he didn't hide from his readers. Albee emphasizes, "Goethe wrote in the modern temple, where all the Muses were real women. He transformed them back to their ancient estate. Thus his temple was of glass, so that the transformation could be seen, [. . .] In Goethe's case all is open, all is revealed." The new epoch brings forth new sinners such as Faust and Wilhelm Meister. But, according to Albee, their transgressions aren't truly sins. In their endless search "for wisdom by means of self-cultivation [. . .] they have taken wrong roads." We cannot use old moral standards, because "our age has outgrown the interpretations of the good parish priest" says Albee, thereby trumpeting a fundamental Transcendental belief. "Goethe came, and having first taught and saved himself, in a manner demanded by modern life, he then left us the method and the useful precepts." Wherein, however, does this salvation exist? Not in self-culture for its own sake. "The great human effort and act is renunciation; the final issue, reconciliation. For these self-culture in its broadest meaning is the instrument and preparation, and its purpose justifies its means." This is a wisdom for which we are indebted to "the great intellectual and spiritual physician of mankind."

In contrast to Albee's somewhat poetical remarks, we have Thomas Davidson's on Goethe's titanism. Davidson, a professor from Orange, New Jersey, delivered a lecture with a distinctly scholarly character.[30] He carefully distinguished between the titanism of Kronos and that of Prometheus. Identifying Goethe's titanism with that of Prometheus, Davidson quotes from the Prometheus fragment, finally concluding in the spirit of Alcott, that Goethe's titanism can be explained as a revolt against the gods of tradition and dogma and as an affirmation of the God of one's own heart.[31]

Goethe's life was "a Titanic struggle against the god of the world."[32] But Goethe's god, which is essentially the god of *Faust*, displayed a lack in Davidson's eyes that Emerson had lamented earlier, namely holiness. Because Goethe relied solely upon his own experience, he is incapable of surrendering to what Emerson called "moral sentiment"; neither Goethe nor his readers can tremble before God in *Faust*. Later in life Goethe's titanic struggle was "tamed and soothed."[33] Instead of "Titanic revolution" under the eyes of an authoritative God of absolute truth and absolute law, Goethe's ideal now favors more a quiet evolution that makes him "more desirous of finding a reconciliation between the world-spirit and the supreme inward God." Certainly there was much sympathy for such thinking in Concord. "Only the pure in heart see God," Davidson concludes his lecture, "and for the reason that the heart is the eye wherewith God is seen. [. . .] Goethe struggled manfully during his long life to remove the film from his eye, and obtain a clearer and ever clearer view of the Divine. If he did not at any time entirely succeed, that was his misfortune, in the garb indeed of fortune, rather than his fault."[34]

As the lectures in the Summer School session proclaim, the spirit of Emerson was abroad in Concord. With few exceptions the speakers adopt Emerson's conception of Goethe; only Goethe's idea of self-culture receives a new and more sympathetic interpretation. Margaret Fuller, on the other hand, seems to have been forgotten. How else could the Boston minister Cyrus Bartol have completely ignored her methodological admonition not to play Goethe and Schiller off against each other, but rather to see them as the complimentary friends that they were?[35] Fuller had always warned against a sterile division of readers into the camps of the Goethe admirers and the Schiller adherents. In the case of Bartol, her counsel was in vain. This Goethe enthusiast amassed comparisons between Goethe and Schiller that consistently denigrate Schiller. He presents Goethe as the force that re-created the German language and the German nation, the prophet of Bismarck and Moltke: "Emerson and Darwin are anticipated, exceeded, and included by Goethe." By contrast, Schiller, who thought as a philosopher, emerges as a second-rate writer, whose "philosophy entangles and drowns his Muse":

> Why are the moth and rust at work on compositions which the schoolgirls thirty years ago were mad over, Don Carlos, Marie Stuart, the Robbers, and William Tell, while Wilhelm Meister, Elective Affinities, Hermann and Dorothea, multiply their constituents and strengthen their hold, [. . .] Schiller has fared better than Goethe on the playhouse boards; but the world is the stage on which Goethe's men and women are players of his *dramatis personae*, the scene being life, and society the panorama unrolled.

Not even Schiller's character remains spotless when Bartol presents him as jealous of Goethe in his youth. For Bartol, even the sleepless nights Schiller spent pacing and smoking in his study seem to have left unpleasant traces in his work. He views Goethe, on the other hand, awakened from sound, healthy sleep by "Musagetes, [. . .] the flies that bring the

Muse as they buzz and sting. Schiller thunders and lightens, Goethe brings music and light."

Franklin Benjamin Sanborn, the school commissioner for the town of Concord, was an objective observer of Goethe, as his lecture on Goethe and English literature shows.[36] Sanborn was later the editor of the progressive journal *The Republican* in Springfield, Massachusetts, and as biographer of John Brown, Emerson, Alcott, and Thoreau, was truly someone who cared for and preserved the literary heritage of Concord. His essay does not set out to argue Emerson's dependence upon Goethe, but rather to demonstrate that Emerson came independently to his insights about the unity of nature and the activity of the spirit. Emerson, to be sure, found his ideas reinforced by Goethe and, like Carlyle in Britain, felt compelled to disseminate Goethe's works in the United States.

It is worth noting that Sanborn also emphasizes that Goethe's "modern Satan" had gained importance thanks to the efforts of Emerson and Alcott. Because the founder of the Concord Summer School could no longer participate in the Goethe meetings of 1885, Sanborn therefore lets Alcott speak through his journal passages on the nuances of this modern satan figure, called the "world spirit of the 19th century." Alcott continues, "Our devil has partaken of the cosmopolitan culture; he, too, is a scholar and a gentleman, scarcely distinguishable in a crowd from any mortal else."[37] Alcott regretted that Goethe was born fifty years too soon to see modern western democracy and to describe the Mephisto of the United States. The statesman Daniel Webster, whose support of the Fugitive Slave Law angered Alcott, embodied for him the essence of this character. Goethe's devil "is a friend in the guise of an enemy. We need him to measure our strength and weakness, to prove our virtue. Life, for the most part, is a contest, a devil's duel."[38]

With one other exception, Sanborn was the only speaker that summer to broach the subject that New Englanders often discussed in relation to Goethe, namely "the sexual morality which Goethe at all times considered too lightly, and in his youth and middle life so habitually transgressed." Sanborn notes this aspect with wise foresight and traces the moral deficiency in part back to Goethe's nature, in part to the French, Latin, and Greek writers he read as a youth instead of attending to preferable English and German authors.

Very few individual works of Goethe except the most familiar to American audiences were discussed in the summer school lectures: *Wilhelm Meister's Apprenticeship, Elective Affinities,* the *Märchen,* and *Faust.* William Partridge provided an overview of Goethe's dramatic production.[39] His reactions are not atypical for the entire American reading public, although his estimation of Götz von Berlichingen is higher than that of many readers who had no understanding of the Middle Ages. Partridge suggested that the drama was written during a period when Goethe was under the spell of Shakespeare, but as yet had not developed his own drama theory. Therein lie the flaws and merits of the piece as he saw it: "For so strong in all Germans is the tendency to work according to rules," says Partridge, echoing Mme. de Staël, "that Goethe could hardly have failed to be injured in his work by any such restrictions."[40]

Was Goethe a great dramatist? Partridge's answer is no, and he characterizes the Germans generally as a people lacking a sense of the stage. Schiller, Lessing, and Iffland are superior dramatists to Goethe, while he is superior in the epic genre, an argument Partridge defends by pointing to *Hermann and Dorothea*, which was Goethe's most successful work throughout the United States and the world.

Neither the lecture by Denton Snider, a member of the Cincinnati Hegel group, on "Wilhelm Meister as a Whole," nor William Harris's on the novellas in the same work, were incorporated in the book of printed essays. But the lecture by Harris's pupil S. H. Emery on *Elective Affinities* was published.[41] He makes a case for the work from the aspect of the novel genre, which is "better adapted to a prosaic age and nation. The wider range of incident and more minute analysis of character are more in accordance with the disposition and taste of a highly civilized people."[42] Emery does not seem to expect any knowledge of Hegel's concept of love in the "Chivalry" chapter of his *Aesthetik*. This, Emery says, shows the limits of the kind of love that is the principle force in Goethe's novel, which provides a way to understand "the ethical validity of Goethe's treatment of the situation, [. . .] The obstinacy with which the lover insists that only the one particular individual he has selected can possibly meet the requirements of his nature, lays the foundation for distressing collisions."[43]

Emery responds to American attacks upon *Elective Affinities*. To emphasize the "profoundly moral content" of the novel he invokes Solger, Rosenkrantz, Düntzer, and Herman Grimm as German voices of affirmation; and from the American side, Caroline Sherman, who had lectured the day before on "Child Life as Portrayed by Goethe." Even the two lectures on *Faust* reflected Idealist philosophy. Denton Snider's examination, "The History of the Faust Poem,"[44] included a thorough display of his knowledge of Schelling's and Hegel's *Faust* criticism, whereby his own preference for Schelling is quite clear. He follows his philosophical observations with the historical comments of Kuno Fischer, which give a detailed history of the evolution of the Faust drama. Finally, William Harris offers his Faust interpretation.[45] Following Concord tradition, he ranks his poet the fourth world poet after Homer, Dante, and Shakespeare whereby

Goethe is not so interested in the deeds of the individual nor the effect or institutional reactions of an individual's actions, but rather in the formation of his character.

Harris finds in Faust a seeker of the absolute whose quest he interprets in the context of world events, especially those in French history. "Thus, while the historical process went on in France, as an external phenomenon with deafening explosions, in the still world of German thought there went on a corresponding theoretical process, which more swiftly reached the positive solution."[46] Harris is referring here to Kant's *Critique of Pure Reason,* which had been published eight years before the storming of the Bastille, while his *Critique of Practical Reason* appeared just a year before. "In the world of literature a new world-poet had been born, who was to devote his entire life to the same problem, and to leave its solution in great works of art."[47]

This lecture shows Harris to a great extent as the mouthpiece of his friend Brokmeyer from the Philosophical Society in St. Louis. This debt is clear from his liberal use of quotations from Brokmeyer's partially unpublished "Letters on Faust." He even takes the general structure of his lecture from Brokmeyer's third letter:

> For it is the self-consciousness of that individual, nation, or age in direct conflict with itself, — or with this or that particularity of itself, but with its entire content *in the sphere of manifestation,* [. . .] with the receptivity for, the production of, and the aspiration after the Beautiful, the Good, the True, within the individual himself; *in the sphere of realization* with the family, with society, and with the State; and finally *in the sphere of actuality* with art, religion, and philosophy.[48]

This generalization permits Harris to see Faust in collision with all phenomena of social upheaval, be it the French Revolution, the American War of Independence, the Napoleonic Wars, the Industrial Revolution, innovations in art and modern literature, and the natural sciences. "All these and their like are intimately concerned with Mephistopheles and the victory over him,"[49] says Harris, who even finds Hegelian optimism in Mephistopheles' downfall and in Faust's gradual development from rebel to continued participation in the civilization of one's age — an example of thoroughly positive citizenship." Thus, with the help of Goethe's *Faust,* Harris successfully reconciles Hegel's philosophy with Christianity, thereby making the Concord Summer School a place of mediation between modern thought of the old world and traditional beliefs of the new.

Henry Hedge's lecture on Goethe's *Märchen,* a text he had included in his monumental anthology of German literature, also exploits American knowledge and approval of recent developments in Europe.[50] At the time, the German Empire had been in existence for fourteen years and was growing in power. This political development had consequences for the intellectual life of the nation as shown by changes Hedge perceived in the distinctly nationalistic German interpretations of Goethe after 1871. There was, furthermore, a tendency among many members of the Concord group to force allegorical or emblematic interpretations upon nature and literature.

Hedge uses his lecture as an opportunity to disparage Wolfgang Menzel, a critic whose unpopular opinions of Goethe had first emerged with Margaret Fuller's objections. "Menzel wrote," notes Hedge with satisfaction, "'Mark my words; in twenty, or, at the longest, thirty years, he [Goethe] will hot have an admirer left; no one will read him.' Well, near sixty years have elapsed, and here we are, on the other side of the globe, devoting these summer days to the reverent consideration of the man and his works."[51]

Hedge's interpretation of Goethe's *Märchen* cites Hermann Baumgart's essay of 1875, "Goethes Märchen: ein politisch-nationales Glaubensbekenntnis," according to which poetry provides a prophetic vision and allegorical indication of Germany's future. According to Baumgart and Hedge, Goethe's *Märchen* had predicted the fall of the Holy Roman Empire and the resurgence of Germany. All characters, aspects, and events in the text are forced to fit this reductive system so that by the end of the *Märchen,* the reader is urged to see that Goethe's prophecies have come true:

> The Genius of Germany is no longer a sighing, sickly youth, pining after the unattainable, but, having married his ideal, is now embodied in the mighty Chancellor whose state-craft founded the new Empire, and whose word is a power among the nations.[52]

The Concord Summer School would not have spread much of the spirit of Emerson, Alcott, and their friends if women had not also stood at the podium. Three delivered lectures on themes that specifically concerned women. Caroline Sherman from Chicago spoke on Goethe's images of children.[53] Goethe had said that "what in us women leave uncultivated, *children* cultivate when we retain them near us."[54] Children's roles comprise a significant portion of the whole of *Wilhelm Meister,* and Goethe devotes himself to their interests and feelings, according to Sherman, "with an enthusiasm worthy of Frederick Froebel."[55]

Ednah Cheney, friend of the Alcott family and biographer of Louisa May Alcott, lectured on "Das Ewig-Weibliche" (the Eternal-Feminine), a demanding intellectual exercise.[56] She reads the final words of the first part of *Faust* as Goethe's most important utterance, the pinnacle of his thought and the sum of his experience ("The Eternal-Feminine draws us upward"). But why does he use the formula *das Ewig-Weibliche?* The expression is for Cheney "the supreme abstract idea of womanhood." She reveals how this idea appears in the various female figures in Goethe's works. Nowhere does she find it better represented than in Goethe's review of the "Poems by a Polish Jew" in the pages of the *Frankfurter Gelehrten-Anzeiger.* In that piece Goethe wished for the young poet a girl

> whose soul, all goodness in a form of pure grace, has ripened happily in the quiet family circle of domestic, active love; she is one who is beloved, friend, support of her mother, the second mother of her house; a girl whose ever compassionate soul irresistibly attracts every heart to it; one from whom poets and wise men willingly learned and with delight recognized inborn virtue, inherent abundance and grace.[57]

All of Goethe's female characters, Mrs. Cheney argues, follow the laws of their own nature and exert their influence on others through their strength of character and will-power. The relations they have with men are those of free and independent people, a situation that is possible only because the natures of men and women are not radically different from each other.

This was an idea that was important to Margaret Fuller and not alien to Bronson Alcott. Fuller felt the division of the human race into two sexes as a burden. Writing about the relationship between Mme. Récamier and Mme. de Staël, she wrote in her journal: "It is so true that a woman may be in love with a woman, and a man with a man. I like to be sure of it, for it is the same love which angels felt, where 'Sie fragen nicht nach Mann und Weib.'"[58]

In 1850 when Ednah Dow Littlehale (later the wife of the artist Seth Cheney) lectured at the Summer School, Alcott noted in his journal:

> The company of intellectual women has a certain freshness and zest one seldom tastes from intercourse with cultivated men. Sexual qualities seem as needful to the propagation of thought as of human beings, nor do I like any man who never reminds me of the graces proper to women. It is these qualities that we love in a friend. The best of Emerson's intellect comes out in its feminine traits, and were he not as stimulating to me as a woman, and as racy, I should not care to see and know him intimately nor often.[59]

Ednah Cheney takes up this point, finding in the highest human types an admixture of characteristics of both sexes. She finds, for example, distinct feminine traits combined with masculine strength in Jesus, Buddha, Dürer, Michelangelo, and Dante. The same applied to the biblical figure of Deborah, to Joan of Arc, Isabella of Castile, and Margaret Fuller. For the memorial celebration of Fuller's sixtieth birthday at the Boston

Women's Club in 1870, Alcott wrote that with her male intellect and female heart, Fuller came close to the ideal of womanhood. Mrs. Cheney notes that one could find the "boy-girl girl-boy in almost every family," which doubtless reminded her listeners of Jo March in Louisa May Alcott's *Little Women*. Cheney quotes the "Fair Saint" (Cheney's term for the "Beautiful Soul") in *Wilhelm Meister* when she says, "The father of the Fair Saint 'often with suppressed joy called her his misfashioned son.'"[60]

Ednah Cheney asserts that one cannot differentiate between the intellectual lives of the sexes. The examples she gives span a gallery of creative women from George Sand, George Eliot, through Karoline von Lengefeld (whose *Agnes von Lilien* the critics in Jena mistook for the work of Goethe), to the poems by Marianne von Willemer in the *West-östlicher Diwan*. The American women's movement, then, with its roots deep in the nineteenth century, drew upon important ideals from German literature through the person of Margaret Fuller. Ednah Cheney is an example that this impulse continues in the generation following Fuller.

The last speaker in the Concord Summer School was Julia Ward Howe who used her lecture on "Goethe's Women" as an opportunity to make a political statement:

> I had my Goethe-time long ago, when as a girl I read "Faust," "Götz von Berlichingen," and others of the plays, and when, a young mother, I quieted a baby with one hand, while the other turned over the pages of "Wilhelm Meister" [. . .] I, too, who once adored the Teuton rule, do so no longer. Heaven forbid that my grandchildren should be fed upon the tonic of "blood and iron"! Give me American rule, American training, with its lapses even and its faults. For, though Germany did wonderfully take the lead in critical thought during the first half of this century, when the moment came for liberal action, she shrank away, and lost the world's leadership, and will never regain it. And how did her Nemesis, Bismarck, obtain the mastery over her daring thought and unrepentant speculation? Let me grimly parody, in reply, a line of Robert Browning: "Just for a handful of silver he had us;/Just for a ribbon to stick on our coat."[61]

These harsh words are from the ardent poet, pacifist, suffragette, and author of the first book on Margaret Fuller. Her writings included poems (she is best known for the text of "The Battle Hymn of the Republic"), as well as travel accounts of Cuba and Europe. In 1870 she was a driving force in the women's movement, and a co-organizer of the first women's conference in Seneca Falls, New York. A concrete result of the New York meeting was the creation of the American branch of Women's International Peace Association. After clearing the air with her indictment of militarism in modern Germany, Howe came to her actual subject, which she clearly presents as a return to an earlier time of "social and literary glories which once illuminated two hemispheres from the narrow heaven of a small German principality."[62]

Julia Ward Howe displayed the sort of learning in European, and specifically German matters, that New Englanders had appropriated in the last decades. As Margaret Fuller had done earlier in her "Great Lawsuit," Howe's lecture on Goethe's women describes the female members of his family. It is remarkable to follow Howe's characterization of Goethe's mother as "bürgerlich." She explains this difficult cultural concept to her listeners. The German lies somewhere between Moliere's gently sarcastic "bourgeois" and the English status concept of "upper class," whom Howe describes as someone "who could lend the Court money, but who would not borrow manners from it."[63]

In the series of "lady-loves" of Goethe, which she presents very tastefully, Marianne von Willemer is curiously absent. For this reader Gretchen from *Faust* is Goethe's most overpowering female character. For her Mariane and Philine from *Wilhelm Meister* are ill-bred women "which no one would dare to present in English literature so badly as Goethe has presented them in the phraseology of his mother tongue."[64] She ultimately explains Goethe's weaknesses in light of Christian *caritas,* viewing him as a man for whom there was nothing common, nothing hopelessly impure, a man whose profound Christian convictions led him to proclaim the unity of faith, hope, and love. Thus, a lecture that had begun so critically ended on a note of reconciliation, which as far we know, preserved the atmosphere of harmony that had prevailed at the Concord Goethe meetings.

And yet, no participant demonstrated better than Julia Ward Howe how much the fifty years since Emerson had settled in Concord had changed both New England and Germany. All participants shared this awareness. Most, Henry Hedge being the prime example, regarded the changes in Germany as positive; even Emerson himself congratulated Herman Grimm on Prussia's defeat of France in 1871. But astute younger participants such as Julia Ward Howe came to different conclusions. Their responses make it apparent that the influence of German literature, including Goethe, was changing by the summer of 1885. If one compares the scholarly lectures of the Summer School to the letters that Margaret Fuller exchanged with her cousin James Freeman Clarke, Emerson's journals, or the first articles in *The Dial,* the youthful elan of the early reception is missing. German literature and Goethe had at last become academic subjects.

Notes

[1]   See Frederick C. Dahlstrand, *Amos Bronson Alcott: An Intellectual Biography* (Fairleigh Dickinson UP, 1982), 17–35. Cited in the text as Dahlstrand.

[2]   Amos Bronson Alcott, *The Journals of Amos Bronson Alcott,* ed. Odell Shepard, (Boston: Little, Brown, 1938), 38ff. Cited in text as *Journals.*

[3]   Ralph Waldo Emerson, *Letters,* 2:138.

[4]   Amos Bronson Alcott, *Readings 1833* (Houghton Library, Harvard University).

[5]   *Hamburger Ausgabe,* 7:71.

[6]   *Hamburger Ausgabe,* 7:101

[7]   *Hamburger Ausgabe,* 7:180.

[8]   *The Story Without an End;* Translated from the German of F. W. Carové by Sarah Austin, with a Preface and Key to the Emblems by A. Bronson Alcott (Boston, New York: Joseph H. Francis; Charles S. Francis, 1836), iii.

[9]   Ralph Waldo Emerson, *Letters,* 2:294.

[10]   *Ibid.*

[11]   Margaret Fuller, *Letters,* 2:135.

[12]   *Orphic Sayings* (Mt. Vernon, NY: The Golden Eagle Press, 1939), 3. The following sayings are from this source, pp. 3–27 *passim.*

[13]   *The Correspondence of Emerson and Carlyle,* 269.

[14]   *The Correspondence of Emerson and Carlyle,* 163; 218; 322.

[15]   *The Correspondence of Emerson and Carlyle,* 163; 326.

[16]   *Ibid.*

[17]   Louisa May Alcott, *Transcendental Wild Oats and Excepts from the Fruitlands Diary,* Ed. William Henry Harrison (Harvard, MA: The Harvard Common Press, 1975), 13. For a contradictory account, see Richard Francis, "Circumstances and Salvation: The Ideology of the Fruitlands Utopia," *American Quarterly,* 25 (1973), 202–234.

[18]   *Transcendental Wild Oats,* 22.

[19]   *Transcendental Wild Oats,* 25–26.

[20]   Ralph Waldo Emerson, *Journals,* 8:433.

[21]   Amos Bronson Alcott, *Concord Days* (Boston: Roberts Brothers, 1872), 158.

[22]   *Concord Days,* 159.

[23]   *Louisa May Alcott, Her Life, Letters and Journals,* Ed. Ednah D. Cheney (Boston: Little, Brown & Co., 1905), 321.

[24] William T. Harris, "Emerson's Relations to Goethe and Carlyle," in *Genius and Character of Emerson,* 390.

[25] *William T. Harris, "Emerson's Relations to Goethe and Carlyle,"* 393–394.

[26] Ralph Waldo Emerson, *Poems,* Centenary Edition, (Boston, New York: Houghton Mifflin, n.d.), 9:223.

[27] Horatio S. White, "Goethe's Youth," in *The Life and Genius of Goethe: Lectures at the Concord Summer School of Philosophy,* ed. Franklin B. Sanborn (Boston: Ticknor & Co., 1886), 1–36.

[28] Horatio S. White, "Goethe's Youth," 28.

[29] John Albee, "Goethe's Self-Culture," in *The Life and Genius of Goethe,* 37–68. The following section quotes and paraphrases from this essay.

[30] Thomas Davidson, "Goethe's Titanism," in *The Life and Genius of Goethe,* 68–106.

[31] Thomas Davidson, "Goethe's Titanism," 79.

[32] Thomas Davidson, "Goethe's Titanism," 92.

[33] Thomas Davidson, "Goethe's Titanism," 92.

[34] Thomas Davidson, "Goethe's Titanism," 102.

[35] Cyrus Bartol, "Goethe and Schiller," in *The Life and Genius of Goethe,* 107–134. All references to this essay, *passim.*

[36] Franklin B. Sanborn, "Goethe's Relation to English Literature," in *The Life and Genius of Goethe,* 157–188.

[37] Franklin B. Sanborn, "Goethe's Relation to English Literature," 173.

[38] Franklin B. Sanborn, "Goethe's Relation to English Literature," 176.

[39] William D. Partridge, "Goethe as a Playwright," in *The Life and Genius of Goethe,* 189–217.

[40] *Ibid.,* 202.

[41] S. H. Emery, Jr., "The Elective Affinities," in *The Life and Genius of Goethe,* 251–289.

[42] S. H. Emery, Jr., "The Elective Affinities," 254.

[43] S. H. Emery, Jr., "The Elective Affinities," 281–282.

[44] Denton J. Snider, "The History of the Faust Poem," in *The Life and Genius of Goethe,* 313–344.

[45] Denton J. Snider, "Goethe's Faust," in *The Life and Genius of Goethe,* 368–445.

[46] Denton J. Snider, "Goethe's Faust," 382.

[47] *Ibid.*

[48] Denton J. Snider, "Goethe's Faust," 389.

[49] Denton J. Snider, "Goethe's Faust," 425.

[50]   Frederic Henry Hedge, "Goethe's Märchen," in *The Life and Genius of Goethe,* 135–156.

[51]   *Ibid.,* 137.

[52]   *Ibid.,* 156.

[53]   Caroline Sherman, "Child Life as Portrayed by Goethe," in *The Life and Genius of Goethe,* 290–312.

[54]   Caroline Sherman, "Child Life as Portrayed by Goethe," 296.

[55]   Caroline Sherman, "Child Life as Portrayed by Goethe," 299.

[56]   Ednah D. Cheney, "Das Ewig-Weibliche," in *The Life and Genius of Goethe,* 218–250.

[57]   *Goethes Werke,* herausgegeben im Auftrag der Grossherzogin Sophie von Sachsen (Weimar: H. Böhlau, 1896), 37: 224.

[58]   "They do not ask whether man or woman." Margaret Fuller, *Memoirs,* 1:283.

[59]   *The Journals of Amos Bronson Alcott,* 221.

[60]   *Hamburger Ausgabe,* 7:360; Ednah D. Cheney, "Das Ewig-Weibliche," 231.

[61]   Julia Ward Howe, "Goethe's Women," in *The Life and Genius of Goethe,* 345–346.

[62]   Julia Ward Howe, "Goethe's Women," 346.

[63]   Julia Ward Howe, "Goethe's Women," 347.

[64]   Julia Ward Howe, "Goethe's Women," 353.

Louisa May Alcott
Courtesy of Concord Free Public Library

5: The Pragmatist: Louisa May Alcott

IF EVER THERE WAS A FIGURE IN AMERICAN literature who could have inherited the legacy of the Concord circle, it was Louisa May Alcott. Born in Philadelphia on her father's thirty-third birthday, she spent most of her life by her father's side, surviving him by only two days. She and her three sisters grew up in the transcendental atmosphere of Boston, Concord, and the various New England towns where their father's calling led them.

Bronson Alcott's daughters enjoyed an abundance of talent and imagination: they wrote poetry (as did so many in the Concord circle), painted, and put on dramatic performances. Of the two younger sisters, Elizabeth, died at age twenty-two of tuberculosis. May became a successful painter who travelled frequently to Europe where she studied art and exhibited her work in Paris in 1877. She married a Swiss merchant, but died after the birth of their first child, a girl whom Louisa for a time brought up in the United States. The oldest Alcott sister, Anna, was left a widow with two sons at an early age. This unhappy series of family circumstances furnished Louisa with important formative experiences for her literary development.

The Alcott children were raised in material poverty and intellectual wealth. As daughters of the man known as the American Pestalozzi, they were under the watchful eye of the pedagogue Alcott from the moment they saw the light of day. He gave them lessons in the house and garden and, as soon as they reached school age, included them in his progressive classrooms. For Christmas and birthdays the Alcott parents presented their children with poems, illustrated epigrams, and letters. These were exchanged throughout the year; in Fruitlands, however, they became a daily ritual. The notes were put into a special post-box for such correspondence and then read aloud in the evenings. In addition, family members kept journals, those of the children also being accessible to their parents.

Louisa and her sisters certainly knew their father's friends from the Transcendental circle. Margaret Fuller, who often recalled the happy company, viewed the Alcott children as the embodiment of a youth she had never had. When Louisa attended school in Concord for a time, she encountered Henry David Thoreau for a teacher. The eccentric loner left a deep impression upon her and more than once appears disguised in her novels.

But it was Emerson who exerted the most significant influence on Louisa. When the Alcott family moved to Concord after the Fruitlands disaster, his presence became quite perceptible. About this formative phase in her life she later wrote:

> My romantic period began at fifteen, when I fell to writing poetry, keeping a heart-journal, and wandering by moonlight instead of sleeping quietly. About that time, in browsing over Mr. Emerson's library, I found Goethe's "Correspondence with a Child," and at once was fired with a desire to be a Bettine, making my father's friend my Goethe. So I wrote letters to him, but never sent them; sat in a tall cherry-tree at midnight, singing to the moon till the owls scared me to bed; left wild flowers on the doorstep of my "Master," and sung Mignon's song under his window in very bad German.
>
> Not till many years later did I tell *my* Goethe of this early romance and the part he played in it. He was much amused, and begged for his letters, kindly saying he felt honored to be so worshipped. The letters were burnt long ago, but Emerson remained my "Master" while he lived, doing more for me, — as for many another, — than he knew.[1]

Ednah Cheney added her editor's comment on Bettine von Arnim's *Correspondence:*

> It may be difficult for readers of to-day to understand the fascination which this book exercised upon young minds of the last generation, yet it is certain that it led more than one young girl to form an ideal attachment to a man far older than herself, but full of nobility and intellectual greatness. Theodore Parker said of letters addressed to him by a young New Hampshire girl, "They are as good as Bettine's without the lies." This mingling of idealism and hero-worship was strongly characteristic of that transcendental period when women, having little solid education and less industrial employment, were full of noble aspirations and longings for fuller and freer life, which must find expression in some way.
>
> (Cheney, 58–59)

When she turned seventeen Louisa started writing a new journal, which she entitled "The Sentimental Phase." During this time in her life she immersed herself in Goethe's works. Emerson, who lent her *Wilhelm Meister,* was again the mediator of this formative intellectual experience. The result, as she recorded, was that "from that day Goethe has been my chief idol" (Cheney, 48). At the age of twenty Louisa swore an oath to read henceforth fewer novels and to concentrate on what she called "the best books." Her list of favorite works and authors included Carlyle, Goethe (poetry, drama, and novels), Schiller's dramas, Bettine, Plutarch, *Uncle Tom's Cabin,* and Emerson's poems (Cheney, 68).

Louisa's time had to be divided between housekeeping and contributing to the family income. As she wrote herself, "I was born with a boy's spirit under my bib and tucker. I *can't wait* when I *can work;* so I took my little talent in my hand and forced the world again, braver than before and wiser for my failures" (Cheney, 85). She would have preferred to become an actress. As a child she had written plays, which she performed with her sisters, and later she enjoyed acting in amateur performances in Boston and in the country. This daughter of the American Pestalozzi even tried her hand as teacher, without finding much satisfaction in that calling. Sewing offered some small financial rewards: twelve pillowcases, twelve sheets, six neckties, and two dozen handkerchiefs brought in four dollars. "But," she noted, "I can plan my stories while I work, and then scribble 'em down on Sundays" (Cheney, 84).

Louisa May Alcott's "little talent," as she put it, lay in storytelling. When she was sixteen she wrote a series of tales for Emerson's daughter Ellen, which were published (along with several poems) six years later under the title *Flower Fables.* These pieces, inspired by Carové's *The Story Without an End,* were well received, but Louisa soon turned from fairytale material to contemporary themes. These she treated in short stories that found eager publishers like the *Courier* and *Atlantic Monthly* in Boston, or *Frank Leslie's Illustrated Newspaper* in New York — journals that catered to the instruction and entertainment of a large reading public. Louisa perceived the opportunity not only to free herself from poverty — which no Alcott had ever been able to do before — but also to help her needy family. She felt she had to rescue her youngest sister, who always wore the older girls' hand-me-downs, and particularly Betty whose declining health incurred ever higher doctors' bills over the years. The financial woes of the family are captured in a vignette from Louisa's journal where she describes Bronson's return home after one of his lecture tours. Hungry, tired, and half frozen he arrived in the middle of the night to be embraced by "five white figures" who warmed and fed him. When the youngest finally asked, "Well, did people pay you?", their father responded by pulling out a dollar bill from his pocket, with a smile "that made [their] eyes fill." He explained: "My overcoat was stolen, and I had to buy a shawl" (Cheney, 69–70). Such experiences turned Louisa May Alcott into a pragmatist who could say, "Goethe puts his joys and sorrows into poems; I turn my adventures into bread and butter" (Cheney, 262).

Her productivity was extraordinary, drawing as she did on her own experiences of New England life and of her own family as the basis for many of her stories. But her breakthrough came from the book *Hospital Sketches* (1863), which are accounts based on her nursing experiences in a Washington military hospital during the Civil War. She worked with the wounded and dying soldiers for six weeks until she literally collapsed from fatigue. "I was never ill before this time, and never well afterward" (Cheney, 137).

The Alcotts' material fortunes changed with the success of Louisa's sensational tales that she produced in great number during the 1860s. When a two-volume edition of these thrillers — which she called "blood and thunder tales" — appeared in 1975, many disappointed readers of *Little Women* felt their ideal image of a writer of juvenile fiction had been destroyed.[2] These stories were either published anonymously or under the pseudonym A. M. Barnard. The tales had titles like "Pauline's Passion and Punishment," "A Woman's Power," "The Abbot's Ghost, or, Maurice Treherne's Temptation," and are set in the exotic jungles of Cuba or in crumbling English abbeys where *femmes fatales* work their mischief and experiments with hashish receive harsh punishment.

But stories in this vein did not satisfy their author. Setting her intellectual sights higher, she wrote her first novel — one that represented a summation of her intellectual experience. *Moods* (1864) is clearly a piece of juvenilia, but despite the implausible plot and unnatural dialogues, the book conveys the impression of the talent behind it, which even the 23-year-old Henry James had to admit in his otherwise sharply critical remarks in the *North American Review*: "With the exception of two or three celebrated names, we know not, indeed, to whom, in this country, unless to Miss Alcott, we are to look for a novel above the average."[3]

Moods is the story of 17-year-old Sylvia Yule who must choose between two men. Although she loves the independent free-thinker Adam Warwick, she follows a mood and chooses the domestic aesthete, Geoffrey Moor. When she reveals to her husband her true feelings for Warwick, he is no longer able to live with her. He leaves for Europe — with Warwick as travelling companion no less — where, fighting for Garibaldi in the Italian war of independence, Warwick single-handedly saves an entire village. When Sylvia calls for her husband, he returns with Warwick to America after half a year. Shortly before landing, their ship is wrecked and Warwick sacrifices his life for Moor, not suspecting that Sylvia is mortally ill.

The novel understandably aroused considerable surprise, which was albeit minimal compared to what was to confront readers of the second, revised version. In her reworking of *Moods,* Alcott eliminated the motivation for Warwick's hesitation toward his beloved Sylvia by leaving out the Cuban beauty Ottila, to whom he is engaged but wishes to leave. Nor does Sylvia die in the second version, but is instead reunited with Moor to begin a new life built this time not upon moods, but principles. Furthermore, the second version also contains all the material that Alcott had omitted from her first version at the behest of her publisher who insisted on a dramatic plot. These details included passages in which Alcott paid homage to her masters Goethe, Thoreau, Emerson, and Bettine. In 1882, when the famous author of *Little Women* returned to her earlier work *Moods,* nobody dictated literary form to her, and she restored the cuts.[4]

One of these textual restorations presents the following episode in the revised novel: Sylvia, who lives with her family in the house beside Geoffrey Moor, purloins a copy of *Wilhelm Meister* from his library. When Moor asks her why she has taken this of all books, she responds with words the 17-year Louisa May might have used to answer Ralph Waldo Emerson: "I heard some people talking about 'Mignon,' and I wanted to know who she was."[5] When she finds the other volumes in a special bookcase of favorite authors, her eye falls upon a portrait. This exchange between Sylvia and Moor follows:

> Please tell me who that is? It looks like Jove, but has not eagle nor thunderbolts.
> That is a modern Jove, the writer of the book you like so well, Goethe.
> What a splendid head! I wish he lived now, I would so love to see and know him. I always envied Bettina and longed to be in her place. People nowadays are so unheroic and disappointing, even the famous ones.
> I can show you a man who resembles this magnificent old fellow very much. He is not so great a genius, but sufficiently "many-sided" to astonish and perplex his friends as much as young Wolfgang did his during the "storm and stress period." I hope to see him here before long, and I am sure you will not find him unheroic, though he may be disappointing.
> (*Moods,* 233)

Warwick appears to Sylvia as a hero at his first entrance. He rescues her from a rock in the sea near her house where she has climbed to sing undisturbed her song that is "Ariel's dirge mingled with the Lorelei's song" (*Moods,* 235). Endangered by the advancing tide, she soon finds herself in the strong arms of an unknown man, carrying her through the water with the warning, "Next time you play Undine have a boat near, for there may be no Kuhlborn at hand to save you" (*Moods,* 237) — evidence that he too has read Fouqué's *Undine.*

Adam Warwick is generally seen to be a disguised portrait of Henry David Thoreau, an identity that is supported by the character's love of nature and his unconventional mode of expression. Warwick speaks his mind with a disarming directness, without thought of whether his candor injures his listeners. He lacks the polite conventions that Victorian society of New England relied upon. He is a connoisseur of people, nature, and literature. One evening Sylvia and her friends play a game of characterizing each other as familiar books. Warwick reminds her of *Sartor Resartus,* "a fine mixture of truth, satire, wisdom, and oddity," which amuses Warwick who knows the author Carlyle personally. His report pleases Sylvia "for she was a hero-worshipper and loved to find new gods to look up to and love." When she asks Warwick which book she is, he names Carové's *The Story Without an End,* to which Sylvia responds like the true creation of an Alcott daughter: "I wish I might be as lovely, innocent, and true as that is" (*Moods,* 241–242).

Like Thoreau, Warwick is also a great nature lover and walker. This is evident in the most famous chapter in *Moods* (present in both versions), which describes a week-long river trip taken by four young people (Sylvia; her brother, the jocular painter Max; Geoffrey Moor; and Adam Warwick). The homage this section pays to Thoreau's *A Week on the Concord and Merrimack Rivers* is striking. Louisa Alcott has her romantic band listen to Warwick's evening song: "Leaning on his oar he lent the music of a mellow voice to the words of a German Volkslied, and launched a fleet of echoes such as any tuneful vintager might have sent floating down the Rhine" (*Moods,* 35). Sylvia, this "modern Mignon" then regales her companions with recitations from Shakespeare.

The figure of Warwick also embodies Louisa's views on Goethe. These are evident when Sylvia's brother describes his friend Adam, a fellow who is a head taller than Moor, "broad-shouldered, strong-limbed, and bronzed by wind and weather. A massive head, covered with rings of ruddy brown hair; gray eyes, that seemed to pierce through all disguises, an eminent nose, and a beard like one of Mark's stout saints (Mark being Sylvia's brother, whose name in the second version of *Moods* becomes Max). Power, intellect, and courage were stamped on face and figure, making him the manliest man that Sylvia had ever seen" (*Moods,* 36). With the exception of the beard (which Goethe hated but Thoreau wore) the figure is an idealized fusion of the two men. Even Warwick's character blends the two "masters." Sylvia's brother, who had met Warwick in Germany, describes him to his sister as a "violently virtuous," man who lived according to his principles no matter what the cost. "He studies [the world], as we do books; dives into everything, analyzes character, and builds up his own with materials which will last. If that's not genius it's something better" (*Moods,* 37).

Warwick, it seems, will never gain fame, for his radical reforms are even more extreme than those of Thoreau. As Sylvia's brother says, "He is too fierce an iconoclast to suit the old party, too individual a reformer to join the new" (*Moods,* 37). In the chapter entitled "Sermons" Warwick tells his friends their character weaknesses to their faces. His catalog begins by calling Max prideful, Moor as self-sacrificing, Sylvia as romantic dreamer, and finally ends with a veritable flood of progressive ideas:

> Such an audacious onslaught upon established customs, creeds, and con-stitutions, [Sylvia] had never heard before; for, as Warwick charged, down went the stern religion that preaches heaven for the saint and hell for the sinner, the base legislation which decrees liberty to the white and slavery to the black, the false public opinion that grants all suffrages to man and none to woman yet judges both alike, — all knavery in high places, all gilded shams, all dead beliefs, — and up went the white banner of infinite justice, truth, and love. (*Moods*, 254–255)

Sylvia is stunned by this invective. "Mr. Warwick has pulled my world to pieces, but has given me no other, and I don't know where to look" (*Moods*, 256), she says in frustration to Geoffrey Moor. Her wise friend assures her that when seen through Warwick's telescope, the world may appear magnified, but not in correct perspective. Warwick must first over-come his Storm and Stress period before he can calm himself. But Sylvia cannot follow her father's advice ("Keep happy, dear, and no fear but you will get to heaven."), nor her sister's ("Read your Bible and talk to the Bishop."), nor her brother's ("fall in love"), and therefore chooses Moor as her true guide and advisor. He counsels her, "Take Nature for your friend and teacher. [. . .] Watch the harmonious laws that rule her, imi-tate her industry, her sweet sanity; and soon I think you will find that this benignant mother will take you in her arms and show you God" (*Moods*, 258). Geoffrey Moor's teachings, of course, memorialize Emerson.

Warwick also criticizes marriage, another institution that in New Eng-land was all but holy. Once Sylvia and Geoffrey Moor have married, War-wick visits them in the company of his friend Faith Dane. This female character is an extraordinary woman who lives alone in the country and combines elements of Beautiful Soul and Makarie from *Wilhelm Meister*. Their conversation turns to Helen Chesterfield who has "run away from her husband in a most disgraceful manner" and formed an attachment with one of her admirers. According to Sylvia's sister Prue, such behavior could only happen in Paris where she was married to a rich old man. There ensues a lively debate about marriage, which is retained in both ver-sions of the novel. Alcott's publisher actually wanted to make this dimen-sion, rather than the moods of a young girl, the main theme of the work. One almost suspects that with her ambitious first novel Louisa wished to compete with Goethe's novel about marriage, *Elective Affinities*. Her work also treats affinities among three main characters (not four, as in Goethe) where the fourth makes possible the dissolution of two relation-ships and the formation of two others.

This is another of those "complicated cases," which Goethe calls the "most interesting." In the conversation in his novel *Elective Affinities* about the mutual attraction of chemical compounds, we read: "In these [compounds] one meets with degrees of affinities that show closer, stronger, more distant, less powerful relationships; the affinities become interesting once they cause separations.[6]

The discussion about marriage in *Moods* never reaches such daring extremes as "marriage of convenience" as suggested by the Count in Goethe's novel, or even the indissolubility of a third marriage. Yet, Warwick does scandalize Sylvia's sister, the New England conservative, Prue, who views the sanctity of marriage as absolutely necessary to the order of the state:

> for with her marriage was more a law than gospel; a law which ordained that a pair once yoked should abide by their bargain, be it good or ill, and preserve the proprieties in public no matter how hot a hell their home might be for them and for their children. (*Moods*, 145–146)

In Warwick's opinion, the faithless Helen Chesterfield should have followed her heart and admitted the error to her husband that they had both made. Then she should have either married her lover and born the reproof of the world or, if he was not an honorable man, she ought to have lived alone as an "honest woman in God's eyes, whatever the blind world might have thought" (*Moods*, 145). Warwick thus considers marriage neither the only goal nor the sole fulfillment of life — a truth young people must be taught. But as long as this is not done, unhappy marriages remain "the tragedies of our day." People ought to know that it is not always wise or safe to marry out of love: "Often what seems the best affection of our hearts does more for us by being thwarted than if granted its fulfilment and prove a failure which embitters two lives instead of sweetening one" (*Moods*, 146).

The last word of this lengthy discussion is given to the wise and generous Faith. In their frustration Geoffrey Moor and Sylvia seek her out for advice to couples trapped in loveless marriages. Faith says, "If both find that they do not love, the sooner they part the wiser; if one alone makes the discovery the case is sadder still, and harder for either to decide" (*Moods*, 147). She then gives an example that corresponds precisely to Geoffrey and Sylvia's situation, leaving them with the advice to separate, for without love their marriage had become a sin. Warwick, of course, hangs on her every word: "And the lover, what of him? ," he asks. Faith Dane responds, "I would have the lover suffer and wait; sure that, however it may fare with him, he will be the richer and the better for having known the joy and pain of love" (*Moods*, 147).

With this gesture Faith alludes to Goethe's highest ideal of renunciation. Adam Warwick, it will be remembered, embodies Goethe in that he forswears Sylvia three times: first when he sees he has excited emotions too powerful for a 17-year old girl; the second time when he follows Faith's advice and goes to Europe; and the third time when he gives his life for Moor.

Louisa May Alcott did not write *Moods* "for money, but for its own sake," as her biographer Ednah Cheney suggests. Cheney did not recognize that Alcott invested more in the work than literary inspiration from other books, nor could she even find traces of Alcott's own life in New England in the novel. She dismisses as imported from Germany the "golden wedding" chapter in which the group of friends take part in a farmers' wedding anniversary, finding this episode out of place in a New England farmhouse (Cheney, 116–119). Nor did Cheney realize that here for the first time in American literature was an effort to recount the reception of a foreign literature, and to transform what had been gained into something new.

By contrast to her experience with short stories, Louisa had difficulty finding a publisher for her novel. Every one suggested new changes. Nonetheless, the work did sell — thanks in part to the reputation of her *Hospital Sketches* — and the second version did even better. Despite the difficulties Alcott encountered with *Moods,* she essentially wanted to write more novels like it. In 1860 she had discovered Jean Paul, which proved to be a reading experience that left its mark even in *Moods.* For example, when Moor returns to Sylvia after Warwick's death, the reconciliation of the two comes about through a dream of the proportions of Jean Paul. She dreams of the apocalypse when she and Moor stand with hosts of people beneath a black heaven, illuminated on the horizon by the word "Amen." Once the sea has swept everyone away, Moor and Sylvia find themselves alone on high ground as Warwick's smiling face disappears in the shining waves.

"On my thirty-second birthday received Richter's Life from Nan and enjoyed it so much that I planned a story of two men something like Jean Paul and Goethe, only more every-day people." (Cheney, 162). This plan was never realized. By contrast Louisa did something that nobody else from the inner circle of Concord had done, neither Emerson, Margaret Fuller, nor her father: she travelled to Germany.[7]

In August 1865 she journeyed as a lady's travelling companion through London and Brussels down the Rhine to Koblenz. Like so many travellers to the river, she was completely captivated by the romantic scenery, feeling herself to be a richer, better person, full of images that she would never forget. From Koblenz the journey continued to Bad Schwalbach for a spa cure and then to Frankfurt via Wiesbaden. She records her impressions in Frankfurt:

> Here I saw and enjoyed a good deal. The statues of Goethe, Schiller, Faust, Gutenberg, and Schaeffer are in the squares. Goethe's house is a tall, plain building, with a marble slab over the front door recording the date of Goethe's birth. I took a look at it and wanted to go in, as it was empty, but there was no time. Some Americans said, "Who was Goethe, to fuss about?" (Cheney, 176)

Before returning to America, Louisa went from Heidelberg to Baden-Baden, Freiburg, and via Switzerland and France back to England. On her second European trip in 1870, this time with her sister May, they were hindered by the outbreak of "this silly little war between France and Prussia," as she writes home where the anxious relief over the end of the U.S. Civil War is still felt. She continues to assuage the concerns of her family: "It won't trouble us, for we have done France and don't mean to do Germany" (Cheney, 240–241). That did occur, however, as they travelled through Switzerland north through all of Germany, with the result that Louisa was able to see Munich.

At this stage of her writing, the German influence leaves less obvious traces than in the novel *Moods*. Yet subtle vestiges are always present. Evidence for this is the particular configuration of characters in all of Alcott's work, her short stories, sensational tales, and juvenile novels. The primary pattern that recurs is the relationship of a young girl to an older man. The most familiar couple of this nature can be found in *Little Women* in which the hoyden Jo March marries the German professor Friedrich Bhaer. The older, paternal friend in these novels is often a legal guardian or uncle, sometimes given evil, not to say diabolical, traits. Madelon Bedell has traced these patterns in Alcott's works and concluded that they represent an "American translation" of the relationship between Goethe and Bettine. Indeed, the description from Goethe's *Correspondence with a Child*, which shows the Olympian poet on an elevated step receiving the young Bettine, is repeated in Alcott's novels and stories.[8]

Louisa's literary success enticed her to write more for an eager market, making it possible to cover her family's debts. And so she supplied the popular journals with sensational material for years. Her parents had become used to a comfortable home, her sister was thriving in her art studies, and her father's free time was spent in transcendental musings. To support these activities she let herself be persuaded by her publisher to write seven more books in a series that were modelled on *Little Women*. Because she disliked the work, however, she wrote these in haste, sometimes completing as much as a chapter per day.

Twice more she was able to free herself from the weight of this labor. In 1873 she published the autobiographical novel *Work,* which describes her experiences as servant girl, actress, nurse, and seamstress. Then in 1877 she retreated to the Boston Hotel Bellevue to write a book "that has been simmering ever since I read Faust last year" (Cheney, 296). On December 20th, 1875 she wrote to her father that she had just received the second part of *Faust* to read. "So I said 'Not at home' to everyone & for a week have lived with Goethe's hero. What a wonderful book it is? *[sic]* I admire the grand old gentleman more than ever, & forgive him his fifteen sweethearts, for I've no doubt they helped him do his work, unconsciously. He seems to have believed in the worth of experience & gone to find them; so I feel set up as that always has been my idea & practice too."[9] That whetted Louisa's appetite. Eleven days later she wrote to her mother, "I wish Papa would tell me how many of Goethe's books we own. As Mr Heath (who is a book man) can get me a complete set of Bohn for $1.25 a vol. I want the whole of Faust, Meister & Affinities. We have the plays & a part of Faust & W.M. Take a look & let me know if they are ours or R.W.E's."[10]

The novel, *A Modern Mephistopheles,* appeared anonymously in the No-Name Series of the Roberts Bothers publishers and became a sensation that readers attributed to various authors, among them the son of Nathaniel Hawthorne. It is a so-called "artist-novel" in which the young poet Felix Canaris (a man of more ambition than talent) is rescued by a character with the allegorical name of Jasper Helwyze. Helwyze discovers Canaris half starved and half frozen, burning his manuscript in an attempt to induce death by asphyxiation. Once Helwyze promises to publish his manuscript, Canaris agrees to belong to him "body and soul" as he has nothing left to offer.[11] This literary figure represents Louisa's version of an idea held by both Emerson and her father, namely that the Prince or Darkness is a gentleman best portrayed as a member of proper society.

Helwyze takes Canaris to his house to meet Gladys, the Gretchen figure of the novel. The book actually takes for its epigraph the closing words of *Faust II:*

> The indescribable
> Here it is done:
> The Woman-Soul leadeth us
> Upward and on![12]

Gladys, the companion of Olivia, is a woman Helwyze once loved, but who rejected him. She returned to him after an unhappy marriage only to find his feelings have cooled. His only pleasure now lies in studying "the mysterious mechanism of human nature," with the intention of gaining power over it. Helwyze refers admiringly to Goethe's manipulation of characters: "Goethe's boyish puppet-show was but a symbol of the skill and power which made the man the magician he became."[13] Alcott's configuration mirrors Goethe's in *Faust,* as she gives Helwyze the role of Mephistopheles and Olivia the part of Martha.

Despite the sensational elements in the plot (for example, Helwyze's administering hashish to Gladys and then hypnotizing her), Louisa's main purpose seems to be to edify her readers. To achieve this goal, she has Gladys read aloud to Helwyze from Montaigne, Voltaire, Carlyle, and Heine. One's curiosity is piqued by comments like the following:

> Equally fascinating to him, [Helwyze] and far more dangerous to her [Gladys], were George Sand's passionate romances, Goethe's dramatic novels, Hugo and Sue's lurid word-pictures of suffering and sin; the haunted world of Shakespeare and Dante, the poetry of Byron, Browning, and Poe.[14]

Gladys and Olivia entertain Helwyze and his ward with *tableaux vivants,* the subject of one which is Goethe's mythic-erotic poem "Der Gott und die Bajadere" ("The God and the Bayadere"). Helwyze even once tries to transform Gladys into an oriental beauty, which this pure soul rejects: "My Hatem does not need that sort of inspiration, and had rather see his Suleika in a plain gown of his choosing, than dressed in all the splendors of the East by any other hand."[15] This is another reference to Goethe, this time to figures from the *Der west-östlicher Diwan.* The figure of Hatem (the older man) that Gladys envisions, is obviously Canaris whom Helwyze forces to marry her. After the great success of his epic poem the poet cannot decide to write a drama or a novel, whereupon Helwyze advises to try his hand at the former. A novel would tax his strength to its utmost. He supports his advice with a long quotation from *Wilhelm Meister's Apprenticeship,* which this diabolical and educated man seems to know by heart:

> Because you [Canaris] have neither patience nor experience enough to do it well [write a novel]. Goethe says: "In the novel it is *sentiments* and *events* that are exhibited; in the drama it is *characters* and *deeds.* The novel goes slowly forward, the drama must hasten. In the novel, some degree of scope may be allowed to chance; but it must be led and guided by the sentiments of the personages. Fate, on the other hand, which, by means of outward, unconnected circumstances, carries forward men, without their own concurrence, to an unforeseen catastrophe, can only have place in the drama. Chance may produce pathetic situations, but not tragic ones."[16]

It is interesting to note that Helwyze does not actually quote the last sentence, although the narrator inserts it into the commentary that follows: "For the memory which served him so well outran his tongue, and recalled the closing sentence of the quotation, — words which he had no mind to utter then and there, -'Fate ought always to be terrible; and it is in the highest sense tragic, when it brings into a ruinous concatenation the guilty man and the guiltless with him.'"[17]

The guiltless character in the plot is Gladys who, dominated by her husband, suspects a secret behind the relationship between Canaris and Helwyze. When she at last discovers that Canaris's coveted fame is not owed to a work written by him at all, but by Helwyze, the blow is fatal. Felix's confession of his crime hastens the tragic miscarriage in which both mother and baby die.

When Helwyze suffers a stroke and Canaris forsakes him and the promise of fame, what remains is a broken, modern Mephistopheles. "Goethe could make his Satan as he liked; but Fate was stronger than I."[18] And so ignominious failure comes to Helwyze whose weakness — what else can be expected in a novel by Louisa May Alcott — was love. He loved and lost Gladys and although she will save her Faust with her prayers, he is condemned to eternal damnation.

The Faust theme had occupied Alcott once before. She had considered the title *A Modern Mephistopheles* for a different novel that was so incredible and sensational and contained so many dramatic episodes that even she probably thought it unworthy of publication. It contradicted the precepts of Goethe that Helwyze quotes (especially at the novel's end), precepts that Louisa wanted to make her *Modern Mephistopheles* follow. At any rate, this title was rejected at the manuscript stage and changed first to *The Fatal Love Chase*, and finally to *A Long Love Chase*.

It is hard to date *A Long Love Chase* with precision, but it must have been after 1865 for the plot takes place (among other places) in Koblenz and Wiesbaden, cities Louisa visited on her first European trip. Furthermore, everything that connects the protagonist Philip Tempest with Faust's Mephistophelian traits was deleted in the manuscript, Even the sentence, "Poor little Margaret, no hope for you when Faust and Mephistopheles are one."[19]

Tempest exerts a captivating charm over the beautiful Rosamond who must care for her embittered grandfather in their house by the sea. Tempest lures her away from America on his yacht to a life of wealth and splendor in Europe. When Rosamond, who is a veritable Bettine figure, lets herself down from her balcony with a belt and overhears Tempest's conversation, she discovers that he is already married. She then begins her escape across half of Europe from the man she still loves. Traversing all the countries that Alcott herself visited, Rosamond is constantly overtaken by Tempest who even traces her to a nunnery on the Rhine before she can finally return to America.

Overworked and sick from her tireless writing, Louisa May Alcott did not have the strength to include an enthusiastic reception of the sort of German literary inspiration (despite its shortcomings) that was in *Moods*. Now and then she would read in Henry Hedge's *Anthology of Classic Prose Writers of Germany* or a book on Goethe, about whom she always bought the latest publications. But during the summer of 1885 that she spent in Concord, she did not participate in the Summer School devoted to Goethe. In March 1888, Louisa May Alcott died, two days after her father.

Reception of German literature in the Concord circle came to an end with her death. But what sort of an end was it? Did the previous half century show a constant decline from the transcendental heights that Emerson had reached, only to descend to the relative depths represented by Louisa May Alcott's novels? There is certainly evidence to support this assertion, and yet it hardly does justice to the whole picture of this development. What was achieved here could be called unintentional collaborative work to which many talented people contributed their unique energies. While the reception of German literature certainly owes its primary impulse to Emerson and Margaret Fuller, it owes them completely different things. Emerson's critical encounter with German literature produced a new quality of American thought inspired by the German, while Fuller's critical advancement of German letters produced spirited and ingenious interpretations. As a thinker, Henry David Thoreau cannot be compared to either of these, for he led his American readers to inspirations from German literature by very indirect paths. The enthusiastic eccentric Amos Bronson Alcott presents a different situation, for it was through his conversations that he was most influential in communicating his impressions of German literature. His work in the Concord Summer School, especially the Goethe Summer of 1885, can be called the high point of American Goethe reception. By contrast, the immense success of the popular novels and children's literature from the pen of Alcott's daughter Louisa, were rich in references to German literature and quotations from German authors. The wide readership of these books make them the most far-reaching and influential conduits of German literary material in America. In a sense, then, Louisa May Alcott's contribution brought this reception to a point of democratization and made it into a thoroughly American phenomenon.

Notes

[1]   Louisa May Alcott, *Her Life, Letters, and Journals*, ed. Ednah D. Cheney (Boston: Little, Brown & Co., 1905), 57–58. Cited in text as Cheney. The original entry in Alcott's journal of April 27th, 1882 reads: "Mr Emerson died at 9 p.m. suddenly. Our best & greatest American gone. The nearest & dearest friend father has ever had, & the man who has helped me most by his life, his books, his society. I can never tell all he has been to me from the time I sang Mignon's song under his window, a little girl, & wrote letters a la Bettine to him, my Goethe, at 15, up through my hard years when his essays on Self Reliance, Character, Compensation, Love & Friendship helped me to understand myself & life & God & Nature. Illustrious & beloved friend, good bye!" *The Journals of Louisa May Alcott*, introduction by Madeleine B. Stern, eds. Joel Myerson and Daniel Shealy, assoc. ed. Madeleine B. Stern (Boston: Little, Brown & Co, 1989), 234.

[2]   *Behind a Mask: The Unknown Thrillers of Louisa May Alcott*, ed. Madeleine B. Stern (New York: Morrow, 1975).

[3]   Henry James, Review of *Moods*, (1865) in *Critical Essays on Louisa May Alcott*, ed. Madeleine B. Stern (Boston: G. K. Hall & Co., 1984), 73.

[4]   The manuscript of the first version does not survive, but it is apparent from the foreword to the second that several chapters have been restored to their original form because the author wished to preserve the "love, labor, and enthusiasm" of the original.

[5]   Louisa May Alcott, *Moods*, ed. Sarah Elbert, (New Brunswick and London: Rutgers UP, 1991), 228. Cited in text as *Moods*.

[6]   *Hamburger Ausgabe*, 6:273.

[7]   See Shirley Foster, "Germany in Fact and Fiction in the Writings of Louisa May Alcott," in *Images of Central Europe in Travelogues and Fiction by North American Writers*, ed. Waldemar Zacharasiewicz (Tübingen: Stauffenburg, 1995), 60–67.

[8]   Madelon Bedell, *The Alcotts: Biography of a Family* (New York: C. N. Potter, 1980), 240–243.

[9]   *The Selected Letters of Louisa May Alcott*, introduction by Madeleine B. Stern, eds. Joel Myerson and Daniel Shealy, assoc. ed. Madeleine B. Stern (Boston: Little, Brown & Co, 1987), 209.

[10]   *The Selected Letters of Louisa May Alcott*, 216.

[11]   Louisa May Alcott, *A Modern Mephistopheles*, No Name Series (Boston: Roberts Brothers, 1880); Rpt. *A Modern Mephistopheles and Taming a Tartar*, Introduction by Madeleine B. Stern (New York, Westport, CT & London: Praeger, 1987), 17.

[12]   Critics have stressed a feminist aspect of the novel. Gladys revises, from a woman's point of view, a woman's role in the script of her feminist writings. See Rena Sanderson "*A Modern Mephistopheles:* Louisa May Alcott's Exorcism of Patriarchy" in *American Transcendental Quarterly* 5 (March 1991), 1:41–45.

[13]   *A Modern Mephistopheles,* 46ff.

[14]   *A Modern Mephistopheles,* 122.

[15]   *A Modern Mephistopheles,* 128.

[16]   *A Modern Mephistopheles,* 236; *Hamburger Ausgabe,* 7:307ff.

[17]   *Ibid.*

[18]   *A Modern Mephistopheles,* 288–289.

[19]   Louisa May Alcott, *A Long Fatal Love Chase,* Ed. Kent Bicknell (New York: Random House, 1995), 37. The original manuscript of *A Long Fatal Love Chase* was found, edited, and published by Bicknell in 1995. This manuscript consists of 290 pages written and subsequently revised by Louisa May Alcott.

Index

"The Duty of Men to Judge
Men only by their Actions," 14;
Encyclopedia, 25; "The Uses of
Natural History," 29; "The
Relations of Man to the Globe,"
29; "Water," 29; "The
Philosophy of History," 30;
"Literature," 31; "Thoughts on
Modern Literature," 33, 113;
"The Eye and Ear," 33; *Nature*
(1836), 34, 40, 59, 142; "Art of
Life, — The Scholar's Calling,"
44; "Thoughts on Modern
Literature," 44, 168; poems, 46;
"The Transcendentalist," 48, 53;
Selected Poems, 52; "The Test,"
52; "Goethe: Or, The Writer,"
53; "Nominalist and Realist,"
52–53; "The Poet," 56–57;
"Written in a Volume of
Goethe," 57; "To J. W.," 57;
"Waldeinsamkeit," 57; "Persian
Poetry," 58
Emerson, Waldo, 36
Emerson, William, 11, 12; meeting
with Goethe, 12–13; and
Thoreau, 146. Works by: *Journal
of a Tour from Göttingen to
Dresden,* 12
Emery, S. H, 174
Engels, Friedrich, 124. Works by:
*The Situation of the Laboring
Class in England,* 124
Ertheiler, Moritz, 120
Etzler, John Adolphus, 146;
influence on Thoreau, 146–147.
Eutin, 124
Everett, Edward, 12

Farrar, John, 82
Felton, Cornelius, 96
Fichte, Johann Gottlieb, 84, 102,
116, 167
Fischer, Kuno, 174
Florence (Italy), 128

Follen, Charles, 12, 36, 52, 73, 85,
104, 138, 159. Works by:
German Reader for Beginners,
138
Folsom, Abigail, 5
Foreign Review, 53, 75
Foreign Quarterly Review, 16
Forkel, J. F., 109
Fouqué, Friedrich de la Motte, 189
Fourier, Charles, 91, 92, 120
Fox, John, 29
Francis, Converse, 117
Frank Leslie's Illustrated Newspaper,
187
Frankfurt am Main, 123, 194
Frankfurter Gelehrten-Anzeiger,
170, 177
Frankfurter Chronik, 103
Fraser's Magazine, 16
Freiburg, 117, 194
Freiligrath, Ferdinand, 47
Friends of Universal Reform, 5
Freischütz, Der, 120
Froebel, Frederick, 176
Frohschammer, Jakob, 140
Fromann, Friedrich Johann, 125,
126
Frothingham, Octavian Brooks, 7
Fruitlands, 163, 185, 186
Fugitive Slave Law, 2
Fuller, Margaret, vii, 4, 6, 26, 31,
41, 46, 51, 155, 161, 165, 170,
172; and Ralph Waldo Emerson,
37; writes to Bettina, 42; knowl-
edge of German language and
literature, 44; early education,
72–73.; reads German, 75;
correspondence with Clarke, 76–
78, 83; on Körner, 81; as trans-
lator and scholar of Goethe, 82–
83, 95, 99, 107; compares
Goethe and Schiller, 89–90; at
Brook Farm, 92–93; holds her
Conversations, 93–95; and *The
Dial,* 95–105; *contra* Menzel,